Kubrick's Total Cinema

Kubrick's Total Cinema

Philosophical Themes and Formal Qualities

Philip Kuberski

B L O O M S B U R Y
NEW YORK • LONDON • NEW DELHI • SYDNEY

Bloomsbury Academic
An imprint of Bloomsbury Publishing Plc

1385 Broadway
New York
NY 10018
USA

50 Bedford Square
London
WC1B 3DP
UK

www.bloomsbury.com

Bloomsbury is a registered trade mark of Bloomsbury Publishing Plc

First published in 2012 by the Continuum International Publishing Group Inc
Paperback edition first published 2014 by Bloomsbury Academic

Library of Congress Cataloging-in-Publication Data
A catalog record for this book is available at the Library of Congress.

ISBN: HB: 978-1-4411-5687-7
PB: 978-1-6289-2947-8
ePDF: 978-1-4411-4956-5
ePUB: 978-1-4411-6591-6

For my wife Eileen Cahill

Contents

Preface

Stanley Kubrick (1928–99) was one of the greatest filmmakers of the second-half of the twentieth century and a worthy descendant of the great modernists of the first half of the century. The director of 13 films over the course of nearly 50 years, Kubrick continues to reveal himself to us in his depth, subtlety, beauty, humor, and surprise. There is something distinctive, even unique, about the best films he made: an intellectual edginess, a Dionysian explosiveness, an apocalyptic inventiveness, an intractable ambiguity, and an undeniable originality. But there is something else.

Kubrick's films *think*. His work is not simply a celluloid or digital canon, a collection of films: It is a cinema, more properly, a kinetics, an energy, that thinks through forms and themes. The audience is the necessary complement to this thinking cinema: We are carried along and into this kinetic expression of embodied thought.

The making of a film, in this sense, is a widely distributed event including many people over a course of several years. The film that emerges is not simply the record of a lot of beard-scratching, rewrites, and takes: It continues with each of its showings in the minds of millions of viewers. So the thinking is not something that precedes the film—it is not a concept, a shooting script, a storyboard, a series of sets and actors. The thinking never really stops and it is always available and present.

By thinking we usually mean cognition, calculation, and abstract reasoning. But in truth, most of our thinking is embodied by our senses. We think through forms, images, sounds, and motion. In this respect, all of the arts think in and through their media: If a painter thinks in images, a composer thinks in sounds, and a poet thinks in words, so a film director thinks in all three. The greatest directors exploit these forms in ways that sustain potentials over time. This is one way of recognizing a classic film: Its cinematic thinking never comes to an end.

So, all films think, some more and more thoroughly than others. Kubrick's films are distinguished by their conceptual consistency, intellectual coolness, and formal inventiveness. But by "thinking," I do not mean that his films present "arguments" or "philosophies." Rather, they work as visual, verbal, musical, and intellectual provocations to the mind and emotions. They work against expectations, "thinking" through cinematic conventions to address fundamental questions: What is human nature? Are human beings fundamentally violent? Is war intrinsic to civilization? Is "love" really possible? Where do we come from? But of course Kubrick's films are not philosophical discourses. Like any major artist, his concerns are rooted in the facts of human experience, in characters, stories, conflicts, and—oftentimes—enigmatic or provocative resolutions. Some see his films as antihuman or cynical. I see them as tearing away the bogus and artificial and pointing ahead to something else, different, and frighteningly authentic.

If cinema is a thinking carried on via different but synchronized media—speech, image, music—its meaning is a matter for a similarly ongoing process of interpretation. In the other arts, intention is often determined by the biographical and historical record and qualified by psychological and philosophical suppositions. In the end, though, a single artist, composer, or poet would appear to be the source of a work's ambition, intention, and meaning. But a film director is not in a comparable situation, even if he writes, lights, films, and edits the work. His art is inevitably one of delegation and appropriation. Individual contributions from the crew are easily absorbed by the director. More than the other arts, the intentions, origins, and meanings of a film are widely distributed among a corps of artists, craftsmen, and businesspeople. The film director can only be an *auteur* in a highly qualified way. He signs the work, but it is countersigned by the work of others.

So Kubrick's ways of thinking are likewise a distributed event and not confined to anything so neat as a philosophy of life or a single style of filmmaking. In order to present my own thinking about this thinking cinema, this book treats Kubrick's films to a conceptual and formal analysis rather than a biographical and chronological survey. My approach is to study his philosophical themes and cinematic qualities and suggest the ways in which the first are related to the second.

The formal qualities I have chosen are Kubrick's embodiments of time, light, speech, music, and finally what I call *poiesis*—the final synchronization and mixing of media into the film itself. Other qualities could have been used—Kubrick's predilection for symmetrical and geometric uses of space, for instance—but these are his most distinctive. The conceptual themes I have chosen are corporeality, war, eros, technology, and transcendence. These choices highlight the dominant conflict in Kubrick's films between instinctual drives and conditions—the embarrassments of the body, the organization of violence, the insistence of sexuality—and the redemptions offered by culture and manners, civilization, romantic love, and technology. The central conflict in Kubrick is between the insistence of the instincts and the dream of transcendence. Thus, Kubrick's work employs the formal esthetics of film as a modernist artist does: to recreate the form of his art, to dismantle the ideological clichés of its usual deployment, and to present both scathing critiques and visionary possibilities.

* * *

I give my thanks to the Provost's Office of Wake Forest University for a Reynolds Leave for the years 2007–8 that allowed me to fashion several essays into a book-length argument. Chapters 2 and 11 appeared originally in a different form in *Arizona Quarterly* 60.4 (2004)/64.3 (2008), reprinted by permission of the Regents of The University of Arizona. I would like to thank Maja-Lisa von Sneidern of *Arizona Quarterly,* as well as Scott Berry of Wake Forest University for editorial assistance. I would also like to thank Frederick Dolan of the University of California, Berkeley; Dennis Foster and Nina Schwartz of Southern Methodist University; and Howard Needler of Wesleyan University for invitations to give talks on Kubrick at Berkeley, Southern Methodist University and the University of Helsinki. I also owe a debt of gratitude to Katie Gallof of Continuum, the press readers, and the production staff. For conversations about Kubrick that go back at least to *The Shining* in 1980 and more recently for a commentary on my manuscript, I owe a debt of gratitude to Frederick Dolan. My greatest debt is to my wife Eileen Cahill. This book is dedicated to her.

1

Thinking

Can the cinema think? This study proposes that it can—but that it rarely does, less out of incapacity than inclination. It proposes, moreover, that the distinguishing characteristic of Stanley Kubrick's cinema is that it thinks. I do not mean that it offers views, opinions, messages, or arguments. I mean that it searches through the media of sound and light, words, music, and image to find insight and illumination. Much in traditional cinema, even of so-called classic cinema, has stood in the way of thinking: sentimentality, patriotism, complacency, actors, prudery, didacticism, and a nearly concealed contempt for the audience. Kubrick cuts through these obstacles, making way for a cinema that discovers unprecedented and challenging combinations of beauty and knowledge, satirical critique and visionary possibility.

Critics have realized for some time that one of the distinctive qualities of Kubrick's cinema is its intellectual and conceptual coherence. Alexander Walker points to intellectual coherence as one of Kubrick's distinctive characteristics: "Only a few film directors possess a conceptual talent—that is, a talent to crystallize every film into a cinematic concept."[1] Walker pinpoints this conceptual focus: "a persistent interest in the symbolic analysis of society through its enduring myths and fables."[2] For Kent Jones, Kubrick is "a metaphysical story-teller," a filmmaker capable not only of moving his audience but evoking and meditating on the great questions.[3] Thomas Allen Nelson claims that "Kubrick's conceptual universe" is informed by a pervasive

> awareness of contingency [which] arises whenever there is a loss of faith in teleological explanations, in the received or discovered validity of meaning in the rational structures of nature or the signifying power of mind and language. Once meaning has lost the authority of teleology we then perceive how many different ways there are to create meaning through the expressive extensions of language and form.[4]

In their seminal works, Walker and Nelson firmly establish the relationship between Kubrick's deconstructive vision of modern life and his formal inventiveness and brilliance.

If Walker and Nelson see Kubrick as a kind of cinematic deconstructor of "pieties" and "teleology," James Naremore sees him as a satirist whose subject is human folly and barbarism; in the interest of satire, he is drawn to a family of "estranging effects—the grotesquely mistaken, the uncanny, the fantastic, the Kafkaesque—and he repeatedly conjoins methodical orderliness and horrific absurdity."[5] Penetrating as his assessment is, Naremore leaves out two essential elements of Kubrick's cinema: the visionary and the beautiful. Satire, even when practiced by masters like Swift or Kafka, has a fantastic aspect that distorts the world in order to expose its absurdity. The formal beauties and complexities of Kubrick's cinema go beyond caustic critique to potential transformation.

Kubrick told Alexander Walker, "Naturalism finally does not elicit the more mysterious echoes contained in myths and fables; these resonances are far better suited to film than any other art form. People in the twentieth century are increasingly occupied with magic, mystical experience, transcendental urges . . ."[6] In this sense, the surreal or hyperreal aspect of Kubrick's films is less satirical, per se, than a response to cinematic traditions of realism or naturalism that reflect and attempt to enforce cultural norms of family and nation.

A thinking cinema is something less and more than a conceptual or a satirical cinema—it is a cinema constantly alive to possibilities of representation and vision. It is less concerned with contingency, per se, as it is with the ways in which cinematic reality can be an ongoing criticism and revelation of material reality. Although governed by narrative, character, and theme, it is at the same time—and more importantly for some—a material thinking, a thinking that transcends words, themes, and concepts and enters the delightful realm of the ineffable and endlessly interesting. In a way, Kubrick was able to fuse the cinema's power of enchantment with the power of relentless investigation and exhibition, continual critique, and surprising revelation. For this reason, Kubrick's cinema invites thinking through that draws out an implicit phenomenology of its strikingly original formal qualities. It also merits a conceptual analysis that treats its concerns as more than merely thematic. This study thus approaches Kubrick's cinema through philosophical categories (corporeality, technology, war, eros, and transcendence) and formal qualities (time, light, music, speech, and poiesis). In turning away from a chronological, film-by-film analysis, we can perhaps establish the distinctive and coherent nature of Kubrick's cinema.

The Search for Illumination

Kubrick's films were made through a process of search and discovery: they were not produced so much as they were expressed through the long process of scripting, set and costume design, casting, filming, improvisation (especially Peter Sellers's performances in *Lolita* and *Dr. Strangelove or: How I Learned to Stop Worrying and Love the Bomb*), editing, and scoring. As Saul Bass observed,

> Stanley is very monastic. He's a great beard scratcher. He thinks; he rubs his beard. He expresses himself quietly. I can't say he's reasonable . . . There has to be a certain unreasonableness in any serious creative work.[7]

Kubrick taught others this art of thinking and brooding, of beard scratching and chess-playing, of sudden shifts of course and rewritten dialogue. This made for long shoots, countless takes, and surprises. The thinking never stopped, and this thinking is reflected in the ineffable and the willing collusion of media that a film is or ought to be. It was all in the service of the film's mysterious heart, less an intention or a point of view than a commitment to illumination. During the writing of *Eyes Wide Shut*, his last film, this consummate aim was represented for Kubrick by Arthur Schnitzler, the author of *Traumnovelle*, upon which the film was to be based. In adapting the novel to cinema and translating it from Vienna to New York, much had to be discovered. In practice, Schnitzler became the oracle who provided directions for the making of the film. It was an oracle that only Kubrick could understand. He called him, simply enough, "Arthur." His hired screenwriter, Frederic Raphael, wrote in his notebook on May 31, 1995: "[Kubrick] has convinced himself that our salvation lies in keeping to Schnitzler's 'beats'; if anything goes wrong, deviation from 'Arthur' has to be the reason for it."[8]

For Kubrick, films begin with questions he could not begin to formulate. Making a film was a process of embodied thinking, thinking *toward* a mystery that could not initially be framed. In a sense, the thinking was not directed at the solution of a mystery: it was directed toward that mystery's cinematic realization.

This kind of esthetic search is complemented by Kubrick's conception of cinema as a spiritual instrument. In his article "Words and Movies" (1961), Kubrick argues that action in a film must act as an "objective correlative" of the source novel's "psychological content." Drawing on T. S. Eliot's famous argument from his essay "Hamlet and His Problems" (1919), Kubrick's article is a modernist and formalist defense of the work of art: "For a movie or a play to say anything really truthful about life, it has to do so very obliquely."[9] Where Eliot argued that poetry had to be "difficult" if it were to dislocate language into meaning, Kubrick believes that a film needs to remain remote from explicit statement and rely on the medium:

> You use the audience's thrill of surprise and discovery to reinforce your ideas, rather than reinforce them artificially through plot points or phony drama or phony stage dynamics.[10]

Thus, in defending his choice to adapt a highly verbal novel like *Lolita*, Kubrick argues that a film, like a novel, discovers its own style as a manifestation of its thematic concerns. "Style," he writes, "is what an artist uses to fascinate the beholder in order to convey to him his feelings and emotions and thoughts."[11] The style realized in the making of a film may begin in service to a novel, but it cannot be confined to that sense of commitment:

> Any art form properly practiced involves a to and fro between conception and execution, the original intention being constantly modified as one tries to give it objective realization. In painting a picture this goes on between the artist and his canvas; in making a movie it goes on between people.[12]

Kubrick's statements about his films fall into the tradition of esthetic formalism dominant in academic literary criticism at mid-century which was largely devised to justify the difficulties of modernist literature: If his films violated genre expectations, that was because they were poetic and resistant to summary and explanation. As James Naremore has pointed out, Kubrick's cinema is "modernist" or "late modernist" in orientation and esthetic: We note an authorial detachment, a cool mode of presentation, and a formal ineffability.[13] Likewise, T. Pipolo has argued that Kubrick was "an important modernist artist" whose films are characterized by a "perplexing conflation of aesthetics, technology, and narrative."[14] These qualities in modernist writers had inspired New Critics such as Cleanth Brooks and W. C. Wimsatt to speak of the literary texts in spatial terms such as a well-wrought urn and a verbal icon.[15] Similarly, Kubrick claimed that "it is . . . misleading to try to sum up the meaning of a film verbally."[16]

Like paintings, his films cannot, he maintained, be understood in terms of explanation. Leonardo did not provide an interpretation of *La Giaconda*, and neither will he provide an interpretation of his works. Although such an esthetic was largely prompted by *2001: A Space Odyssey*, Kubrick invoked the same formalism to characterize *Full Metal Jacket* 20 years later:

> Truth is too multifaceted to be contained in a five-line summary. If the work is good, what you say about it is usually irrelevant . . . The work is bigger than one's capacity to describe it.[17]

Any attempt to summarize a real work of art is "hateful conceptualizing."[18] In *2001*, Kubrick did not attempt ambiguity for its own sake; "it was inevitable." "A certain degree of ambiguity is valuable" because it allows the viewer his own "visual experience."[19] Rather than a verbal art that is susceptible to summary interpretation, the film

> operates on a level much closer to music and to painting than to the printed word . . . The basic purpose of a film is one of illumination, of showing the viewer something he can't see any other way.[20]

Thus, like a true modernist, Kubrick denies that art has a social responsibility: "I don't think that any work of art has a responsibility to be anything but a work of art."[21] Kubrick's esthetics recognize the intrinsic complexity of an art form that combines a simultaneous juxtaposition of music, image, and speech. The distinctively stimulating and pleasurable qualities of Kubrick's are the product of an intensification of this complexity.

The "illumination" that Kubrick believes to be the "basic purpose of a film" may be interpreted in many ways. My own approach will be to explore the ways in which Kubrick's art illumines the visible world but also, and equally important, what lies behind and within it—culture, psychology, philosophy, and ideology. His work, even as it avoids conceptual intentionality, is deeply conceptual, philosophical, and analytical in nature. Kubrick was a popular film director who was also an intellectual, an exile (though he denied it), and a technical artist. Kubrick's own ambitions and accomplishments are admirably suggested in his praise for two fellow filmmakers:

> I am always reluctant to single out some particular feature of the work of a major filmmaker because it tends inevitably to simplify and reduce the work. But in this book of screenplays by Krzysztof Kieslowski and his co-author, Krzysztof Piesiewicz, it should not be out of place to observe that they have the very rare ability to dramatize their ideas rather than just talking about them. By making their points through the dramatic action of the story they gain the added power of allowing the audience to discover what's really going on rather than being told. They do this with such dazzling skill, you never see the ideas coming and don't realize until much later how profoundly they have reached your heart.[22]

For cinema to have such purchase on the imagination it has to be living, unpretentious, and yet somehow suggestive of something eternal or primordial, something "archetypal" in the terminology of C. G. Jung. In a way, Kubrick was able to join the heightened or exaggerated aspect of satire to the profounder aspect of the archetype. Sergeant Hartman in *Full Metal Jacket* is a satirical caricature, but more importantly he is an archetype—the Ogre or the murdering Father. Humbert Humbert in *Lolita* is a caricature of a scheming pedophile, but more importantly he is an archetype—the impassioned lover of courtly romances. Kubrick's central and enduring works are, at the same time, transgressive and archetypal, satirical and visionary.

The form of enigma

This point of ineffability indicates another quality of Kubrick's films—an irreducible ambiguity or, more grandly, an undeniable mysteriousness. This is certainly true for *2001*, and also for *The Shining*, *Full Metal Jacket*, and *Eyes Wide Shut*. And this quality points to—and accounts for—another characteristic of the films: Their reputations continue to grow and deepen with time. *2001* mystified and frightened MGM executives and the New York City newspaper critics, but connected with audiences—and yet not even a loose consensus has ever emerged about what its conclusion "is," let alone what it means. One observes, then, a two-part invention in Kubrick's major films: a risky devotion to a project not easily assimilable through generic expectation and closure and a slowly accruing cultural reception and recognition.

While *2001* triumphed not only in spite of but also because of its apocalyptic mysteriousness and grandeur, *The Shining* proved an especially bitter pill for many of Kubrick's admirers at the time of its release in 1980. To them the film seemed, on first viewing, to be an overacted, confusing pastiche of horror films from the seventies such as *The Exorcist* (1973), *The Omen* (1976), and *Carrie* (1976). Thirty years later, it is one of his most popular and critical successes. *Full Metal Jacket*, constructed in two discrete sections at Parris Island and South Vietnam, refuses to answer to standard expectations for artistic closure, and yet continues to grow in esteem, outstripping the reputation of earlier Vietnam War films such as *The Deer Hunter* (1978), *Apocalypse Now* (1979), and *Platoon* (1987). And both films, despite these difficulties, are firmly lodged in collective popular memory and speech. *Eyes Wide Shut*, his last film, was a financial and a critical failure in 1999. By 2002 it was the subject of a monograph by Michel Chion in the British Film Institute's Modern Classics Series and has gone on to stimulate dozens of critical studies. Following his death just before the release of *Eyes Wide Shut*, it became clear that Kubrick's canon was a uniquely rich and rewarding subject of continuing scholarly inquiry and popular interest.

The mysterious or enigmatic aspect of Kubrick's films derives from a certain obliqueness of presentation and a corresponding trust in the ability of mass audiences to experience and accept ambiguity. Kubrick told Alexander Walker: "I'm sure that there's something in the human personality which resents things that are clear, and, conversely, something which is attracted to puzzles, enigmas, and allegories."[23] Executives and newspaper and magazine critics have a vested interest in "knowing" what a film is "about": the first in order to sell it and the second in order to provide a kind of consumer report. Both institutions were based on cultural norms that had begun to disappear in the sixties. Audiences were able to deal with ambiguity because society itself was becoming more and more fraught with complexity and competing narratives. And in succeeding decades, the nature of the film audience continued to change, along with the culture at large. Cable television, VHS, DVD, and internet exhibitions transformed films from theatrical events to something closer to reading and rereading. Kubrick's films were ahead of this transformation, as well as contributing to it.

The crucial element to Kubrick's enigmas is his devotion to ellipsis: leaving things out of the film means leaving them "in"—for the audience's own consideration. While cinema relies on ellipsis and montage to carry the narrative forward, Kubrick's most enigmatic films leave out a good deal more. *2001* leaves out millions of years of its narrative. *The Killing* leaves out a single line of narrative, providing instead an *analysis* of the events. *Full Metal Jacket* leaves out narrative connections from the basic training narrative, the Da Nang narratives, and the conclusion in the City of Hue. Only two characters from the opening sequence find their way into the last. Thus a kind of macro-montage binds the film together rather than a sequential unfolding of narrative. In these films, ellipsis introduces a manifest discontinuity that shifts the syntax from narrative to a modernist montage of the sort first observed in modernist works such as *Ulysses*, *The Waste Land*, and *Citizen Kane*. Kubrick's use of ellipsis includes a tendency to leave out explanatory scenes that would close other narrative gaps. Thus, Kubrick does not clearly dramatize the means by which Alex is deconditioned in *A Clockwork*

Orange; he does not provide a clear-cut explanation—as Stephen King does in his novel—for Jack Torrance's absorption by and into the Overlook Hotel in *The Shining*; he does not resolve the identity of the "mysterious woman" in *Eyes Wide Shut*. There are other instances of elliptical narrative that have the effect of turning the film from transparency to enigma.

Ellipsis is both bridged and deepened by Kubrick's use of title cards and narrators: The effect is to create films that appear in panels. Paneling in *2001* was introduced after the first screening in order to clarify the narrative. In *The Killing* and *The Shining*, it would appear to be ironic, appearing to provide assistance but instead adding to a sense of ambiguity, ambivalence, and enigma. To provide time cards in *The Shining* is curious indeed, since the film is concerned with the metamorphic and permeable aspect of time itself. The paneling and cards in *Barry Lyndon* appear as mannerist devices, meant to stress a neo-classical striving toward manifest order and symmetry. Ellipsis and panelling provide a nice example of Kubrick's ambivalence about narrative coherence: It must be provided and recognized, but it should appear to have more cogency in films than it does in life.

Another characteristic of this form of enigma is the screening of a symbolic tableau: a manikin warehouse, a clown's mask, a carnival mask, sculptured furniture in the forms of naked women, an oil painting punctured with bullet holes, a frozen frame of a one-legged man, a photograph of a July 4 celebration in 1921, a montage of atomic clouds, an astral fetus turning in space. These symbolic tableaux act to conclude or compress the films' themes and narrative in a mute, inviting way, ranging from moral certitude to comic nightmare or enigmatic promise. Such symbolic scenes act like still points in the interrupted flows of narrative, still points that concentrate the picture language of Kubrick's cinema in a moment outside of time. It is this interplay of ellipsis and archetype that most clearly establishes a link between Kubrick's cinema and modernism.

Modernism comes to the mall

Kubrick was, strictly speaking, neither a purveyor of mass entertainment, like Steven Spielberg or John Ford, nor an art house auteur like Bergman or Godard. Like a popular filmmaker, he worked with film genres—science fiction, horror, noir, war—only to deepen and extended their potentials; like an auteur, he put demands on his audience, demands of attention, comprehension, and interpretation. And yet his films are almost always entertaining, diverting, and often hilariously funny. And more than many strictly popular filmmakers, images, music, and dialogue from his work have become a familiar element in world culture: bikini-clad Lolita looking over her sunglasses; Major Kong riding a nuclear bomb like a bronco-buster; the astral fetus looking at us enigmatically from space; Jack Torrance with his axe and grin; the prelude to Richard Strauss's *Also Sprach Zarathustra*; Walter Carlos's synthesized version of Beethoven's *Ninth Symphony*; "Me love you long time"; "Look, Dave, I can see you're really upset about this." These and many other words, images, and musical passages have become aspects of the world media ecology. Kubrick's films often began as enigmas, but they have had a deep and continually growing reception and recognition. They end by growing into the culture.

When they were not enigmatic—like *2001*, *The Shining*, and *Eyes Wide Shut*—they were perceived as a threat to contemporary values. *Paths of Glory* was banned in France for 17 years because of its portrayal of the French Army's General Staff. *Lolita* was studied minutely by industry censors and the Roman Catholic League of Decency in 1961 and was approved only after many negotiations with Kubrick. At the height of the Cold War, *Dr. Strangelove* satirized the US military, Department of Defense, and the presidency, prompting a condemnation in *The New York Times*—which the critic, Bosely Crowther, later retracted.[24] Just as the counterculture began to wane in 1971, Kubrick foresaw a bleaker aspect of youth culture by adapting Anthony Burgess's novel *A Clockwork Orange*. The film was assailed in print for inspiring violence and contriving to find the seeds of violence even in such cultural capital as Beethoven. *A Clockwork Orange* was given an X rating, usually reserved for pornographic features, and prompted a refusal by some 30 American newspapers to publish advertisements and reviews.[25] And *Eyes Wide Shut* proved that even in 1999, a film could go too far: It was threatened with an X rating unless Kubrick altered certain scenes: Thus, perhaps the greatest living director was forced to deface his last work in order to recoup investors. (Subsequent DVDs, of course, restored Kubrick's original cut.)

His enigmas challenged the audience's intelligence and imagination, while his provocative themes challenged its values and shibboleths. Like the modernists, Kubrick claimed the artistic right to a position outside the known and revered world of respectability to challenge intellects and morals, all the while entertaining and amusing his audiences—and securing artistic independence over his work, huge budgets, and big profits—at least during the sixties and early seventies. This anomalous fusion of modernist license and mass cultural appeal reached its apogee with *2001*, which set out apparently to revive the nearly dead genre of science fiction but became an unprecedented tone poem about the great metaphysical mysteries, a work which developed and extended the modernist tradition initiated by Joyce and Pound of revising Homer's *Odyssey*.

Kubrick's deepening of film genre, evident in all of his mature films, is in essence a modernist reinscription of the commercial categories of the movie business. Kubrick's films worked with and against the grain of commercial cinema to discover new and unexpected qualities in genre. *Barry Lyndon*, rather than a historical or costume drama, is a cinematic reflection on time and light, as well as a historical analysis of the last decades of the premodern world. *The Shining*, rather than simply a horror film dedicated to sensation, thinks through the American family and the passing of the patriarchal age. And *Full Metal Jacket* played against the genre of the training and war film and thought through the nature or production of masculinity. None of these films satisfied those who expected generic experiences: instead Kubrick enticed his audience into different kinds of pleasure—esthetic contemplation, ideological critique, and interpretive closure. Some were more profitable than others, but Kubrick's insistence on furthering his own vision was evident even to those who were baffled or disappointed.

Their cinematic significance derives in large part from what these films do not do. In other words, it is the ideological values in which genres are steeped that come into play. The historical drama should provide for grand gestures, high romance, and heroic sacrifice—*A Tale of Two Cities*, in other words. But *Barry Lyndon* has other interests and different pleasures to offer: It opens on a world of candle light, symmetry, and painterly composition never seen before in cinema. And the same could be said for Kubrick's deconstruction of the horror and war films. The publicity leading to the release of *Eyes Wide Shut*, drawing on the tabloid interest in the love lives of two big stars, prepared audiences for something private and perhaps scandalous to be played out between Tom Cruise and Nicole Kidman. Instead of a sex romance about the Beautiful People, Kubrick gives us a dream film that manages to go beyond love and romance and even sex—to the mysterious, impersonal, and dangerous will-to-life.

This was one of the missions of the modernists—to introduce and stimulate an appreciation and involvement in the critical pleasures offered by the various art media and then to reimagine the world on new and different terms. Modernists like Joyce, Stravinsky, and Picasso were not only inventors of new forms of writing, composition, and painting, but they also showed that the arts not only represented experience or expressed emotions, they think *through their media.* Each of these modernists made his medium absolutely present and accessible to affect and to reflection. Joyce's works are made out of words, Stravinsky's out of sounds, and Picasso's out of images. Their readers, audiences, and witnesses cannot leap ahead to story, melody, and representation without discovering how these have been mediated. Illumination, enigma, threat, and form: These are the elements of a modernist art. They can equally well be used to characterize Kubrick's thinking cinema.

Kubrick's attention to formal fundamentals acts to bring the circumstances of film reality into play. Light becomes a player in the drama, not a dumb purveyor of reality. We see that it does not pour from an extra-real studio source: It is part of the real, streaming from windows, candles, lamps, and the sky. Time, in a similar fashion, is not a given, a premise of life, but a medium that reflects the psychology and the drama of the film: It slows down and speeds up, jumps forward or back, or, in some cases, is transformed into space. Music, often the pathetic amplifier of emotion, gains independence and actively comments and participates in the drama from an unknowable position beyond the scenario. This independence came at the cost of a traditional score composed as a unified musical parallel to the action. In its place, Kubrick devised the collage score, drawing most often on the classical repertoire. The effect is to activate a rich field of musical reference, allusion, and counterpoint. This liberation of the elements of the drama and character can also be heard in speech—in dialogue and narrative—as it breaks past the task of exposition and expression. Speech in Kubrick's films is often a character in its own right—the NASA jargon of *2001*, the Nadsat (Russian "teen") argot of *A Clockwork Orange*, the Nam-speak of *Full Metal Jacket*, the mythic ventriloquism of *The Shining*, and the inspired improvisations in *Dr. Strangelove*. Speech in Kubrick's films achieves an opacity and a physicality that enlivens and frustrates attempts at communication and understanding. When these elements are orchestrated in a scene and a series of scenes, we experience a simultaneous *poiesis*—an integral overlay of imagery, music, speech—that exceeds rational exegesis or paraphrase. It is the illumination that Kubrick aimed for in his films.

This freeing of the elements of representation provides a formal foundation for Kubrick's deconstructive vision—which has often been understood by critics as cold, indifferent, or remote. This view seems dependent on the constitutional sentimentality and sensationalism of ordinary cinema. Kubrick pushes past this scrim. Kubrick's characters, despite their flat presence on the screen, displace space, achieve weight and embody appetites: they are corporeal; they copulate; and they defecate. Their satiric aspect, to a large extent, depends on the discrepancy between their mental or spiritual pretentions and their corporeality. In response to this evident antagonism, Kubrick is constantly engaged by these corporeal beings' attempts to forge extra-human, technological agents and legacies. Technology emerges as a dominant and ironic theme in these films and comes into powerful conflict and convergence with corporeality and eros—the supra-human drive of the Will, in Schopenhauer's terms.[26] This supersession of the individual will by the implacable nature of the machine, the body and the impersonal Will of eros, can also be observed in Kubrick's lifelong study of war. Kubrick demonstrates how martial culture and civilized values arise at the same moment in time—and go hand in hand through history.

In the final chapter, this study will examine how corporeality, technology, eros, and war point to the possibilities of self-discovery, realization, and transcendence. *2001* takes all these elements and transforms them into a mythic, poetic technology of self-discovery and surprise. Grounded as it is in corporeality, war, and eros, Kubrick's cinema has a kind of discontinuous teleology directed at ultimate forms of realization. David Bowman is reborn, in *The Shining* Jack Torrance escapes from time, and in *Eyes Wide Shut*, Bill and Alice Harford hope to awaken from the dreaming sleep of domestic life. Because of—and not despite—his unblinking attention to human corporeality, war, and blind eros, Kubrick remained a deeply spiritual artist.

In thinking through Stanley Kubrick, I have made reference to literary and philosophical figures more often than to cinema—directors, films, critics, and theory. My purpose in doing this is to establish a cogent intellectual context for Kubrick's modernist esthetics and his conceptual vision. For, in a sense, modernist thought paved the way for its own mass cultural appropriation—and dispersal—in the sixties. Philosophical concerns with consciousness, epistemology, metaphysics, psychology, mysticism and the like burst from academic and artistic milieux into the general cultural scene in those years.

In a sense, Kubrick's cinema rode this countercultural wave from the late fifties to the early seventies, from the critique of the State and the military in *Paths of Glory* in 1957 to the black comedy of *A Clockwork Orange* in 1971. If we see the elements of the counterculture as a mass manifestation of critical features of modernism—cultural and moral critique, sexual license, transformation of consciousness, the deconstruction of artistic convention—then Kubrick's films, more than Godard's, Bergman's, and Antonioni's, extended modernism into the popular imagination. This popularization of modernism was accomplished through Kubrick's mass appeal at the height of his popularity in the sixties and early seventies, while the great European auteurs attracted art house audiences already familiar with the modernist tradition and certain of its prestige. Kubrick managed to transform the tradition of popular American films into a modernism of rare intelligence, flexibility, and beauty.

2

Corporeality

Kubrick's temperament led him to leave no aspect of his film world as a mere fact: Everything had to be questioned and put into thematic play. Eating is always more than a datum of reality or simply a dramatic occasion for exposition, repression, tension, and an eruption of conflict and violence, as it often is in literary fiction and films. Kubrick's characters often eat at inappropriate times or places or in inappropriate ways that introduce a complex of humor, pathos, and irony. And just as the dining room scene and scenes of alimentation are subverted and dramatically stylized, so the room at the other end of the alimentary journey receives a constant and curiously oblique attention. The dining room and the bathroom are granted a necessary and elusive polarity in Kubrick's films that acts to subvert and ironize human pretentions to super-corporeal existence.

Yet, as Mervyn Nicholson has pointed out, food is neither "subject nor object: it is food because it subverts this distinction."[1] Because of this uncanny positioning, food and eating can ground Kubrick's action in corporeality and point ahead to possible visionary transformations: "eating discloses the divine and the infinite."[2] At the same time, urination and defecation insist on a reversal of the divine and the infinite: they are in a sense exhausted matter, alive with bacteria but depleted of their former lives. The journey from the anterior to the posterior orifice is of course a constant in human life, a kind of interior odyssey for which the living body is a world. In her analysis of the "abject" in *Powers of Horror*, Julia Kristeva writes:

> Excrement and its equivalents (decay, infection, disease, corpse, etc.) stand for the danger to the identity that comes from without: the ego threatened by the non-ego, society threatened by the outside, life by death.[3]

Food and excreta, while aspects of the abject, are of course central to both life and custom in positive and negative forms: the dining room and the "bathroom" mark the poles of the abject in day-to-day life. Kubrick's interest in the staging of these corporeal scenes has to do with their repressed roles in founding culture. As Kristeva writes

> A massive and sudden emergence of uncanniness, which, familiar as it might have been in an opaque and forgotten life, now harries me as radically separate, loathsome. Not me. Not that. But no nothing, either. A "something" that I do not recognize as a thing. A weight of meaninglessness, about which there is nothing insignificant, and which crushes me . . . There, abject and abjection are my safeguards. The primers of my culture.[4]

While the abject marks the frightening exterior which we unaccountably contain within ourselves, it also prompts the formation of custom and propriety, the openly celebratory and the privately reviled. Human customs clearly evolved as bulwarks against the threatening forces of abject. It is here that Kubrick finds a point of access to the fundaments of culture. His attention to eating is manifest; his attention to defecation is oblique—for this would seem to be the best way to evoke its omnipresent yet repressed presence as a reminder of something no one really wants to recall.

Distasteful

In *Dr. Strangelove*, the communication officer Lt. Goldberg is eating a sandwich when he suddenly tells Major Kong over the intercom, "I really think this is crazy, but I just got a message from base over the CRM 114. [Takes another bite.] It decodes: 'Wing Attack, Plan R. R. for Romeo.'" When Kong accuses him of joking, Goldie continues, chewing his food, "I'm not horsin' around, sir, that's how it decodes." Swallowing his food, Goldie's enunciation is comically exaggerated on the last word. As the crew check out the CRM 114, Lt. Kivel also finishes his snack. Alimentation complete, within moments Kong has his cowboy hat on and the crew has put their bomber on a heading that will lead to the destruction of all "human and animal life on earth." Later, in the war room, the Russian Ambassador DeSadesky orders a late night snack from an opulent buffet. There is a fruit bowl with a pineapple, rolls, wine, roasted turkey, coffee in a silver pot, cream pies, and more. DeSadesky, incredulous about the absence of "fresh fish," orders poached eggs and Cuban cigars. Kubrick's satire is accomplished by such incongruity—and yet we do not see it as unrealistic depiction so much as an uncensored one.

These men are presiding over the destruction of the planet, the immolation of billions of people, and the incineration of human history—yet there is still time for a bite. If we find these scenes funny, it is perhaps because of a sense of incongruity and disproportion. The fact that human beings need to internalize once-living morsels of the outer world can be seen as funny, especially when highlighted with exaggerated chewing or choosy tastes. Or it can be seen as monstrous. How funny is it, after all, that everything on the planet can survive only by demanding the death of another plant, animal, or man? Perhaps it is better to laugh than to be revolted, and much better than thinking about it. Eating, however crude or polite, is something quite distasteful, if the action is dislodged from its transparency and seen for what it is.

This fact is quite evident in Kubrick's first treatment of the theme in *Fear and Desire*. The four hungry soldiers, 6 miles behind enemy lines, come across a shack in the forest where enemy soldiers are eating stew. They break in and beat them into submission. The fists smashing into faces are intercut with shots of a hand squeezing cut potatoes and thick sauce oozing through the clenched fingers. Mac announces that he will have some of that cold stew. When an enemy soldier comes in with firewood, Sydney shoots him with an enemy rifle. This first of many scenes of rough alimentation in Kubrick alternates shots of violence, food, and eating in a manner that echoes the early Soviet director Dovzhenko's treatment of peasants. It is both vital and crude and shows us how fundamental and physical life can be when far from the customs that transform eating into a social ritual. Watching a hungry man eating is rarely an edifying sight; watching a sated man eat is a refined one. Kubrick's intention being to represent the timeless drama of fear and desire, the scene is brutal and elemental in establishing the brutish aspect of corporeality.

In a civilized state of affairs, violence is kept far from the act of alimentation, a custom that the English language maintains by distinguishing between animals in the yard and an animal on a table, the pig in the sty and the pork on the plate. The same division is followed in war, when the planners, properly attired, sit far from the front lines where the killers go about their tasks in more informal attire.

When, in *Paths of Glory*, Corporal Paris and Privates Ferol and Arnaud are served a last meal before their execution on trumped-up charges of cowardice, Ferol is torn between impulses. Picked as a scapegoat because his officer considers him as a "social undesirable," he is the least compromised by social pretense. Looking at the roasted duck brought in, he tears off a leg and is about to eat when a dark suspicion seizes him:

Ferol: You suppose they put anything in the food?
Arnaud: First, they poison us, then they shoot us?
Ferol: I think they put something in it . . .

While the men in the brig renounce their last meal, afterward Gen. Mireau, who had insisted on their sacrifice, eats his breakfast with Gen. Broulard without a qualm. Seated cheerfully over the silver service, with coffee, eggs, and scones with jam, he acts as fastidiously as Ferol had acted naturally:

> Mireau: This had a kind of splendor, don't you think? [. . .] The men died wonderfully. There's always that chance . . . that one will do something that will leave everyone with a bad taste. This time you couldn't ask for better.

Never a very observant officer, Mireau ignores that, of the three men executed, one was weeping and begging for mercy and one was unconscious and strapped to a litter leaning against a post. Since the execution left no bad taste in his mouth, he cheerfully eats a scone with jam. When Col. Dax joins them, he praises his men ("Your men died very well") and tosses the rest of the scone into his mouth.

The origins, triumph, and atrophy of table manners

In *2001*, once Moon-watcher has discovered via his confrontation with the monolith that a bone can be used as a weapon, he slaughters one of the tapirs that his clan had lived with peacefully in the past. The slaughter will send a fissure between what will become human beings and what are now animals, as well as demonstrating the physical advantages that arise with a protein diet. So for the first time, the hominids enjoy the taste of raw meat, chewing single-mindedly in two discrete parties. The feasts are silent and solemn and, we can guess, suffused with historical resonances. Moon-watcher eats his meat alone, the bone, now a fetish and a symbol of his dominance, at his feet, while the others eat in the ravine below with the tapirs. The first weapon leads to the first blood meal and the first division of the organic clan into sections: the mob below and the king and his scepter above. Two divisions have come as a consequence of the first flesh meal: that between animals and men, and that between rulers and the ruled.

Hundreds of thousands of years later, we see the descendants of Moon-watcher and his clan flying on the moon bus toward the uncovered monolith. Michaels brings Floyd and Halvorson a cooler with a choice of sandwiches:

> Floyd: What's that? Chicken?
> Michaels: Something like that. Tastes the same.
> Halvorson: Any ham?
> Michaels [rummaging in the box]: Ham, ham, ham.

As they eat, Halvorson tells Floyd that his presentation to the staff at Tycho base "beefed up morale a hell of a lot." Their conversation then shifts to the monolith and its mysterious provenance. Like Goldberg and Kivel, these men equably snack while confronting, in effect, the beginning and the end of human civilization. The meat they eat is synthetic, not hunted, and the development of human speech leads to chatting, flattery, and bogus bonhomie. And again there is something oddly comical about eating that Kubrick brings out: a sense of corporeal atavism that delimits and ironizes the sublime technology that has brought men to the moon in the first place.

The same can be said of Bowman and Poole as they eat their synthetic TV dinners and watch the BBC report about their own Jupiter Mission. Side by side, they eat from trays with differently colored but identically textured dishes and watch themselves on a television beamed from earth and edited to remove the 7-minute time lag. They are caught up in a reflexive loop of eating and watching TV, just like the millions of human beings back on earth. In sharp contrast to this banal captivity, Bowman is in the end transported "Beyond the Infinite." He has changed from an uptight astronaut to a kind of aristocratic pensioner in smoking jacket and ascot. Situated in the alien hotel or observation room, he eats alone, as Moon-watcher did. Formally dressed before a formal table setting with white cloth napkins, silver serving dishes, dinner rolls, and a plate of what seems to be beef, he turns around twice, anticipating yet another transformation. Reaching across the table, he accidentally knocks off a glass and looks up to see an even older version of himself in bed—about to achieve his final transformation to astral fetus. This meal is at the end of human history, at the point where the physical and organic human being has been supplanted by HAL (the Heuristically programmed ALgorithmic computer)—who consumes only electricity.

In *Lolita*, Humbert is musing on the "eerie vulgarity" of "this nymphet" at precisely the moment that Charlotte asks Lolita to take his breakfast up to his room, but not to "disturb him." As she goes up the stairs, she picks up and eats the bacon from the tray, licking her fingers—despite having just been instructed by her mother in etiquette: "We don't eat with our elbows on the table." Putting the tray before Humbert, as he quickly puts his diary away, she confesses she has eaten his bacon and then begins to work on a slice of toast. He reads to her from "Ullalume" by the "divine Edgar" as she sits on the window sill, putting her feet on his desk—so much for American manners before the refined European lodger. The poetry reading over, she begins to improve on her intimacy with

Humbert, but suddenly stops. When he promises never to "blab" about her, Lolita rewards him: she dangles a fried egg above Humbert's mouth, the way one will train a seal, and says, "You can have one little bite." Lolita clearly understands what is in Humbert's diary, and so her breaking bread and egg with him is no less clearly an indication of her willingness, but also her single condition: Humbert's subjection to her.

Drinking and dining in *A Clockwork Orange* tend, unsurprisingly, toward the perverse or the irregular. Alimentation is not a wholesome, human custom and organic necessity, but a paradoxical act that recycles and exhibits violence and lust. For Alex and his droogs, drinking doctored milk in a bar is a prelude to their violent evening activities. Like big babies, they drink tall glasses of milk dispensed by the plastic breasts of the Korova Bar's female decor: "milk plus vellocet or synthemesc or drencrom . . . This would sharpen you up and make you ready for a bit of the old ultra-violence." The "natural" aspect of this imbibing is thus nicely compromised: The minors can legally consume milk, but it is laced with opiates, synthetic mescaline, and adrenochrome, and drawn "naturally" from artificial breasts. That mother's milk should put Alex in touch with the "the old ultraviolence" is Anthony Burgess's allusion to St Augustine's observation that even as a child nursing at his mother's breast, he was tarnished by original sin, enjoying as he did the erotic relation with his mother. The opiates in the milk are thus like traces of original sin.

In prison, Alex discovers a particular interest in the Old Testament: "I like the parts where these old yahoodies tolchock each other and then drink their Hebrew vino, then getting on to bed with their wives' handmaidens." His biblical studies feature a particular fantasy: lounging in a tent with semi-nude handmaidens, who feed him grapes and fan him. But then Alex is himself subject to another biblical theme. For Alex, then, alimentation is implicitly the extension of violence and sexuality. Once he has undergone the Ludovico treatment and fallen into the hands of Mr Alexander and the other "conspirators," who plan to use him to bring down the government, he is given a bath and a meal of pasta and wine. Plied with wine by the maddened Alexander, he begins to think, like Ferol, that he is being poisoned or drugged. They are soon joined by the conspirators Rubinstein and Dolin: together they have planned Alex's Last Supper. So Alex eats alone surrounded by his enemies who plan to sacrifice him to the "greater good" by driving him to suicide.

When Alex survives his attempted suicide, the Minister of the Interior comes to the hospital to win him over to the Government's side in its battle against the conspirators. Now another curious eating scene ensues. Unable to handle his fork, the Minister intervenes and feeds Alex as they work out an arrangement whereby Alex will be compensated with job and salary if he will speak on behalf of the Government. Alex opens his mouth theatrically again and again as the Minister delivers the charged fork. It is like a baby bird being fed by its mother, or like Lolita feeding Humbert. With Alex's mugging, lip smacking, exaggerated chewing, and the strange intimacy between the plum-voiced Minister and the cunning hoodlum, a visual objectification of the film's theme of the relationship of violence to society and art is accomplished. Filled with eggiwegs and steakiweaks, deconditioned from the treatment, Alex is free to enjoy Beethoven and violence once again.

Barry Lyndon provides a point of contrast with the dominant treatment of signs of corporeality, dedicated as it is to an age that aspired to the dominance of reason over the appetites and etiquette over the body. The themes of the film emphasize this ritualized attempt to dominate the passions at all costs, even as the actual world was swamped in offal, disease, sexual violence, war, and colonial conquest. War is organized by the formalities of engagement, mating by the codes of courtship, politics by the manners of Parliament and Court, eating by the ritual of table manners, while excretion and washing are largely left without formal redress, as well as being, ordinarily, addressed in solitude. To a large extent, and in contrast with the other films, *Barry Lyndon* presents the formal aspirations of the century according to its own standards of behavior and even according to its own painterly esthetics—and even its own experience of light: sunlight, candlelight, and moonlight. Where Kubrick is usually committed to a satirical dismantling of social fictions, here he assumes a gentler and more elusive task. Time and again in *Barry Lyndon* one sees how the formality of the dining ritual, of whatever level of society, is ruptured by the forces it was designed to contain.

Barry's career as a wanderer begins with the disruption of a dinner to celebrate the engagement of his beloved cousin Nora Brady to the cowardly British Officer Jack Quin. The emotional pitch of the scene from celebration to consternation, the announcement of matrimony to the demand for satisfaction, is a familiar one, but Kubrick is not interested in satirizing it. Once the nuptials have been announced, Barry refuses to join in the toast, proposing a moment later his own toast, by throwing his charged glass into Quin's face and provoking a duel. The same dynamic can be observed in a different dining scene after Barry has enlisted in the British Army. During outdoor mess, Barry complains that his beaker is filled with grease and provokes general laughter. A beefy soldier stands up and says: "Get the gentleman a towel and a basin of turtle-soup," and then downs the beaker. Told how to vex the red-haired giant, Barry provokes a fist-fight and wins, gaining respect from his fellows. In both scenes, Barry violates dining codes, but he recoups his fault by adverting to another code dedicated to restoring honor. Dining in other words has little to do with nourishment of the organism and much to do with the ceremonial aspects of honor and prestige. Although both scenes are violent, they are not satirical. The body is not shown to be comically needy, but as a bearer and instrument of spiritualized values.

Subsequent dining scenes in *Barry Lyndon* observe this rule. Barry's candlelit dinner with the German peasant girl Lischen and her beatific infant is photographed with great beauty and delicacy. The rupture here occurs at her confession of loneliness. Like Barry, her husband is away at the war. Despite, or perhaps because of the language barrier, whatever formal considerations separating them fall away, and the two become lovers. But the narrator, as always, is out of step with the scene and makes a graceless comment: "This heart of Lischen's was like many a neighboring town and had been stormed and occupied several times before Barry came to invest in it." A similar rupture occurs when Barry, posing as the British Lt. Fakenham, is dining with his Prussian companion Capt Potzdorf. The scene is once again intimate, candlelit but in a crowded Officers' Mess. Both men, apparently drunk, toast their "two great nations," and Potzdorf even tells Barry of a woman in Bremen, presumably a prostitute, to whom Barry may give a message: it is as if the two are doubles. But Potzdorf has been studying him in the candlelight, and we see now that he has been keeping track of various anomalies. The rupture occurs when Barry claims to be carrying a message to General Williams, whom Potzdorf knows to be dead. He stands up suddenly and calls out: "Sergeant. Dieser Mann ist unter Arrest," and then tells Barry: "You are a liar. You are an impostor. You are a deserter." And so Barry is forced to "take the bounty" and join the Prussian infantry. Both of these scenes of Barry dining with the Prussians break down: the first from propriety to sexual passion, the second from camaraderie to military arrest and impressment.

The theme of impersonation easily passes into the theme of social performance, as everyone in the film is involved in the elaborate disguise of private motives and passions behind social masks. Having saved Potzdorf's life, Barry has been promoted to a Prussian spy, posing as Lazlo Zilagy. Told to present himself and then spy on an Irish gambler posing as the "Chevalier de Balibari," Barry finds him at breakfast. The table is set for one, with white cloth, silver service, a plate of meats, an egg cup, butter, and a cup of coffee. The large room and the small table set for one emphasize the Irishman's solitude and readiness for company. Their highly formal conversation in foreigner's German breaks down when Barry suddenly confesses his true identity and nationality and mission. The Chevalier embraces his countryman and the two plan their escape. Barry poses as the Chevalier and is escorted across the frontier by Prussian soldiers and is joined by the Chevalier who had crossed over the previous night. His imposture of the Chevalier is recapitulated later in his life when, his attempt to secure a peerage to guarantee that Lady Lyndon's fortune passes to his son Brian having failed, we see him dining alone at his club.

A final scene will indicate how deliberate the pattern of formal dinner and rupture is followed in *Barry Lyndon*. Formal dinner is served at Castle Hackton for Barry, Lady Lyndon, Rev Runt, Mrs Barry, Graham, and little Brian. No one must wait to be served or is given precedence, as six servants come in at once with plates. Little Brian cannot wait, either, to determine what his birthday gift will be, and he soon wheedles the information from his doting father. Brian wants the horse because it indicates his independence, but he can ride it only when his father is with him. In the next scene Barry learns that his son has broken his promise and been kicked in the head. Once again, formal devices—dinner manners, birthday and gift, promise—all fail to deter the force of desire and will. Barry's gift on his son's birthday kills him, and instead of a birthday an elaborate funeral is organized. Despite all the precautions that a society of custom and manner can take, these forces cannot be contained.

Kubrick's attitude in all these dining scenes is, first, a respectful observance of society's attempts to master the body's needs and replace them with a metaphysical drama concerned with control and custom. Eating, which can be an unsightly and embarrassing scene if not properly performed, must be subjected to an elaborate code of behavior. But even as these precautions are taken, other kinds of appetites assert themselves: for love, prestige, sex, honor, friendship, and independence. These ruptures in dining rituals point toward a more serious failure of congruence between appearance and reality, between what Kubrick's photography shows us and what the narrator tells us. Analytical insights into society are left in the gaps that open between what we see and what the narrator notes, between the aspirations of characters and the rigid, painted world of the eighteenth century. Following the keen satire of *A Clockwork Orange*, *Barry Lyndon*'s ironies are gentler and more nuanced, the former being a warning of a possible future, the latter a reflection on a past that we can never truly know.

The archaic meal

Beyond and before the dramatic interventions into table manners is the original, archaic meal. Mythology is filled with tales of infanticide, patricide, and cannibalism. The authors of *Genesis* claim that God commanded Abraham to seize his son Isaac, bind him, bring wood and tinder, and sacrifice him, as he would a lamb. We learn from *Theogony* that the Titan Kronos ate his progeny until his son Zeus intervened. Laius bound Oedipus's ankles and abandoned him in the wilderness, but Oedipus survived to kill his father, if unintentionally. Kubrick's films are more than a little interested in monstrous father figures and threatened or vengeful sons: Vince Rapallo and Davy Gordon, General Mireau and his men, Sergeant Hartman and Private Pyle, Victor Ziegler and Bill Harford, Barry and Lord Bullingdon, General Ripper and the world, HAL and Bowman, Jack Torrance and Danny.

The psychic competition between father and son that Freud describes as a *fantasy* of the threat of infanticide or castration countered by patricide is nearly realized in *The Shining*.[5] But Kubrick pushes past the nearly domesticated Oedipal drama to its more fantastic and abysmal origin in the archaic meals of myth and fairy tale. At the point where Jack is breaking into the rooms where his wife and son are hiding, his imagination seizes on an analogy for his deranged mood:

Jack as Big Bad Wolf:	Come out, come out, wherever you are . . . Little pigs, little pigs, let me come in.
Jack as Little Pig:	Not by the hair of your chinny-chin-chin.
Jack as Big Bad Wolf:	Then I'll huff and I'll puff and I'll blow your house in!

For *The Shining* is also about the fear of starvation, slaughter, and cannibalism—and the ways in which the Torrances deal with it. It all begins with Jack losing his job and abusing his son and the unstated question in his family's mind: Is Jack a breadwinner or an ogre? He has not only taken a job at the Overlook Hotel in order to feed his family. He has done so in order to redeem himself—by writing a novel.

Wendy and Danny manifest their fears in terms of food and hunger on the drive to the remote Overlook Hotel:

Danny:	I'm hungry.
Jack:	You should've eaten your breakfast.
Wendy:	We'll get you something as soon as we get to the hotel.

. . .

Wendy:	Wasn't it around here that the Donner party got snowbound?
Jack:	I think that was farther west, in the Sierras.
Danny:	What was the Donner party?
Jack:	They were a party of settlers in covered wagon times. They had to resort to cannibalism in order to stay alive.
Danny:	You mean they ate each other up?
Jack:	They had to, in order to survive.

This theme accounts for the pantry scenes with the cook Dick Halloran and later when Wendy locks Jack inside. It is the black man Halloran who seems the proper father to Danny and provider for the family, not Jack, who shares some racist moments with his double Delbert Grady. Halloran provides a Rabelaisian catalog of the holdings of the freezer: "You got fifteen rib roasts, thirty ten-pound bags of hamburger. We got twelve turkeys, about forty chickens, fifty sirloin steaks, two dozen pork roasts and twenty legs of lamb." And the storeroom is equally well-stocked:

> You got canned fruits and vegetables, canned fish and meats, hot and cold cereals. Post Toasties, Corn Flakes, Sugar Puffs, Rice Krispies, Wheaties, and Cream of Wheat. You got a dozen jugs of black molasses. We got sixty boxes of dried milk . . . We've got dried peaches, dried apricots, dried raisins and dried prunes.

This abundance is beside the point if Wendy and Danny are themselves the food for Jack's mad appetites. While Halloran means to reassure them about this abundance, his catalog can only point elsewhere for the source of worry: "You know, Mrs. Torrance, you got to keep regular, if you want to be happy." Happiness or psychic wholeness depends, according to one who shines, on a fully integrated system of consumption and evacuation. To be "irregular" is to be unhappy—or in Jack's case—maddened.

In contrast to the homey meals that Wendy and Danny eat, Jack is seen eating alone only twice. There is something predatory and alienated about his meals. On Closing Day, we see him finishing his lunch when Ullman meets him. A second time, we see Wendy bring him breakfast on a room service trolley, as if he were a guest of the hotel. But Jack is still in bed, and only sits up casually to poke his bacon repeatedly into his egg yolk. There is no custom here, and the formality of the trolley service Wendy manages—Kubrick crosscuts her wheeling it to his room with Danny's manic cycling around the hotel and his moments of "shining"—acts to emphasize Jack's drifting from family life. In the "Tuesday" segment, we see Wendy making dinner (she pours a two-quart can of fruit cocktail into a bowl for the three of them) and then coming to Jack's workroom, presumably to tell him that dinner is ready. Jack drives her away, telling her that she can no longer "interrupt" his writing (or, more properly, his typing), because, whatever she might hear from outside, he is "always working." It is as if Jack has given up ordinary nutrition for his engulfment by the hotel.

But the significant fact in *The Shining* is that Jack fails to realize his mad and mythic ambition to consume his family. Instead, his son destroys him, leaving him like a rack of frozen meat in the snowy maze. So the would-be infanticide is bested by his agile parricide. In contrast to *Barry Lyndon*, *The Shining* utterly deconstructs the codes of dining and returns them to their archaic origins in myths of patriarchal rage, infanticide, and cannibalism. Kubrick discovers this abysmal origin by delving into the blandly tasteless décor and commercial culture of Middle America in the seventies.

Plumbing the abyss

The pantry and the toilet, the dining room and the bathroom—and the activities they imply—indicate the disturbing yet banal polarity of human corporeality—and its nagging reminders of death and decay, of slaughter and digestion, mastication and defecation. It also affects our sense of copulation and childbirth, which in a way are acts of eating and excreting. Our only defenses against these unseemly reminders that life lives on life, that we live by consuming bodies which our own bodies sort out into energy and waste, are silent custom and embarrassed humor. If the dining room is a social theater where the body assumes a dignified remoteness from the facts at hand, the bathroom is a monastic retreat where we confront our natures in solitude.

The bathroom is the first place one enters in the morning and the last place one leaves at night. It is a room for bathing, washing, cosmetics, and self-preparation, but it is also a room for urination, defecation, masturbation, and regurgitation. Like the kitchen, it is usually tiled, curtained, and plumbed, with mirrors as well as toilets, tubs, and sinks. It is a room dedicated to flowing water and shining surfaces, chrome, glitter, and reflection. It is luxurious and clinical, superficial and profound. It supplements faces and eliminates feces. There is an unavoidable duplicity about the bathroom. It is a palace of luxurious hardware and a slum of fetid waste: urine, feces, semen, blood, mucus, dirt, and sweat.

The bathroom has always served a neatly duplicitous purpose in the movies. In the early epics, pagan baths allowed for sensuous titillation coupled with puritanical censorship. In *Cleopatra* (1933), Claudette Colbert chastely and wantonly languishes in a prudently opaque milk bath. Countless other films, pagan, biblical, and otherwise, feature bubble baths in which the same compact is struck between viewer and director, director and the Hollywood production Code. Since the sixties, there has been little need for such antics, so the bathtub has been deprived of its historic uses—and assumed new ones, often of a frankly violent character. The shower, moreover, has been converted from Hitchcockian abattoir to confessional and boudoir. Ever since *The Big Chill* (1983), it has been a place where a woman can go to have a good cry.

Sex is readily dramatized in terms of romance, marriage, procreation, duty, lust, and violence, but excretion has commonly been regarded as uninteresting and therefore unworthy of report. There would seem to be little for it to illustrate dramatically. Perhaps it has been left unrepresented not because it is private or vulgar, but because it does not signify anything—unless, of course, it is because it signifies too much.

But things are changing. Excretion, once the profane par excellence, has been divided into the acceptable and the unacceptable. Urination, in recent years, has been coyly represented and domesticated. Hollywood now admits that if bladders are filled, they must also be emptied. When babies or children urinate, it connotes a cheeky naturalness to which no one can object. When men urinate—it is rarely quite explicit—the suggestion is: "Well, they're men. What do you expect?" When women urinate, matters are not so clear. Female urination can be seen as a form of camaraderie that encourages intimacy and revelation. If a tampon is passed between stalls, we know that sisterhood is flourishing. Defecation, on the other hand, is not yet legitimate. Rabelais and Joyce attempted to bring it into literary respectability, and it plays a role in specialized pornography and in the occasional surrealist film, such as Luis Buñuel's *The Discreet Charm of the Bourgeoisie* (1972), in which people move their bowels together at table and retire to small private rooms to eat. Its sounds and consequences have their comic uses, of course, and during the 1990s, defecation and related acts were successfully mocked in movies for youngsters, such as *Austin Powers: International Man of Mystery* (1997) and *Doctor Dolittle* (1998). The model for this theme may be the Mel Brooks parody *Blazing Saddles* (1974).

In cases like these, however, defecation is simply laughed away rather than explored. Can we imagine a leading man or woman involved in this leaden drama?

Can it be made to signify in any way—to develop character, advance plot, resolve conflict? In fact, and quite unlike the typical uses of such imagery in film, the bathroom and *all* that it suggests as site and symbol is ubiquitous in Kubrick. As Alexander Walker observes, "Bathrooms and their ceramic conveniences occupy a central and ominous place in Kubrick interiors."[6] When we see the commode looming at the end of the hall in *Lolita* or *The Shining*, much more than realistic detail is at stake. An attempt is being made to show us something that cannot be seen. For the fact is that the toilet is the entrance into a labyrinthine abyss of unsuspected unities: an underworld of sewage pipes, channels of deposit, and estuaries of human waste hustled into a great unseen pool, a vast abjection in hidden contrast to the desire for a freeing independence from the necessities that encumber organic existence. That polished white commode, like an obdurate toadstool, signals a distributed underground webwork, a mycelium that does not nourish but expels.

In *Eyes Wide Shut*, for example, several important scenes are set in bathrooms. Alice Harford urinates in the first scene while chatting with her husband Bill. Is this gratuitous "realism"? Or the first indication that things are not quite right with the Harfords' marriage? Perhaps their intimacy has blinded them to each other. The cinematography exhibits Alice's body, but her husband fails to notice: absorbed in putting on his own face, Bill confirms his wife's beauty without bothering to look.

The party for which the Harfords are preparing is a glittering display of artificiality, pretense, deceit—and enormous wealth. Bill flirts with two generic models—a "blonde" and a "brunette"—and Alice flirts with a generic Lothario who speaks of art, poetry, and worldly hypocrisy. In due course, Bill is led into a palatial bathroom. It has a tub, a toilet, a bidet, a sink, an armchair, a fireplace with a mantle, is hung with original paintings—and it also contains Bill's host and patient Victor Ziegler and his prostitute, who is sprawled, naked, and unconscious, on a chair. She would appear to be the last of the bathroom's fixtures, but something has gone wrong with her—a drug overdose, it turns out—and Bill has been summoned, like a plumber, to repair her.

What are the bathrooms of the Harfords and the Zieglers saying to us? The Harfords put on a show of friendly tenderness to their babysitter in the living room, while in the bathroom, the ordinary tensions in their marriage are expressed. The Zieglers play the happy hosts, but we see that Victor has decided, in the midst of his Christmas party, to employ the services of a prostitute. The Harfords' bathroom provides for the expression of routine inadvertences and neglect; the Zieglers' bathroom is a fully furnished brothel and drug den. Later in the film, when Alice goes to her bathroom to retrieve the marijuana that Bill and she keep hidden there in a Band-Aid box, we see that the Harfords' bathroom also doubles as a drug den. But their mild version is comfortably conventional and safely within upper-middle-class norms, compared with the exotic injection that causes the "little accident" with Victor's prostitute. *Eyes Wide Shut* explores the relative merits of a conventional world that maintains a distinction between (private) bathroom and (public) living room, and another, scarier, seductive, powerful world that allows these two rooms to collapse dangerously into one another. Victor's bathroom has given Bill a peek at the world of the truly rich in decadent times. It is his passageway into a secret world.

After his exposure to the threatening spaces beyond their domestic life, Bill indulges with Alice, the next evening, in a convulsive conversation that opens a door into Alice's inner life. The way into this world, as it was for her husband, is through the bathroom, where Alice conceals her stash of dope. The treatment from the medicine cabinet leads her to speculate about what goes on in her husband's examining rooms (or rather, in his imagination), and to confess her private sexual fantasies about a naval officer spotted during a past vacation. Just as Alice has finished her account, Bill learns that he must make a house call. From that point forward, his adventures consist of encounters with a side of life in New York that he has resolutely repressed from consciousness, namely sexual and perverse dimensions that are ruled by a spirit that regards itself as outside or above the laws and rules by which "normal" individuals are pleased to regard themselves as constrained. The worlds represented by public living rooms on the one hand and private bathrooms on the other are elaborated, reversed, and fused in the so-called orgy (in fact, a rich men's sex party with prostitutes) conducted in a Long Island mansion and complete with masks, costumes, nudity, and copulation. In this scene, the public world is mockingly exhibited as a cult, while corporeal activities that are commonly hidden away in the private bedrooms and bathrooms are instead staged in drawing rooms, libraries, and, in the final analysis, in culture itself—an image of Kubrick's cinema at large—metaphors for abject or mysterious states of being just beyond the living room. To plumb the abyss is both to sound the corporeal depths and to render them inoffensive and unthreatening through ceramic hydraulics.

Normality and perversity

The bathrooms of *Eyes Wide Shut* are the last in an elaborate and impressive series of Kubrickian toilets and related places and activities. Consider *Spartacus*. The first bathing scene at the gladiatorial school shows the subterranean society of slaves. The trainees wash their wounds and wipe away sweat after the gladiator instructor has attempted to goad Spartacus into striking him so that he can have the contemptuous slave killed. One slave warns Spartacus, and the Ethiopian slave Draba refuses to exchange names with him since they may have to fight each other. We see the dilemma of slavery: Intimacy and alienation are equally dangerous and equally futile. When the black gladiator stirs the slaves to revolt by refusing to execute Spartacus and attacking his Roman captors, we recognize that Spartacus's attempt at intimacy in the bathing scene has inspired rebellion.

The next bath scene shows us the Roman Crassus in a capacious bath in his private estate. The scene is dimly lit for the attempted seduction of Crassus's recently acquired Greek slave boy Antoninus. As Antoninus enters the bath, Crassus attempts to seduce him through recourse to a Socratic discussion in which he contrasts questions of morality and matters of taste. In presenting another contrast, heterosexuality and homosexuality, as akin to a taste for either oysters or snails, respectively, Crassus hopes to persuade the boy by flattering his intellectual pride. His final appeal, as he rhapsodizes over a view of the eternal city, is to the ultimate law: to "serve" and to "love" Rome; to "abase" oneself to it. The apparently repulsive prospect of homosexuality drives Antoninus to leave his comfortable position in a Roman household and join Spartacus's revolt. Ironically, this scene was cut from the movie in 1960 and only restored in the 1990s: In 1960, homosexuality was too threatening even to be condemned, for that would have required representation; instead, it had to be "eliminated."

Within the moral compass of *Spartacus*, bisexuality is aligned not only with unnaturalness and amorality but with Rome, while heterosexuality is conjoined with naturalness, morality, and freedom. Thus, in the scene that follows, we see slave children frolic as they are washed by their mother. All of the innocence of children, nature, and motherhood is on display. The contrast is deepened in a subsequent scene, when we see a rapturous Varinia bathing in a pond, unknowingly watched by her lover, Spartacus. She is reciting poetry she has learned from Antoninus, who, before his delivery to Crassus, had tutored the children of his previous master. It is in this scene, her breasts coyly obscured by a fern and then by a towel, that Varinia tells Spartacus that she is pregnant. The Roman bath is a scene of unnatural, homoerotic seduction; the slaves' open-air bath is natural, free, and even fecund. This outdoor bath, bespeaking the slaves' "natural" aspiration for freedom and their other richly "human" qualities, contrasts firmly with the last major bathing scene in *Spartacus*. In it, we see the Roman senators, like mobsters in a *film noir* sauna, walking about in towels and talking *Realpolitik*. Crassus attempts to seduce Julius Caesar away from Gracchus's populism, but the latter will not be moved. Speaking in the cavernous baths designed for senatorial discourse and relaxation, Crassus once again imagines Rome as the greatest of all things, "an idea in the mind of God." Bathing in *Spartacus* reveals and contrasts. It shows us what people "really" are: democrats or tyrants, straight or gay, natural or unnatural. We see mid-twentieth-century signifiers, but no naked bodies—for these would perhaps undermine the didactic ideology of the film.

The first scene of *Lolita* disposes the palpable stupidities of *Spartacus* immediately. Tracking down Clare Quilty in his disordered mansion, Humbert Humbert wants to make sure of the man's identity before killing him in revenge for stealing the nymphet Lolita. Quilty rises from a chair and surrounds himself with a sheet that resembles a toga. "Who are you," he asks the twitching pedophile, "Spartacus? Come to free the slaves?" Clearly, Kubrick is recording here his view of the film he had been hired to direct, and announcing the beginning of his own signature work. That the heterosexual, natural, free, democratic, and heroic Spartacus should be seen in the furtive, intellectual, decadent, criminal, child rapist Humbert signals to the viewer that he or she is entering a very different cinematic universe. One can easily entertain the idea that the conventional bathroom ideology of *Spartacus* inspires all of the bathroom explorations and deviations to come. Where in *Spartacus* the baths became the central site for moral and political contrasts of the most conventional and ideological kind, in *Lolita*, they are spaces for other, less legible activities: irony, disguise, and writing.

Our first encounter with the Haze *salle de bain* occurs during Humbert's introductory tour of the house in Ramsdale. As Humbert emerges from his future bedroom, we see the bathroom, its door open at the end of the hall. Charlotte Haze leads Humbert to it and demonstrates the toilet, whose "old fashioned plumbing" is likely, she says, to appeal to a "European" (there seems to be a childish pun here: "You're a-peeing"). And it does indeed appeal to Humbert, for it is in the bathroom that he will relieve himself of his passion for Lolita by writing of her in his diary. And it is there that his new wife stakes him out, as Humbert is pinned between the commode with its European *chasse* and the sink, diary in hand.

After their first marital spat, Charlotte draws a bath and wanders into Humbert's former room to discover the diary that he neglected to properly hide. Trying to smooth things over (Lolita has been sent off to Camp Climax by her mother), Humbert makes Charlotte a martini and tries to persuade her that his fervid confessions are the coolest fiction. Unconvinced, she wanders out of the house and into a thunderstorm. When he is then told that Charlotte has been hit by a car and killed, Humbert realizes with pleasure that he is now positioned to take possession of Lolita. The transfer of the child from mother to pedophile assured, Humbert lounges in Charlotte's bath and drinks her booze to the accompaniment of the mindlessly affirmative "Lolita theme." As his illicit beloved becomes his legal daughter, so the privacy of the bath becomes a public meeting place, as Humbert receives his neighbors and friends there ("I'm perfectly decent," the immoralist assures his visitors), including the father of the man whose car struck Charlotte. And just as the bathroom dramatizes the transfer of Lolita from mother to pervert, so it allows Humbert his first glimpse of Lolita's dalliance with Quilty. It is from the "john" (as he terms it) of a service station that Humbert spots Lolita conversing with the driver of a car. Washing his hands furiously, he peers anxiously through the opened window of opaque glass at the next male to whom Lolita will be given—or gives herself.

Perverse security

Love, in *Lolita*, is polarized: It is either frivolous infatuation or profound *Amor*. The polarity is signaled by the contrast between Nelson Riddell's lushly romantic score that we hear during the opening and closing titles and credits, and the "Lolita" theme signaling the spell under which Humbert has fallen. Where in this polarity is the love of nymphets located? Kubrick indicates clearly enough, in the pathetic last scene with Lolita and Humbert, that it goes along with the romantic love-death tradition: Both characters die soon after they part. In *Dr. Strangelove*, Kubrick widens his understanding of perversion, showing how it can lead, beyond an operatic love-death involving individuals, to nuclear holocaust involving the destruction of whole populations. In both cases, these strange loves evade the conventional pathways of romance, family, and children that society provides for eros, and focus instead on the forbidden child and the inhuman killing machine.

The key to *Dr. Strangelove* is the "double-bind," which is Gregory Bateson's term for the breakdown of a behavioral system featuring two contradictory directives.[7] The Cold War quest for security and freedom is one such double bind, and Kubrick shows how the search for security not only supervenes the possibility for freedom but for life itself: The establishment of complete security leads to nothing less than the destruction of the world. In a more defined milieu, the double-bind is manifest in communication technology. Once again, the same paradoxical development occurs: The "perfection" of communication leads to greater and greater barriers to expression. The B-52's "safeguard" against an enemy's "false" or "misleading" communications—the CRM 114—also insulates its crew from urgent and essential communications sent by their own side. The "Doomsday Machine," an array of automatically triggered nuclear bombs intended to deter war, destroys the world because its makers neglect to inform their enemies of its existence.

The bathroom would seem to have little to do with such themes, but Kubrick assigns it a crucial and suggestive role in the film. The bathroom, after all, is a technical solution to an organic problem. It proposes to meet some of the body's needs, but it does so only by insisting that those needs are superficial, disposable, forgettable, shameful, and unworthy of comment. When Col. Butridge (unseen and unheard by the viewer) calls him about an order to attack Russia that has been sent by Gen. Jack D. Ripper, the commander of Burpelson Air Force Base, to a group of airborne B-52s, General "Buck" Turgidson is apparently at stool, though also offscreen. The communication is relayed by his mistress, Miss Scott, but it is also filtered, euphemized, and delayed by her; indeed, the principle parties to this act of communication are opaque to the film's viewer, who neither hears Butridge nor sees Turgidson. Miss Scott informs Butridge that she and Turgidson are "catching up" on some "paperwork" and that he is currently "tied up." (We also infer, from her tone, that Butridge is another of Miss Scott's lovers: She is not only the two men's shared communication conduit but their shared paramour.) When Miss Scott finally reveals that Turgidson is in the "powder room," we cannot fail to reread her clichés as euphemisms, understanding Turgidson's "paperwork" as toilet paper (and its use) and "tied up" as a reference both to the state of his intestines and to the organic constraints that prevent him from rising to take Butridge's call. The bodily needs of the turgid general must be met first, even if he is a critical link in the command–communication structure. (His verbal turgidity interferes with clear communication, as well as thought, throughout the film.) In the war room, perhaps recalling his recent indisposition, Turgidson tells President Merkin Muffley that if the United States joins in Ripper's attack with all its strength, it might be possible to "catch [the Russians] with their pants down." Defecation unifies everyone in a moment of vulnerability that is also a momentary inability to assume the persona of the rational subject of clear and distinct communications. Turgidson's eagerness to exploit this vulnerability attests to a militarized disposition toward anal sadism.

If Buck is turgid, Ripper is fluent, verbally and emotionally. He orders the attack against Russia because he believes that America's "natural fluids" have been tainted by the communist conspiracy of fluoridation (a notion seriously propounded in the fifties and sixties by the extreme right-wing John Birch Society of Southern California). Our bodily fluids can be "sapped" and "impurified" unless we are on call for constant and natural purification. Ripper prefers grain alcohol and rainwater to the water dispensed by bathroom faucet and tub and compromised by the international communist conspiracy. Singing the praises of water to Group Capt. Lionel Mandrake, Ripper celebrates its purgative and cleansing powers, now lost to the communist usurpation of America's plumbing. It comes as no surprise that when he commits suicide (fearing that, under torture, he might reveal the "recall code" that is needed to stop the attack against Russia and which only he knows), Ripper chooses to die in the bathroom. As Mandrake tells him just before we hear the blast of his pistol offscreen, a "wash and brush-up does wonders for a man."

Yielding to necessity

A Clockwork Orange explores the philosophical foundations of the bathroom's symbolic ambivalence. Anthony Burgess's novel, a theological allegory written in an invented English dialect, is concerned with the nature and value of free will. Following an Augustinian interpretation, it insists that man's capacity for goodness is dependent upon his freedom to sin.[8] Free will is given us that we may discover our limitations, above all our inclination to sin, and on the basis of direct experience come to understand our dependence upon divine grace. Attempts by the state or by the professional therapeutic community to "make" people better behaved with incentives, drugs, conditioning, or other such measures are therefore deeply immoral – just as immoral (if not more so) as the wrongs done by those who are allegedly being "improved."

Kubrick's film, by contrast, does not defend free will; on the contrary. In the world Kubrick shows us, everyone is "conditioned" in some way or another, explicitly, implicitly, or by self-interest; freedom of any kind is either a cynical ideology or a self-destructive illusion. The wanton violence in the first third of the film is less a reflection of a deliberate choice than it is the expression of blind impulse. Alex acts not by conscious decision so much as unconscious inclination. That he loves Beethoven suggests, of course, that Alex possesses an esthetic sensibility. But esthetic rapture is for him only a goad to acts of sadistic violence—a markedly primitive understanding. The images we are shown of Alex urinating in a bathroom with yellow décor, and then wandering his apartment while scratching his posterior, like one of the hominids in *2001*, sums up his "subject position" succinctly and exhaustively.

Alex ends up a convict, and the first prison scene takes place in the reception room, where the inmates' street clothes are kept along with a row of tubs. Prison, it quickly transpires, is simply another society with its own incentives, economies, roles, and modes of conditioning. Alex immediately accepts these ways, working for the chaplain in order to curry favor and perhaps gain time off for good behavior. And yet, all his biblical reading, like his appreciation of Beethoven, only serves to conjure visions of rape and murder. He has not chosen to "reform." With Alex, conformity under these circumstances is also an instinct, a conditioning laid down by the body itself, as it were, in the form of its built-in arts of adaptation and survival. The Ludovico treatment too is simply another kind of conditioning, but one that is directed against the self-conditioning that had served Alex well in society and prison because it deprives him of the ability to participate in society's struggle for comparative advantage in the only way he knows how. "Free," Alex wanders the streets of London subject to the vengeance of his victims. They too are bearers of unreflected instincts, having been conditioned by the evils perpetrated upon them by Alex to seek their repetition and reversal. Alex, relaxing in the bathtub at Home, repeats "Singing in the Rain" and so exposes his identity to the right-wing propagandist Frank Alexander, whose wife had been raped and beaten to that tune by Alex and his companions. Alexander, conditioned by this attack to hate Alex, devises a plan to use Alex to advance his anti-government politics but also revenge himself by driving Alex to commit suicide. When the plan fails and the government again conditions (or deprograms) him, Alex is once more "himself." He can again listen to Beethoven and fantasize about rape and murder without discomfort. In allowing the film to culminate with this event, Burgess complained that Kubrick had missed the point of his novel. But Kubrick saw Burgess's point; he simply disagreed with it. For anyone but a Buddha, free will is an illusion. We are always conditioned and controlled, if only to oppose some form of conditioning or another. It is better to accept that, for the price of not doing so is the bitterness that goes with the pursuit of unrealizable and dehumanizing goals and the suffering experienced by those to whom "agency," "deliberation," and "choice" are cynically imputed.

A world of shit

In *Full Metal Jacket*, the bathroom is the "head" of the barracks housing the training platoon on Parris Island. We see two recruits, Private "Joker" and Private "Cowboy", methodically mopping the head's floor, and observe that they have been so well-trained by their drill instructor, Gunnery Sergeant Hartman, that they cooperate in the task without even needing to speak to one another about it. Together they mop, rinse, and move the bucket as necessary with skill, economy, and above all with utter resignation. Their unconscious performance of this labor places it on a par with whatever else one might take to the bathroom for elimination; it has certainly been eliminated from conscious reflection. Only we, the viewers, see it. From the point of view of Joker and Cowboy, they are not cleaning the head but having a conversation about Private "Gomer Pyle," the incompetent scapegoat of the platoon who himself is about to initiate some eliminative activities, and in the appropriate location. Cowboy shows no interest in Joker's concerns about Pyle's mental health, and, giving up, Joker changes the topic of conversation: "I wanna slip my tube steak into your sister," he says. "What'll you take in trade?" "Whadda ya got?" replies Cowboy. The equation of money and feces seems too obvious until we note that we are being presented with a barter economy, not one based on money. Barter being a less developed stage of economic exchange than a money economy, the allusion here is to the primitive, the archaic, the natural, the masculine, and the repressed, and as such it blends effectively with its appearance in what Pyle later (but in the same location) calls "a world of shit." This point is further reinforced by another aspect of the head that the recruits have learned not to see. The rows of toilets that face each other in the head are not separated by stalls or walls, and that, of course, removes any possibility of privacy, thus foregrounding the recruits' natural or primitive equivalence to one another. Even as this material is being released and revealed, however, we cannot forget what Joker and Cowboy are doing, namely removing all evidence of same by keeping the head clean.

From the beginning of *Full Metal Jacket*, we learn that excretion and feces are the central terms in the formation of a Marine. When the men first enter basic training, Hartman informs them that they are "amphibious shit," "pukes," and that even their mouths are "filthy sewers." Hartman threatens to "unscrew" heads and "shit down necks," and to pull out eyes and "skull fuck" the men until they are able to "shit . . . Tiffany cufflinks." (Later, in Vietnam, a senior officer disgusted by Joker's ambivalence toward Marine ideals threatens to take "a giant shit" on him.) The recruits are *both* feces *and* toilet, and their primary task is to become "hard." The recruits must be constantly reminded of the abject facts of organic existence so that those facts can be faced and then manfully overcome and transformed. At the same time, sacred or transcendental values are presented in the basest terms: the Virgin, God, Jesus, and motherhood are all subject to obscene imaginings. The abject is humanized and the sacred is profaned: Like a Nietzschean psychologist of the "human, all-too-human," Hartman must achieve a revaluation of values in order to create his supermen.

The recruits are broken down and remade as Marines through physical and psychical violence mediated by excretory and sexual imagery. The psychical violence is rooted in two expressions of an abject and ruinous existence: toilet and vagina. In order to become "men," the recruits must learn how not to be receptacles for feces or semen. They must become "men" by moving from receptivity to repulsion; they cannot attract, they must only repel. At the same time, paradoxically, they must become receptive to the Marines: "skull-fucked" by Hartman, bedmates to their phallic rifles, and shorn of all private fantasies ("Mary Jane Rottencrotch in her pretty pink panties"), which are to be replaced with the romantic illusions of *esprit de corps* and war.

In this process, Pyle plays the role of feces that can neither be shaped into Marine flesh nor flushed down a toilet, a pile (*Pyle*) of intractable fat and receptive femininity. And yet, his special hell—perpetrated both by Hartman and by his fellow recruits—transforms Pyle into a fighting Marine, very much like another murderer that Hartman holds up as a model Marine, John F. Kennedy's assassin Lee Harvey Oswald. In the final scene of the first part of *Full Metal Jacket*, Joker discovers Pyle in the bathroom late on the recruits' last night on Parris Island. He is sitting on a toilet and loading his rifle, in whose use he has become highly skilled. Joker warns Pyle that he will be in a "world of shit" if Hartman discovers him. "I am in a world of shit," Pyle emphatically replies. Training has driven him mad, like Jack Torrance in *The Shining*, like Ripper, like Alex. Pyle has become an utter primitive, and now consists of nothing but unconscious, automatic actions that have been drilled into him, together with his dumb rage and pain. Like a trained monkey, he stands, performs his rifle drill, shoots his tormentor (who has rushed to the head drawn by Pyle's disturbance, comically clothed in skivvies and hat only), and then, seating himself back on the toilet with an expression that might be either relief or determination, turns his weapon on himself and pulls the trigger—spraying blood from his head all over the Marines' head. We have been well-prepared for this scene, so much so that it is impossible to imagine that Pyle's murder–suicide could have taken place anywhere else. It is quite as if the Marine "Corps" or body has absorbed what was of use in Pyle (primarily, his role as scapegoat to create unity among the other members of the platoon), transformed the rest into waste, and excreted that in the appropriate location. The viewer feels certain that this mess will be quickly flushed out by the next batch of recruits, who will render the head so clean that, in accordance with the late Hartman's standard, "the Virgin Mary herself would be proud to take a dump in it." In a film where the sacred is always in close touch with the profane, Hartman's words should occasion no surprise, any more than his contention that "God has a hardon for Marines."

Monstrous and mystical bathrooms

At the Overlook Hotel in *The Shining*, the bathroom is, more specifically, the *men's room*, and indeed the *gentlemen's* room. No (heterosexual) couples will cross paths here to reveal otherwise obscured tensions, ties, and omissions, as in *Eyes Wide Shut*, but confidences of a more exclusively masculine sort will be solicited and revealed. We are introduced to it when Jack Torrance is led there by a ghostly but substantial waiter from the hotel's Gold Room. The waiter has spilled Advocaat on Jack's jacket, and insists on preventing a possible "stain"—that is, we understand, removing the barriers to manhood and freedom, which Jack nostalgically associates with the good old days of white, male-dominated America. The pristine men's room features two symmetrical rows of urinals, above which on both sides of the room run long mirrors. The mirrors facing each other double the duplicity that, as we have observed, is inherent in the bathroom. At times, Jack's eyes dart away from the waiter, who may or may not be a figment of Jack's imagination, and toward his own reflection in the mirror opposite him. But then, in looking at the "waiter," who is also Delbert Grady, the murdering caretaker, Jack is already looking at himself, since, as Grady says to him: "You've always been the caretaker. I should know, sir. I've always been here." The conversation between Jack and Grady is enacted in a meticulously sculpted, studied, iconic style that is exemplary of the mannerist direction that Kubrick prefers, a colloquy of the imposing allegorical figure of duty and the cowering allegorical figure of abjection. Each of the urinals in the Overlook men's room is flanked, for the sake of privacy, with bright orange moldings, which not only remind us of the instinctual violence of *A Clockwork Orange* but also resemble streams of the blood that have flowed at the Overlook in the past and will flow again once Jack is sufficiently aroused. The orange contrasts boldly with the rest of the men's room's pure white tile, which is like the racial purity of the men of power whose rule went unquestioned *avant le déluge* of the sixties that prefaced the initial Overlook rampage of 1970.

At the manifest level, however, this bathroom shelters neither murder nor holocaust nor drugs nor sex, not even urination or defecation, but only the cleansing of a minor blemish—and a provocative conversation between a servant in black tie and tails and a former schoolteacher and failed writer who dreams of the privileges once accorded to wealth, whiteness, and masculinity. The servant fawns at first, reminding Jack that he is "the important one" and confirming the "wisdom" of his banal utterances. Jack enjoys an opportunity for false joviality, slapping Grady on the back and colloquially getting on a first-name basis with him ("Whadda they call ya round here, Jeevesy?") in a melancholy display of artificial bonhomie. Here the bathroom may seem to support a ritual of equalization, in which men whatever their social status or financial position are forced, penis in hand, to acknowledge their basic sameness before nature if not God. In reality, the bathroom is performing its function of supplementing the actual individual with a cosmetic persona, as Jack becomes a rich white man delicately catered to by a servant who knows his place and among whose duties is that of going along with the *pretense* of equality and mutual respect—a pleasure, that of condescension, reserved for the powerful. The bathroom's hygienic, supplementary, doubling function is, however, quickly superseded by its other aspect as a place where refuse is perhaps safely disposed of but also dangerously revealed, indulged, and concentrated. Jack identifies the "waiter" as the caretaker–murderer Grady, but the waiter, abandoning his servile manner, firmly rejects this identification, insists that *Jack* is the caretaker, and then takes the lead in the conversation by informing Jack of his son's disobedience and encouraging him to act on his rage against Danny and Jack's wife, Wendy. When Jack leaves the Overlook's men's room, his "stain" has been removed, but he has not relieved himself. Instead, he has acquired a heavier load of unconscious and uncontrollable urges, resentments, and prejudices that should more properly have been "eliminated." When Jack comes after his wife and child, it is to the bathroom of their living quarters that they flee. When he places his face through the hole that he has hacked in the door with an axe, Jack announces his appearance with the tag "Here's Johnny." Ed McMahon's signature introduction of *John*ny Carson, the host of NBC's *Tonight Show* almost from its beginnings until 1992 and a paragon of white male normality, authorizes Jack's breaking into the John.

But there are other, more mysterious bathrooms in *The Shining*. Indeed, the bathroom might very well be the crucial space in the movie, for it is there that one enters the maze of nonlinear time and post-Newtonian space: It becomes an uncanny and visionary site. Thus, it is in the bathroom, while brushing his teeth, that Danny has a psychic experience that puts him in touch with events at the Overlook while his father is being interviewed for the caretaker's job. Danny sees torrents (*Torrance*) of blood and the murdered Grady girls, and passes out from shock. When the family arrives at the Overlook, they are given a tour of the hotel and of their tawdry living quarters—including the bathroom. When Wendy sends Jack to search room 237, where Danny claims a woman has wrung his neck, he undergoes a psychic experience of his own. Jack sees a figure bathing, the bathtub curtain half closed. A naked young woman steps out of the tub and the two embrace. But during the embrace, the young woman suddenly becomes old and ulcerous, breaking into laughter at Jack's revulsion and fright. She then reimmerses herself in the tub. Like a Buddhist or Christian fable of human transience and the futility of desire, Jack's vision indicates a posttemporal perspective: The bathroom is a passageway beyond the present moment but is nonetheless inflected with the paradoxes of waste and hygiene, remembering and forgetting, fear and desire.

Taken together, these scenes outline incursions into temporality from the atemporal. Why should this mystical passageway be located in the bathroom? Because it is the passage to the subterranean world of *materia abjecta*, and also the redeeming site where human bodies can be relieved of their connection to that world and enjoy, at least momentarily, a buoyant freedom from corporeal necessity. Even so, while the bathroom sees to the voiding of the abject, it cannot help also being a monument to it, symbolizing it through the implications of its contrastingly opposed terms: glass, metal, white plastics, and ceramics. In *The Shining*, corporeality, the past, violence, dependence, and constraint are one by one overcome by the metaphorical technology of the bathroom: eliminating, purging, forgetting, correcting; but they return via the same route. At first, only Danny sees the torrents of blood that gush, as filth gushes from a ruptured sewer main, from the elevators of the Overlook and all that it represents. Then Jack sees them, and finally Wendy does. By the end of the film, all the repressed, expelled, and forgotten have returned, and time itself is no longer past. It has come gushing back in torrents, like a backed-up john—or Jack.

Illusion and necessity

Barry Lyndon focuses not on the denied abject but rather on the refined arts and conventions of English landscape and portraiture. Everything is depicted in a gorgeous and leisurely manner, much as if a gallery of paintings had come to life. But if the film is a series of *tableaux vivants*, it is also an unsparing analysis of corruption—the innate corruption of the mores of the time, and the particular vices acquired by Redmond Barry as he climbs the social ladder. In a film devoted to the claustrophobic stasis and entrapment that is suggested by eighteenth-century landscape and portrait painting, the bathroom is merely noted, not explored. We see Lady Lyndon, following her discovery of her husband's dalliance with a servant, bathing in a partially closed tub while a servant reads to her in French. Wearing an open, transparent gown, she is naked and dressed, private and public. Into this cloistered chamber, Barry intrudes—not unlike the neighbors in *Lolita*—to offer his apologies and regrets. Where Humbert must conceal his joy, Lady Lyndon gratefully accepts Barry's apologies, and they kiss. Again, viewing this scene in light of the other films' more extended explorations of the bathroom allows us to find in it a new depth, as it calls to mind everything that is denied in human relationships but that must inevitably, one day, spill out. In this context, the scene offers a muted foreshadowing of Lady Lyndon's eventual madness, self-destruction, and ultimate captivity at the hands of her son, Lord Bullingdon.

According to a long tradition, everything having to do with necessities imposed on human beings by virtue of their being embodied must be hidden away in the private realm, and only expressions of freedom, choice, independence, agency, and power are permitted to see the public light of day. This logic, one that denies or denigrates all that is blindly compulsive and acknowledges and celebrates conscious agency alone, is both normative and, as Kubrick's cinema chronicles, enormously destructive, though perhaps unavoidable. Kubrick's work explores the costs, in psychic self-mutilation and pain inflicted on others, of this denial. In it, the imagery of the bathroom is exploited in order to foreground elemental and recurrent themes concerning intractable polarities of the human condition: consciousness and the unconscious, reason and organic embodiment, will and instinct, individuation and species-being, immanence and transcendence, freedom and necessity. Even more surprisingly, Kubrick is able to turn the "utopian" pretensions of the bathroom in a direction that allows it to figure the desire for (or illusion of) transcendence and transfiguration. Considered as a unitary device running through his work from 1960 to 1999, Kubrick's bathrooms assumes a depth, significance, and expressiveness that makes one want to look upon them not as a mere set or settings but as virtual characters and even as a symbolic order in their own right.

Identifying the major uses to which Kubrick puts the imagery of the bathroom makes it possible to fully appreciate the more restrained appearances of this trope in his *oeuvre*. In *2001*, Dr Floyd calls home from a space station in orbit around the earth. His wife is out and the babysitter is—in the bathroom. Floyd is forced to ask his small daughter to deliver news of his whereabouts to his wife, and so, as in *Dr. Strangelove*, powerful technologies of communication yield to the vagaries involved when a message is to be relayed by an unreliable third party because a more mature subject was compromised by biology. We are reminded, as we will be throughout this part of *2001*, of the similarities rather than the differences between prehistoric ape-men and twenty-first-century scientists. Accordingly, on his way to the moon, Floyd visits a "zero gravity toilet" and is stymied by a plaque of lengthy instructions in fine print. When Dr David Bowman arrives, at the end of a virtually inassimilable experience, at the mysterious chambers where he will live out his life in a rapid montage, and very much like anyone's first encounter with new living quarters (and like other Kubrick protagonists such as Humbert, Jack, and Hartman), he comically seems most keen to inspect the bathroom first. Bowman finds a coldly immaculate room that feels very much as if it were designed to specifications by creatures who had no need for or understanding of such a space. Like a sarcophagus, the bathtub gleams in unreal light, menacing in an eerily unspecific way. Considered generally in the light of Kubrick's bathrooms, these moments, slight as they are, are seen to contribute powerfully to *2001*'s ambivalence toward technologies that are valued because they seem to deny or suspend elemental features of human corporeality.

3

Time

While modern literary artists may have approached time skeptically because the linguistic medium is so clearly conventional, artificial, and steeped in the linearity of the sentence, film artists approached it with a marked duplicity. The film medium, at least with respect to each continuous shot, is a physical record of space and time. An individual film is, however, a purely artificial construction of an experience of time. Cinema nevertheless eclipsed the "realism" of nonmechanical media and produced a "reality effect" that drew on the objective authority of photography. Cinema masked this disparity through the rhetoric of realism, drawn from conventions of the novel and theater, which created an illusion of the unfolding of real events in time. It is this duplicity, the reality effect and the dream effect, of cinema that makes it such an attractive and a deceptive medium.

The fascination exercised by verbal, theatrical, and plastic media is modulated to some extent by the evident conventions and artifice of print, staging, and tradition. The fascination of cinema is less modulated, not just because of the virtual immediacy of photography and phonography, but because all of us have grown up internalizing cinematic convention. Even the most fabulous film narrative is accompanied by a reality effect that acts to objectify and justify it to viewers who would never give themselves to a narrative or dramatic poem. Perhaps, the chief pleasure that the reality effect justifies is an escape from our ordinary sense of the relentlessly linear nature of time. A film lasting 120 minutes can relate a narrative lasting a week, several years, a lifetime—or, in the case of *2001*, 2 million years, and "beyond." Cutting and montage is the cinematic technique which accomplishes this escape from the tedium of linear time to a poetics of juxtaposition. It is the forgotten gaps in time that entice and liberate us. The reality effect justifies and even dignifies these pleasures.

Watching a film, then, is in effect a virtual experience of time dismantled and translated by a poetics of fragmentation and juxtaposition. Films can eradicate dead time through montage and give us the spiritual pleasures of timelessness. They can also insist upon time and immerse us in a time that seems not to move at all. Kubrick's films can race through time or reveal it in all its leaden deliberateness. When Dr Frank Poole goes outside *The Discovery* to retrieve the AE 135 Unit, the audience becomes extremely conscious of time. The sound of his breathing, the absence of dialog and music, the slowness of his movement—all these give us a pure, undistracted perception of time as incremental progression. The realistic or documentary aspect of the scene foregrounds the dimension of time and throws it into contrast with limitless space. Indeed, throughout *2001*, Kubrick subjects his audience to a nearly unprecedented experience of the elasticity of time: from a 2 million year jump or match cut to elaborate, explicit, and nearly static scenes. Thus, at the end, the "time" of David Bowman's life in the baroque suite of rooms is absolutely indeterminate. Do the cuts edit out minutes or decades—or centuries? In this dialectic of montage and linearity, time appears to be real and unreal, inescapable and arbitrary.

Kubrick's films thus exploit the medium of film and create a reality effect—not to justify fiction, but to relativize time and to promote an intuition of alternative kinds of order and vision. We see that time, rather than being an absolute standard of narrative order underlying the scenario, has been formally reimagined and thematized. Although few directors are as concerned about verisimilitude, consistency, and detail as he is, Kubrick's films are less "realist" than "critical" acts of mimesis. Kubrick both draws us into his world and reminds us that it is a world, not *the* world.

Time as pure chronology is a meaningless progression; time as illumination occurs in moments, or stilled time, when the film accomplishes a synthetic moment of insight. Thus, narrative in Kubrick's world is often a scheme of conceptual variations leading to an epiphanic conclusion: the whirlwind of cash in *The Killing*, the bullet-riddled painting in Clare Quilty's mansion in *Lolita*, a chain of nuclear explosions in *Dr. Strangelove*, the astral fetus in *2001*, Jack Torrance in the photograph from July 4, 1921, at the end of *The Shining*, Marines marching in darkness and singing the anthem of the Mickey Mouse Club in *Full Metal Jacket*. Thus, even the purely conventional three-part arc of *A Clockwork Orange* and *Barry Lyndon* come to a conclusion in summary steps outside of time: the one-legged Barry Lyndon stepping out of a coach into the frozen-frame of a cinematic painting; the deconditioned Alex imagining himself making love to a girl in the snow, surrounded by an approving audience—dressed in the height of Regency fashion.

Fictions of linear time

Kubrick's account of a horse track heist in *The Killing*, his first fully accomplished film, is organized by a nonlinear sequence of scenes, each punctually timed by an authoritative-sounding narrator. Kubrick explained that he and his producer James Harris "weren't worried about fragmenting time, overlapping and repeating action . . . It was the handling of time that may have made this more than just a good crime film."[1] The question then is: What is it about "overlapping and repeating action" that turns a genre film into something more? Although *The Killing* initially appears, despite its structure, to be firmly rooted in time and narrative authority, the viewer begins to see that the failure of the heist is the result of a naïve commitment to time as a knowable and measurable medium.

The Killing works familiar film noir material, a race-track heist pulled off by a ragtag collection of outcasts and criminals that goes wrong in the end. But Kubrick and James Harris wanted to treat this material in a novel way, by presenting the failed heist from a number of different perspectives and starting times, within the strict organization of an overall fixed timeline. Not only was Kubrick picking up on Orson Welles's deconstructive narrative perspectives in *Citizen Kane*, he was showing that there are other forms of suspense than the straight-telling of story that can end either with success or failure. *The Killing* arouses suspense not just to "find out what happens," but "to know what happens"—to delve into the complex working of many fallible people trying to work together—much like a film crew—to accomplish a common goal. *The Killing* provides the familiar trappings of the film noir world, but then it cinematically "thinks" about them, goes over them, tries to discover, by retracing its steps, the point where things went wrong. Each time we see the starting gate wheeled into position for the Seventh Race, the thinking begins again. In doing so, Kubrick discovered a curious pleasure aroused by the repetition of a scene—it is as if the film presents itself as a rehearsal for something that finally cannot be represented. Where forward moving scenes teach us to forget, repetition allows us an opportunity for contemplation and detached esthetic pleasure—an escape from time.

Kubrick's attention to the mysterious nature of time is evident in *The Killing*, yet there seems to be a joke being made about the possibility, or even the value, of exact chronology. Much of the narrator's noting of time is needlessly precise and seems to have no real consequence. The Saturday, a week before the heist, the narrator notes the precise time (3:45 p.m.) when Marvin Unger makes a bet and passes a message to George Peatty about the gang's meeting. The rest of the day's activities are as minutely recorded as the day of the heist. That day, strangely, the bartender at the track, Mike O'Reilly, picks up the flower box with the rifle inside at a bus station locker. The narrator notes that the time is 11:29 p.m. Clearly visible in two different shots is the face of a clock above the doorway: It is completely blank. [In *Killer's Kiss*, shot on location in Manhattan, there are clear discrepancies between the time of the action and the time on the city clocks in full view.] Why is this clock blank? Is it to recall time outside the story? Or does it anticipate the fact that time is already up for Mike and the others, since Sherry has already tipped off Vince, and Vince will come gunning for the gang? Whatever the reason—and it could be purely trivial—the blank face of a clock throws the film's time consciousness into doubt. Is it a search for truth or the expression of anxiety?

In fact, the suspense is tightened, not with respect to a particular moment of truth, but through a hyper-consciousness about time and nervousness about its movement. Kubrick shows the preparations for the Seventh Race, the $100,000 Added Landsdowne Stakes, four times, to further tighten the sense of anticipation—unless it is to suggest a mind going over and over again the failure of the scheme. In a sense, the dramatic concentration on exact time is a red herring. The gang members have, as the narrator knows, already been killed or arrested, and the greenbacks have already been blown all over the Los Angeles International Airport. The face of the clock is blank, and the title of the film reverts from its metaphorical meaning—a huge financial success—to its literal meaning, the killing of everyone involved in the caper, except for Maurice and Johnny. While human beings subject themselves to the relentless movement of time recorded or invented by machines, the movies can suspend, repeat, reverse, and anticipate that movement. Since *The Killing* has no particular perspective on the events it depicts, what unfolds is the curious freedom that ensues from the undoing of chronology.

In *Paths of Glory* and *Dr. Strangelove*, Kubrick would observe and exploit the intrinsic drama in an approaching deadline—the execution of the three scapegoats, the detonation of the doomsday machine—by intensifying the tragic and the satirical potentials of time determined by inhuman mechanisms such as clocks and cybernetic systems. The dictatorial nature of alienated time falls into a significant contrast with cinematic time. We see, then, Kubrick working against the forward-moving rhetoric of cinematic realism toward a cinematic poetics that, in an implicit way, is also a critique of alienated, or machine, time.

Of course, all films are made by eliminating insignificant time and juxtaposing a nonlinear sequence of dramatic or significant scenes. In Kubrick, we see that the very texture of the films and scene sequences is suffused with temporal elasticity. In Kubrick's films, "time" is no more immune to critical representation than the "family," the "nation," "manhood," "love," and other familiar themes. Time is not a given in these films; it is a projection or a cinematic reification of personal and cultural attitudes toward human identity, freedom, and mortality. As the media and meanings of these concepts change, "time" changes and in so doing becomes "visible."

Thus, *Barry Lyndon* unfolds a sumptuous account of the life of a social climber according to the opposite technique of forward moving narrative, giving the illusion that we can understood his ultimate failure in terms of temporal progression. Working silently against this reliance on time as a revealer is Kubrick's photographic and painterly spatialization—slow zooms from a single figure to a panorama—and a worldly narrator who misjudges and frequently anticipates the action. In this way, time is annulled by space and we see that Barry's aspirations in the prerevolutionary climate of eighteenth-century Europe lack a temporal medium for realization. The "slowness" of *Barry Lyndon* is a manifestation of eighteenth-century decorum and hierarchical rigidity that is most explicitly presented through a focus on architectural symmetry, formal gardens, spas, and military formations.

The ritualized time of the duels that drive Barry's fortunes—first as a love-struck boy, then as a heartless collector of gambling debts, and finally as a tyrannical stepfather—is a case in point. The time of the duel opens up a space for movement off, up, and down the social ladder. In the last duel with Lord Bullingdon, as Nelson has observed, Kubrick allows nine minutes to elapse (out of the film's 185 minutes):

> For the first time in *Barry Lyndon*, screen time and "real" time are brought into conjunction. Barry's journey through the byroads of his ambition and into the dreamy parlors of splendor now ends in the existential actuality of time.[2]

If the leisurely perusal of landscape and architecture slows time down as a reflection of the dominance of social space in prerevolutionary Europe, the duels—which can punctuate or accelerate social movement—are revealed in dead or real time. In both cases, time would appear to be insuperable.

By contrast, the increasingly shorter shifts between the time cards in *The Shining* show us a culture in crisis, a culture in which patriarchy and time have become fragmented and cast adrift. Castle Hackton makes way for the Overlook Hotel. Rather than having a mellow and reflective narrator as in *Barry Lyndon*, *The Shining* is framed by cards—"The Interview" and "Closing Day" to "A Month Later," "Tuesday," "Thursday," "Saturday," "Monday," "Wednesday," "8 am," "4 pm," and finally a photograph dated July 4, 1921. The five weeks of action is treated in increasingly frequent but longer time segments as Jack Torrance's madness deepens. "The Interview" panel, which includes Mr Ullman's meeting with Jack, Danny's consultation with "Tony" and the Doctor, as well as Wendy's, takes up over 14 minutes. While "Closing Day" takes up over 16 minutes, the next month is skipped over. The next week is treated in about 15 minutes, while the last Wednesday is given over 38 minutes. The events between 8 a.m. [Thursday] and the events after 4 p.m. are granted 18 minutes and 45 minutes respectively. Although there is nothing unusual about the dramatic treatment of time, Kubrick's scheme draws our attention to it, suggesting there is more involved than the battle between a devouring father and his wife and son: Time itself is the devourer and Jack's homicidal rage is driven by an escape to escape from it. Consequently, time as objective and linear progression is gradually supplanted by space, as the past of the Overlook Hotel becomes present – at which point Jack Torrance steps outside of time into space.

So in *Barry Lyndon*, we see the spatial rigidity and deliberateness of the eighteenth century headed toward the ruptures of 1789—the date is noted in the last scene—and the discovery of the Napoleonic dynamisms of time, revolution, and social crisis. In *The Shining*, we see a world in which authority collapses and reverts to patriarchal violence. Time, in other words, is in crisis and finally yields to the pure space of the Overlook Hotel, where past, present, and future are always present.

Eyes Wide Shut prepares us for a paradoxical experience of waking time suffused with dream time: A chain of serial sexual temptations plays out before Bill Harford but none of them can be (or are) acted on. The reiterative dialog and pauses indicate that the "time" of the film is speculative, unreal, and oneiric. What made this texture difficult for some critics to recognize is that Kubrick refused to present a waking frame story. [Fritz Lang does this in *The Woman in the Window* (1944), a film with a similar theme; the result trivializes the dream story.] Time in *Eyes Wide Shut* has no authority or motive, except as a medium for the revelations of the unconscious. In filming Schnitzler's *Traumnovelle*, Kubrick discarded the rhetoric and urgency of dramatic time for the dream time of pure cinema.

The romance of the closed circle

With *Fear and Desire*, Kubrick began his feature film career by opting out of time and history altogether. This archetypal study of "man" positioned between fear and desire, insight and aggression, is introduced by a narrator, speaking from a point of timeless and esthetic disinterestedness, who informs us that the drama is "outside history." The opening shot of a forested mountain side is repeated once the drama is completed, stressing the existential and irremediable nature of the human condition. Time as a medium for transformation or insight has been tied into a circle: The three days and two nights of the narrative of the men's struggle to return home and to reconcile themselves to their own finitude are absorbed into an endless and archetypal cycle.

This closed circle is inflected by romance in *Killer's Kiss* and *Lolita*. Both begin at the end of the action and come round to the same point and then resolve the story: Davy begins his narrative in Penn Station, waiting to see if his girlfriend Gloria will join him as he escapes from the corrupt city for the innocent West of his childhood. As he tells his story, however, Kubrick's directing overtakes it and presents it from different perspectives. The doubling of Davy and Gloria is established not only by their apartments and their jobs, but by a temporal synchronization. The first night they leave their apartments for boxing ring and dance club at 6:50 p.m. They vaguely acknowledge each other outside the apartment building and head into the labyrinth. He ends his narrative as she suddenly appears at Penn Station, ready to escape with him. *Lolita* begins with Humbert stalking Clare Quilty and ends, after the narrative of his failed quest to possess his faithless nymphet, with his exacting revenge on her faithless lover. Despite their quite different conclusions, these dramas present romance as a closed circle. They recycle endlessly without ever pointing to a life beyond New York City or Quilty's mansion.

Ellipsis

Kubrick's most distinctive structural device is the juxtaposition of discrete temporal and topical panels, a persistent ellipsis with or without establishing cards. *2001* is organized according to temporal displacements, the effect of which is to isolate and then abandon characters and settings without further explicit reference. The hominids in the first panel are suddenly replaced by Dr Heywood Floyd and other upper-level technocrats, who are in turn abandoned and replaced by Bowman, Poole, and HAL. The overall concern is not with characters but with concepts and archetypes, with the nature of time, conceptualization, technology, and transcendence. *Full Metal Jacket* falls into three largely discrete panels: Parris Island, Da Nang, and Hue. Only Private Joker, the narrator, appears in each sequence, but his own development does not dominate the narrative. The focal conflict in the first panel is between Private Pyle and Sergeant Hartman, and Pyle and the platoon. In the Da Nang panel, the tension is established between the official line on the Vietnam War and its lived reality. Since Private Joker is a marine journalist, he is squarely placed between two versions of reality, and opts typically for an ironic remove from it. In the Hue panel, Joker and Rafter Man join a new platoon as reporters, with only Cowboy as a link to Parris Island. The thread of Joker's education brings the film to a conclusion. Once the platoon has wounded and surrounded a lone female Viet Cong sniper, only Joker is willing to put her out of her misery, and so he is finally formed, educated, and unafraid—such are the costs of autonomy in Kubrick's world. We can see, then, that the narrative per se is less important than a conceptual movement across different settings, changing characters, and modulating themes. Kubrick's most significant and radical exploration of this structure takes place in *2001*. Here juxtaposition eclipses narrative and yields a novel kind of cinematic poem that takes as its theme the discovery of time, the discontents of linear time, and the realization of what may lie beyond it.

Kubrick's form and ambition in the film can be aligned with the modernist dismantling of linear form. In his manifesto for Imagist poetry in 1913, Ezra Pound claimed that the essence of poetry is the "Image" and its motive is an escape from time into a "space" of esthetic contemplation:

> An "Image" is that which presents an intellectual and emotional complex in an instant of time . . . It is the presentation of such a "complex" instantaneously which gives us that sense of sudden liberation; that sense of freedom from time limits and space limits; that sense of sudden growth, which we experience in the presence of the greatest works of art.[3]

Drawing on Ernest Fenollosa's *The Chinese Written Character as a Medium of Poetry* (1918, 1936), Pound elaborated Imagism into a poetics of juxtaposition that became the atemporal structural principle of *The Cantos*.[4] Film directors such as Sergei Eisenstein and René Clair meanwhile realized that cinema was a hieroglyphic or "ideogrammic" medium that realized in the boldest way the potentials of such a modernist poetics of image and juxtaposition. Governed by the modernist logic of montage, *2001* is composed of four discrete episodes: "The Dawn of Man," an unnamed second section set in 2001, a third section "18 Months Later," and a final section, "Beyond the Infinite." These cards were added only after an initial screening of the film, when for once Kubrick lost his nerve and worried that the discontinuities in the film were too confusing—at least to the MGM executives. (When *The Killing* was previewed, Sterling Hayden's agent complained that the time shifting made the film difficult to follow. Kubrick then recut the film to chronology, did not like the result, and then re-recut it to its original form.[5]) Of course, the most remarkable of these montages—the cut from the bone thrown in the air by the exultant hominid Moon-watcher to the orbiting nuclear satellite—required no verbal gloss. In this montage and in the final panel "Beyond the Infinite," we see the boldest manifestations of Kubrick's cinematic poetics of nonlinear time.

Although the film is called a "space odyssey," it is more profoundly a time odyssey, starting with the timeless or cyclical lives of early hominids. Time is brought about through the discovery of the tool/weapon which transforms them into *homo faber* and *homo necans*. The rupture of timelessness and the discovery of the linear confinement by time are presented in purely Imagist terms: The bone hurled into the air is, so to speak, teleologically realized by the orbiting satellite (a nuclear weapon, according to the screenplay and the book). The montage of bone to satellite, in other words, jumps two million years of human time and introduces a vision of a technological utopia—or so it first seems. The technological wonders choreographed to the Strauss waltz soon begin to pall as we see the empty human beings confined and bored by their artificial worlds. What seems like an escape from timeless tedium into historical progress soon looks like a repetition of stubborn human violence: The satellite remains a bone.

After Capt. Bowman has dispatched the cyclopean HAL and becomes the commander of a death ship, he is drawn, like his predecessor Moon-watcher, to a communion with the monolith. Trapped as he is by the purely technological vision of time embodied in digits such as 2, 0, 0, 1, Bowman finds his escape from time-bound existence. In this final panel, Kubrick has moved from nonlinear narrative to a kind of anagogy: The "world" that Bowman sees on his journey through the "star-gate" is both a journey back in time to the origins of the universe and a journey ahead in time to his own death and rebirth.

How can a visual artist accomplish a representation of whatever lies beyond the infinite? Thomas Allen Nelson writes:

> for a start, he can undermine the authority of "objective" temporal structures—that is, the continuities of plot, character, dialogue, narration—and require, as Kubrick does, an audience to scan his images and sounds for an associative or symbolic logic.[6]

Kubrick, in a sense, had to abandon linear narrative for metaphorical or ideogrammic form. The puzzlement that this panel has long caused derives from an understandable attempt by viewers to situate it with respect to the linear narrative of the preceding panels. But it is different in kind from them. It is not strictly the continuation of the narrative, but a leap, via image and music, from temporal determinism to poetic thinking (and being). Thus Bowman's Odyssean return or *nostos* occurs in the Imagist terms of a psychological confrontation with the abyss that the monolith can be said to concretize. The fall into time accomplished by brute technology is now reversed by an imaginative identification with the abyss—out of which a stream of poetic figures emerges. Bowman's aging, death, and rebirth occur in the poetic realm of imagistic juxtaposition in which time, paradoxically, has shed its temporality. His impersonal return to earth as an "astral fetus" is a return to timelessness, but one quite different from that experienced by his hominid ancestors: It is a fearless identification with the abyss which they had shrunk from and sought to escape. In terms of physics, the star-gate can be understood as a passageway from Newtonian space and time—fixed and distinct dimensions—to Einstein's space–time. In cinematic terms, it is a passageway from linear narrative to poetic simultaneity, from metonymy to metaphor, from descriptive realism to anagogic totality.

2001 has a unique position in Kubrick's canon. Not only does it present an overarching vision of human civilization within the broadest possible context, it also establishes the "ground" of time in timelessness. It treats time as a reification accomplished by tools and the world schemes that they bring about. The temporal inflections in his other films each develop particular visions of time as a representation of different stances toward the challenges of existence. Mechanical time such as that supposedly represented by clocks is only one kind of time, one especially useful for a world regulated by computers. The madness of the infallible computer HAL and his homicidal rampage tell us much about Kubrick's attitude toward human attempts to realize absolutes. Thus "time" is not "distorted" by subjective experience or the exigencies of cinematic narrative: We actually see "time" slowing down or speeding up, jumping ahead, jumping back, and finally dissolving into timelessness.

4

War

No other human institution is so reviled and celebrated as war. It has consequently generated "anti-war" films, patriotic films, and films that attempt to represent the tragic necessity of war as a defense of (the audience's) civilization. Kubrick's war films are characteristically different: They are neither antiwar nor pro-war; nor do they imagine that war is a mere instrument for the maintenance or defense of civilization. For Kubrick, war is the complementary face of civilization: its founding institution and its ideological sustainer. It is, at the same time, the art and science of bringing bodies into lethal collision. In fact, Kubrick's films reveal war to be a central expression of civilization, not an aberration from human or civilized values. War is less an institution for the protection of civilization than it is the founder and extension of civilizations—as well as their destroyer. It is, one could say, a kind of lethal custom that has directed and mirrored civilization's development, both its social orders and its technology, from the first hominid wars to our much-imagined nuclear apocalypse. War and civilization are caught up in a generative and destructive polarity.

Indeed, Kubrick's war films provide a satirical anatomy of war, tracking it from its origins in prehistory to its final self-destruction in post-history, dramatizing each salient moment in its history. The energies of war, alien to any kind of inherent order or ideology, assume through history progressive guises or manifestations forming and reflecting human society: the first hominid wars rooted in primary and uninflected violence, the courteous death machines of classical war—in which lines of infantry march slowly and methodically toward their enemies' ranks before firing, all in the service of idealized notions of the State; the industrialization of modern war in the slaughter of some 10 million soldiers between 1914 and 1918; and the post-human robotics of the Cold War through which the entire population of the earth is "protected" and "endangered" by Mutual Assured Destruction (MAD) by nuclear warheads. Through all these manifestations, a "strange love" of war and death can be detected beneath or behind the idealized rationalizations offered by warring states.

Kubrick does not, then, like John Ford, Steven Spielberg, and countless others, depict (and sometimes celebrate) war as a necessary mechanism to "save" or "defend" civilization against barbarism. Rather, Kubrick is concerned to show that "barbarism," in the guise of the war machine and its culture, is the driving, constructive–destructive force within civilization. Again and again, Kubrick dramatizes in the harshest terms the transformation of recruits into soldiers, of men into machines, of citizens into agents of State violence. Likewise, Kubrick does not simply decry war in the tradition of the "anti-war" films of directors like Lewis Milestone (*All Quiet on the Western Front*, 1929), Ernst Lubitsch (*The Man I Killed*, 1932), and Jean Renoir (*La Grande Illusion*, 1937), by appealing to human brotherhood.

Rather, Kubrick's anatomy, although it is never didactic, has a philosophical consistency and trenchancy. It accepts the premise offered, for example, first by Thomas Hobbes that war is the normative human state:

> Hereby it is manifest that during the time men live without a common Power to keep them all in awe, they are in that condition which is called Warre; and such a warre is of every man against every man.[1]

Even less dark theorists of human nature have seen war as an inextricable element of civilization. Kant, Hegel, Deleuze and Guattari, and Victor David Hanson all claim that war forms and expresses civilization. It is not merely instrumental or alien from civilization, but part of its internal logic. War not only repels the outsider, it constitutes the insider—and yet these sides remain locked in polarity. War could be called a violent eruption or exhibition of the State's perpetual war on the freedom of its own subjects or citizens. Similarly, technologies devised to wage war slide easily into "peacetime" uses: All sophisticated modern forms of transportation, communication, and computation were immeasurably assisted by the preparations and practices of war, from the American Civil War through the Cold War to the so-called War on Terror. War has driven technology from the beginning, and without technology, it would be difficult to imagine anything like modern, Western society, with all of its technical advantages and comforts.

There is so much sentimental talk about war that it may be useful to consider what some great enlightenment thinkers have had to say about it. Kant believed war to be a natural energy indispensable to the development of civilization. In his *Idea for a Universal History with a Cosmopolitan Intention*, he concludes, however, that this formative role played by war is finally to be discarded once mankind has accomplished a complete rationality that will usher in "perpetual peace": "*The means which nature employs to accomplish the development of all faculties is the antagonism of men in society, since this antagonism becomes, in the end, the cause of a lawful order of this society.*"[2] This conclusion would indicate that war is an inevitable and necessary expression of any society not completely free of emotion, prejudice, and desire. Hegel believed that war is necessary not only in the formation of the State but for its continued vitality. In *Elements of the Philosophy of Right*, Hegel argues for war's salutary effects on the (German) State. Reluctant to assent to any Kantian cosmopolitan world achieved through rational renunciation, Hegel saw in "perpetual peace" the threat of stagnancy and corruption:

> War has the higher significance that by its agency, as I have remarked elsewhere, "the ethical health of peoples is preserved in their indifference to the stabilization of finite institutions; just as the blowing of the winds preserves the sea from the foulness which would be the result of prolonged calm, so also corruption in nations would be the product of prolonged, let alone, 'perpetual' peace."[3]

For Kant and Hegel, then, war is not the obscene embarrassment it has become to contemporary liberal thought. They see it as an expression of civilization as it currently exists, even as they both point ahead to a state of rational or spiritual transcendence in some distant future.

Two contemporary views of war will provide further context for Kubrick's anatomy.

Gilles Deleuze and Félix Guattari, in their *Treatise on Nomadology—The War Machine* (from *A Thousand Plateaus*, 1980), find in the origins of war something positive and liberating. According to them, war is an invention of what they call "the nomads," primordial peoples who operate without reference to rationalizing justifications. The nomads' practice is a kind of unregulated energy and thought which is ultimately appropriated by the barren and stultifying force of the State, which is an essentially inauthentic institution. For Deleuze and Guattari, the nomads and the war machine that they invented were appropriated by State abstractions that they have never accepted:

> . . . the State acquires an army, but in a way that presupposes a juridical integration of war and the organization of a military function. As for the war machine in itself, it seems irreducible to the State apparatus, to be outside its sovereignty and prior to its law: it comes from elsewhere.[4]

The nomads' practice of war has no foundation in universalizing notions of the good and of justice: These are the locutions that the State invented in order to control the nomadic forces and to ground itself:

> . . . the nomads have no history; they only have a geography. And the defeat of the nomads was such, so complete, that history is one with the triumph of the States.[5]

For Deleuze and Guattari, then, the "sides" in a war are themselves at war: There is a cultural and an ideological conflict between the warriors or nomads and the function that they have in the machinations of the State. The first are guided by atavistic notions of individual courage and honor, the second are guided by baseless principles of advancement and advantage. In Kubrick's films, this theme is often treated in terms of the war between "officers" and "men," agents of the State and the de-territorialized nomads who have been drafted or enlisted into an alien or arbitrary cause.

A contrary view is provided by the noted historian of war, Victor Davis Hanson. Hanson argues instead that the drafted, enlisted, and mercenary soldiers who have always formed Western armies are reflective of the highest or signal ideals of their societies. The Greek hoplites that defeated the Persians had a

> sense of personal freedom, superior discipline, egalitarian camaraderie [and] individual initiative . . . The peculiar way Greeks killed grew out of consensual government, equality among middling classes, civilian audit of military affairs, and politics apart from religion.[6]

Hanson believes that "the polis . . . was innate in all Greek soldiers." Subsequent Western armies all "drew on elements of western culture to slaughter mercilessly their opponents."[7] Where Deleuze and Guattari believe that the nomads express primordial energies that are regulated by the State for alien purposes, Hanson argues that Western "men" are not simply engines of war but agents in their own right and allied with State characteristics.

Kubrick shares the unsentimental views maintained by Hobbes, Kant, Hegel, and Deleuze and Guattari. He satirizes the idealized view of Western apologists like Hanson through bringing it into conflict with the views of the nomads themselves. In *Full Metal Jacket*, a purely nomadic expression of the America's casus belli in Vietnam is provided. It is not to "save" South Vietnam for "freedom," as Rafter Man says tentatively. "Flush out your head gear, new guy," Animal Mother tells him. "You think we waste gooks for freedom? This is a slaughter. If I'm gonna get my balls blown off for a word . . . my word is 'poontang.' "

Hominid war

According to Lawrence H. Keeley, historians of war have too often assumed that early human beings lived a kind of Rousseauvian idyll. His archaeological researches have led him to assert that early men instead lived in a Hobbesian state of "warre." *War Before Civilization* presents material evidence that war is not an aberration brought about by the State but is an essential element in human nature.[8] Kubrick's "Dawn of Man" reveals a brutal world of oafish violence. Out of this "warre" of "every man against every man," violence drives discovery and social transformation. *2001* locates the origin of human imagination, socialization, technology, and the war machine in the same moment—when the hominid called Moon-watcher, inspired by his confrontation with the Monolith, uses an animal bone as a weapon against a neighboring clan. Violence here has entered a new phase, since it is delegated, as it were, to a tool—and much will follow from it: clubs, spears, swords, catapults and finally muskets, artillery, jet bombers, and nuclear warheads. This epochal moment in human development has a grimly comic aspect: Kubrick shows us how after his discovery, Moon-watcher—once a worried and imaginative semi-human—discovers a new identity as a warrior. The bone becomes not only a weapon, but a sign of dominance, not only over the enemy but over his own "men." Thus, the *bâton de commandement*, the inaugural feature of tribal and military dress, is established as a symbol—to which, in time, would be added helmets, armor, braid, ribbons, medals, sashes, riding crops, boots, and the like. But at the moment that Kubrick depicts it, the war machine appears without a single remnant of State rationalization, and it has no purpose other than clearing space for itself. Driving the enemy clan from the watering-hole, Moon-watcher has invented war. From this moment in hominid history to 2001, Kubrick's hyperbolic cut implies, nothing conceptually comparable has occurred: Human history is the history of war.

Classical war

In *Spartacus* and *Barry Lyndon*, Kubrick explores what we can loosely call classical war, war organized according to conventions and rules of engagement that appear, from the perspective of modern war, to be quite mad—because they are so reasonable. The Roman Army and the European Armies of the eighteenth century practiced war according to a kind of ceremonial or theatrical logic according to which violence is staged as a form of polite engagement: largely level ground, open space, an appointed time, and perfectly ruled lines of infantry march toward one another and death—the Romans wielding sword, spear, and bow, the British and Prussians armed with muskets. These armies operate like a preindustrial mechanism—a clock, a mill, or a sailing ship; all of its parts are organized to a single unified effect. They march toward one another like dancers at a cotillion. Subjectivity—fear, dread, despair—is supplanted by the collective force of the State and its unified goals. As the two war machines become meshed, destruction and discipline are equally in evidence, as if the participants had agreed that war and civilization were so intimately related that it is unthinkable to engage in one without the other. Even so, nomadic warriors labor beneath the weight of State rationalization so considerable that violence and death are transformed into a kind of political calculus—which comes into its own only in the twentieth century.

Spartacus shows how an army of freed slaves—a contradiction in terms—engages the Roman legions. It is as if the slave army led by Spartacus were a kind of return of the repressed, a war machine motivated entirely by its own survival, while the Roman legions fight to maintain State myths and prerogatives. When Spartacus captures Glabrus's legions, he breaks his baton (the symbolic descendant of Moon-watcher's weapon), shoves the pieces into the coward's jerkin, and sends him back to Rome to report his defeat. Later, Crassus is enraged by Spartacus's refusal to address him after the noble Roman has divined his opponent's identity. Glabrus and Crassus can see in Spartacus natural nobility, a nomadic dynamism that undermines their code of Roman nobility.

It is a curious convention of popular cinema that ancient Rome—whether as Republic or Empire—should be presented as corrupt, decadent, and under constant challenge from the virtuous and the weak. *Spartacus*, produced by Kirk Douglas and representative of Cold War liberalism, follows this tradition, but instead of dwelling on Christian heroics, according to convention, it treats a rebellion of gladiators, one century before Christ, who go about Italy liberating slaves to form an army and a kind of nomadic slave State. The Roman institution of gladiatorial theater can be seen, in terms of our discussion, as a localized exhibition of the "exteriority" or "ungovernable" nature of the war machine. Republican Romans can, within the confines of the State, revisit the nomadic origins and shadow of their civilization at their coliseums and stadia. What is a casual, if gripping, experience for the Roman audience is of course utterly real for the gladiators, who fight to the death. When the Nubian turns his lance on the Roman party visiting Batiatus's gladiatorial school and inspires the rebellion that Spartacus will later lead, it is as if the war machine in all its ungoverned violence has sprung up alongside the State. The war between the slaves and the Republic of Rome thus takes on a quite different significance. It is not simply a war of liberation for Spartacus and his army of slaves and camp followers; it is a war between the State and its own war machine—the people. *Spartacus* concerns itself only with Roman aristocrats, soldiers, and slaves: There is no dramatic role for the plebeians. The decadent and bisexual Roman General Crassus in engaging Spartacus—bold, illiterate, a patriarch-in-the-making—is also engaging the primal energies of Rome's own past, the nomadic sources of the State. From gladiatorial school to slave "general," Spartacus is formed by violence and the organization of violence: His shadowy kingdom of slaves rises out of the battlefield.

The final engagement between the armies of Rome and Spartacus's slave army is a neat expression of the conflicting values of abstraction and pure corporeality. On a plain in southern Italy, the two armies meet, while two other Roman armies stand waiting in the wings. Crassus's army is organized in classic Roman geometries: two rows of squared men with a front line marching on Spartacus's men, who are massed indiscriminately behind their own lines. Crassus sits on horseback behind his legion, while Spartacus chafes before his. As the Romans march deliberately forward, the slave army unleashes its secret weapon: long rollers of flaming pitch (this weapon has no basis in history). After a few moments of misplaced optimism in the ranks, the former slaves simply rush into the disciplined ranks of Roman soldiers. The Romans are then joined by the two other Roman Armies—and a rout ensues.

In a souvenir program provided at the premiers of *Spartacus*, Douglas and Kubrick provided documentation for the battle tactics they had filmed: "This motion picture shows, for the first time in film history, the maneuvers which conquered the world."[9] The brochure went on to describe in some detail the Roman cohorts "fighting in robot formation."[10] The Roman legion, cohorts, maniples, and centuries were designed as a human mechanism, designed to allow 75 minutes of rest for each 15 minutes of combat, a cohort (360 men) being able to fight for a total of ten and a half hours. This instrument of State prestige dominated because it transformed human passions into "robotic" routine. In contrast, the slave army was infused with human passion and operated according to guerilla tactics, and was easily defeated. Yet insofar as the slave army is an expression of human agency and nomadic spontaneity, their defeat is an honorable one: They represent, however sentimentally, the democratic masses celebrated by the Left throughout the twentieth century.

Barry Lyndon provides Kubrick with a second opportunity, now on his own terms, to deal with the formal esthetics of classical war. According to Clausewitz, "War is nothing but a duel on an extensive basis."[11] Kubrick would have taken this claim to heart in shaping *Barry Lyndon*, a historical drama concerned with war, dueling, gambling, and courtship. Dueling with pistols is a test of marksmanship but perhaps more of nerve, especially considering the unreliability of the weapon. This kind of confrontation, like classical war, requires one to "receive" fire without fleeing or firing—a challenge to accept fate. So in this way, dueling is a nice metaphor for controlled violence, the requirements of honor, and of course the play of chance and necessity. Classical war, like gambling, dueling, and courtship, maintains decorum in the context of a large element of chance.

As a young man, Redmond Barry is a spirited idealist who is put to flight by a duel with a British officer, Captain Quin, who has come to Ireland to find a wife. Barry enlists in the British Army, after having been robbed of his mother's fortune, and learns that a soldier in the eighteenth century is nothing like a subject or an agent; he is little more that a cog in the war machine. His youthful heroics—challenging the British officer to a duel—look quaint from the perspective of a cog in the classical war machine. The narrator of Kubrick's film makes clear the nature of the military, its romance, and its reality:

> It is well for gentlemen to talk of the age of chivalry; but remember the starving brutes whom they lead . . . It is with these sad instruments that your great warriors and kings have been doing their murderous work in the world.

Kubrick presents Barry's first "skirmish" with the French Army during which the British Redcoats—"those sad instruments"—march in perfect files into the French fire. The narrator comments dryly: "Though this encounter is not recorded in any history books, it was memorable enough for those who took part." The war machine, organized by the brutalities of training, is indeed a single entity, not a collection of individuals, and it moves without hesitation, well aware that there is no "glory" awaiting them should they fall. As Thomas Allen Nelson observes:

> Barry becomes imprisoned within a military geometry . . . [that] shows how eighteenth-century warfare maintained its formal aesthetics even at the expense of human life and tactical sense.[12]

The code is everything, for it is not only a formal expression of the Age, it is a tactical device. Maintaining the geometric fixity and timed dynamism of the advancing files will result in victory, if the opposing line cannot match it. Tactics are one thing, strategy another, the casus belli yet another and transcends whatever strategic and tactical purpose there may be for the war and any particular battle. Barry and the narrator have no claim to understanding it: "It would require a greater philosopher and historian than I am to explain the causes of the famous Seven Years' War in which Europe was engaged." Insofar as the war was one of the last before the French Revolution, its tactics and motives were analogous: It was about the rigid maintenance of all social codes rooted in hierarchy.

The war machine, in other words, is more an expression of State prestige than the dismal facts of death, survival, or victory. In Barry's case, it is the death of his friend and countryman Captain Grogan that leads him to desert the ranks. By chance and stealth, Barry steals an officer's uniform and mission as a messenger and assumes his identity. No longer an Irish conscript in the British Army, he becomes "Lt. Fakenham," but then marches straight into the Prussian ranks.

Kubrick's picture of the geometrical formation of the army as a mirror of its service to State abstractions of identity and value acknowledges the resistances of the nomads. Barry, although he has no interest in the causes of the war, is hardly an exemplary trooper. No sooner is he in the army than he complains about the rations and boxes another soldier. He carries off his friend Grogan from the field, instead of marching on into the French fire.

Like Spartacus, Barry Lyndon is made and unmade by the practices of war. Born into slavery, the illiterate Spartacus improbably becomes a political philosopher, a slave general, an orator, and an ideal family man. Born into the Irish yeomanry, Redmond Barry becomes a British gentleman and a wealthy one, but in the end, loses everything. Barry can achieve and maintain his individuality and temporary social prominence only by becoming a nomad and a stranger to all States. Within the aristocratic orders of the Roman Republic and eighteenth-century Europe, war is construed not simply as an instrument of State power but of State prestige. War is an expression of social logic, a representation of its hierarchy, codes, and deadly courtesy.

Modern war

Kubrick's screenplay for his unmade film *Napoleon* would have made the transition from classical war to modern war hinge on dynamism. The narrator explains the transition this way:

> Napoleon now introduced a new era of wars of maneuver. Everything would be sacrificed to mobility. The complicated battle formations of the18th century would be abandoned, and the army freed from clumsy baggage trains. War would be made to feed on war. The armies opposing him were still committed to the rigid ideas of the previous era, and their soldiers were treated as automatons. As they could not be trusted to forage for themselves without deserting, such armies were slowed down by their supply trains. The revolution, on the other hand, had produced an army of intelligent citizens, which could move fast by living off the country, and in which courage and initiative were rewarded by promotion.[13]

But this ideal of rational, as opposed to classical, war proved no more tenable than the utopian ambitions of the Revolution. The Great War may have begun with a dynamic movement of men and materiel, but it soon ground to a halt with the construction of trenches and a new kind of war. But even then the railroad was essential in bringing men to the trenches—as well as providing week-end furloughs for officers in Paris and London.

If classical war is absurdly rational and human in its style of engagement and display, modern war is merely rational and inhuman. The magnificent uniforms of the Romans, French, British, and Prussians promote their deadly activities as an expression of noble sentiments and florid abstractions of nation and class. The enlisted men of the Great War were dressed practically for the duties at hand. They were laborers in a factory of death, scuttling through rat mazes—filled with mud, water, and excrement—absorbing shell fire, and occasionally leaping out onto the battlefield to endure the fire of their supposed enemies from the opposing trench. The General Officers of the French Army, by contrast, are magnificently arrayed in capes, caps, and riding crops, and are thus suitably attired for their exertions far from the battlefield. With the coming of modern war, however, the rhetoric of war—the open battlefield, the rules of engagement, the codes of dress—is supplanted by a deadly calculus of mechanized killing. It is here that *Paths of Glory* accomplishes its most chilling exposition of war and its effects.

Based on a true account of the trial and execution of French enlisted men for cowardice during World War I, *Paths of Glory* is widely interpreted to be an "anti-war" film. It was also so powerfully critical of the French Officer Corps that it was thought to be "anti-French." Certainly that is the way the French government saw it, since it did not license *Paths of Glory* for exhibition in France or its dominions until 1974, nearly 20 years after its release. But, as John C. Tibbetts and James M. Welsh argue in *The Encyclopedia of Stanley Kubrick*, *Paths of Glory* and Kubrick's other war films are too complex and elusive to be called simply "anti-war."[14] It would be more accurate to say that *Paths of Glory* uses the theme of war as a representation of civilization. We could equally well claim, then, that *Paths of Glory* is an "anti-civilization" film.

It is well to remember that *Paths of Glory* preceded the histrionic idealism of *Spartacus* and that the "men" who fill the trenches are supposedly "free" French citizens, the inheritors of the Rights of Man won by the Revolution. Largely the descendants of the French peasantry, these free men have been "drafted" into service to the State. But the result of battle is determined by masses not individuals, algorithms not courage: Hundreds of thousands of lives deployed produce hundreds of yards; 8,000 dead motivate a General's promotion. War as practiced in the trenches is a matter of masses of men organized by timetables, artillery, and statistical probability. Dubious at first about the possibility of taking the Ant Hill, Gen. Mireau changes his mind once Gen. Broulard has dangled a promotion before his eyes. Once his personal advancement is factored in, Mireau accepts the mission, devises his disastrous battle plan, and explains it to Col. Dax:

Dax: What sort of casualties do you anticipate, sir?

Mireau: Say, five percent killed by our own barrage. That's a very generous allowance. Ten percent more in getting through no-man's-land and twenty percent more getting through the wire. That leaves sixty-five percent with the worst part of the job over. Let's say another twenty-five percent in actually taking the Ant Hill. We're still left with a force more than adequate to hold it.

Dax: General, you're saying that more than half my men will be killed.

Where classical war is organized according to a geometric logic, modern war draws on the nascent sciences of statistics and systems theory. It is a matter not of lines and formations but of masses and movement. Thus, if the men can be made to move on time in a certain direction and the artillery fires accurately within acceptable parameters, the planned result should be achieved—if the plan has not been drawn up by a "fool" like Gen. Mireau.

The conflict dramatized in *Paths of Glory* is not, then, between the French and the Germans. Indeed, not a single German soldier appears on the screen (although the extras forming the French Army were all German policemen). The conflict is between the French Command—represented by the social life and polished manners at the Chateau—and the enlisted men—represented by the subterranean but material world of the trenches. (This is a spatial organization that *Spartacus* will repeat: The gladiators are confined to subterranean cells; the free men walk above them.) The conflict is between the State's Commissioned Officers and the "men" drafted or recruited from the "masses," between the ahistorical abstractions of "France" and "Glory" and the existential fact of human bodies and death.

As Alexander Walker observes, "Only by implication is *Paths of Glory* a protest against war as such; it is much more pertinently an illustration of war as the continuation of class struggle."[15] Yet, as Frederic Raphael observes, the film "neither called for the overthrow of the ruling class nor did it advocate the brotherhood of man, in the facile style of Jean Renoir's *La Grande Illusion.*"[16] Rather, it gives its audience a nearly intolerable experience of polite and fatal hypocrisy.

What is striking about *Paths of Glory* is the clarity of the conflict between a completely corrupt Officer caste and an innocent and largely admirable enlisted caste. Only Col. Dax, the humanist, can touch both sides of the divide. Kubrick's direction makes this situation cinematically palpable through the ceremonial activities in the Chateau and the violent exertions in the field and in the trenches. The camera work in the castle is calculated and static; the camera work in the trench is dynamic, rousing, and frightening. When we see Dax dealing with Mireau and Broulard in the Chateau, his energies are curtailed, his anger confined—until the end—to questioning remarks and suggestive tones. When we see Dax in the trenches before the assault, he is like a dynamo. The camera tracks him from the front, showing his fully cognitive awareness of the scene around him. It then shows us his point of view of the shelling, the men clearing room for his passage, the gathering smoke, and the ominous combination of fear, dread, and readiness. Four times Kubrick alternates between Dax's point of view and the camera's frontal view of his intelligent, deeply concentrated attention. The contrast with Mireau's earlier tour through the trenches is striking, emphasizing the distinct differences between the static platitudes of the State and the dynamic intelligence of the war machine.

When the action switches from the battlefield to the Court Martial, the viewer can see how war is conducted according to the rules of the State. The Court is indeed "Martial," a ruthless machine directed to the conviction and execution of three "examples" of "cowardice." When the State wages war on its own terms, ceremony and theater dominate and the mitigating facts that Dax provides for his men are irrelevant: The State cannot see or hear. The Brigade is assembled in the neoclassical garden before the Chateau and stand at attention as the three men are shot down after proper words from Church and Army. At breakfast, and before Broulard reveals that he will face an inquiry because of his illegal order to fire on his men, Mireau applauds the "splendor" of the execution.

Guerilla war

The Cold War provided Kubrick with two subjects, guerilla war as explored in *Full Metal Jacket* and nuclear war as imagined in *Dr. Strangelove*. In both films, the range of war is extended beyond classical and modern war to include civilian populations, all according to a philosophical difference between two economic and political systems. In this sense, these two films elaborate and extend the conflict in *Paths of Glory* between the abstractions of the State and lived reality. In *Full Metal Jacket*, every human being in Vietnam is, so to speak, drafted into an army of citizenry, insofar as they are either sympathizers or allies of the Viet Cong, North Vietnam, or the United States and South Vietnam. In *Dr. Strangelove*, everyone on the planet is enlisted into a war in which whole populations serve as targets, and finally will perish when the secret Soviet doomsday machine is triggered. But just as the earth's human population is drafted into service, so the State apparatus is no longer limited to its officers and executives: It is now located within the irreversible and mindless actions of a computer-operated technology, a technology symbolized by Dr Strangelove, a neurotic intellectual confined to a wheelchair. When, at the end, Strangelove "can walk," we witness the final accomplishment of war's autonomy.

While the enlisted men in *Paths of Glory* are invested with a certain traditional dignity, the men in Kubrick's film of the Vietnam War reflect convulsive changes in American society during the sixties. The men of Lusthog Squad, having discarded their civilian names, style themselves as they please and form an army of nomads. Like the liberated slave army in *Spartacus*, they are free to fashion their own identities according to their own codes or whims. The marine uniforms, helmets, and weapons all bear indications of their own particular interpretation of war. Animal Mother's helmet states: "I am Become Death," Krishna's words as cited by Robert Oppenheimer at Los Alamos. Joker's helmet affirms his genesis: "Born to Kill," but a peace symbol is also attached to his jacket. Together they affirm, Joker tells the pogue Colonel, "the duality of man." They are "life-takers" and "heart-breakers." The Lusthogs reject State platitudes and affirm their own policy statements and commentaries. The tradition of military regalia—at its peak in the ornamental excess of the uniforms of classical war—is all dismissed as so much nonsense. The nomads invent their own "uniforms" in deeply personal and idiosyncratic ways. In this way, they implicitly reject their role as agents of the State.

War in *Full Metal Jacket*, as in *Paths of Glory*, is waged by the State against its own citizens, and then against the enemies of the State. As in *Spartacus*, *Barry Lyndon*, and *Paths of Glory*, though never in such detail, Kubrick explores the ways in which human beings are remade according to the dictates of a post-human machine. *Full Metal Jacket* benefits from the relaxed censorship of post-sixties' films and so is able to demonstrate the ways in which the physical, sexual, alimentary, excremental aspects of the human body are the constant targets of shaming so that in the end, the human body is refashioned into a transpersonal, molar, metallic formation.

Although the war in Vietnam was predominantly a guerilla or counterinsurgency campaign waged in the rice paddies and jungles, the battle of Hue City is the climax of *Full Metal Jacket*. Once again, the presumed setting of a Kubrick film flips, from the expected jungle dramas of *Platoon* and *The Deer Hunter* to the city. The Vietnam War becomes World War II. Private Cowboy tells a television reporter:

> When we're in Hue . . . when we're in Hue City . . . it's like a war. You know like what I thought about a war, what I thought a war was, was supposed to be. There's the enemy, kill 'em.

The guerilla war—the word itself playing off of an unspoken bestiality of hominid wars—yields to the apparent clarity of "there's the enemy, kill 'em." While they have been trained according to clear-cut abstractions of polar opposition of "us" and "them," the enemy in Vietnam had proven unclearly defined.

Marching into Hue City, they seem finally to have discovered the kind of war they knew from films and television, presumably of World War II. Cowboy presumes that the fire that cuts down Eight Ball and Doc Jay must come from a large force concealed in the gutted buildings they are trying to clear. Animal Mother goes in against orders to rescue the men, when he determines that there is only one sniper. Despite the asymmetrical nature of the war, it still comes as a surprise to the men and the audience that the sniper decimating the platoon is a single, young woman. Since the men's training had been based on escaping or repressing the shame associated with effeminacy and softness, their hardened response to the sniper brings the film and the war itself into focus. Vietnam, "the pearl of the Orient," and Hue City, a French-influenced city on the banks of the Perfume River, are defended against a troop of American men by a lone girl with a rifle. It is as if the real war has been supplanted by a communist propaganda poster—or a well-observed critique of an American propaganda poster.

Even as the men of Lusthog Squad attempt to recover the nomadic warrior's immunity to ideology through their jargon, dress, and signage, they confront a guerilla army that has no State, although they aspire for one. The Viet Cong, although their supposed enemies, are more properly their ideal—a de-territorialized rout of nomads. As Crazy Earl explains to the new guys Joker and Rafter Man before the battle:

> I love the little Commie bastards, man. I really do. These enemy grunts are as hard as slant-eyed drill instructors . . . These people we wasted today . . . are the finest human beings we will ever know.

The code of the nomads transcends any kind of State abstraction: what is respected is individual capacity and endurance. The Officer caste, oftentimes their enemy, is fighting a quite different war. According to the "poge Colonel":

> We are here to help the Vietnamese, because inside every gook there is an American trying to get out. It's a hardball world, son. We've gotta keep our heads until this peace craze blows over.

While the Colonel's views are satirically expressed, they are a more or less accurate paraphrase of anticommunist US policy. The nomadic grunts operate with a range of ad hoc "policies," but their deepest motives are the oldest—the warrior cult of solidarity.

Nuclear war

According to Peter Sloterdijk, the central characteristic of modernity is "explication"—the unfolding or manifestation of the implicit dimensions of the life world. He finds this explication at work in the arts, product design, and war. Explication in war, for Sloterdijk, begins with the gas attacks in World War I, is industrialized by the Nazi death camps, and culminates, at least for now, with nuclear war: In this arc, he observes how the atmosphere, air itself, is weaponized through chemical and physical technology. The atmosphere, which was once the invisible and implicit bearer of life, unfolds its destructive potential. The explication of the air becomes the medium of terror into which all organisms are drafted as strategic targets:

> The fact that the dominant weapons systems since World War II, and particularly in post-1945 US war interventions, are those of the air force, merely betokens the normalization of the state-terrorist *habitus* and the ecologization of warfare.[17]

The weaponization of the environment accomplished by nuclear bombs comes in two stages: the fire-burst that consumes physical structures and the fall-out that turns the atmosphere into poison. The first "explicates" matter and releases its energies; the second "explicates" breathing itself as a medium of suicide. While the vaporizing capacities of nuclear bombs remain, nevertheless, characteristic of previous weaponry, fallout drifts beyond strategic control into a weapon of amorphous terror. For this reason, Sloterdijk considers modern war essentially a form of terrorism because it explicates the life world into a death world. Thus, the subtitle of *Dr. Strangelove—Or How I Learned to Stop Worrying and Love the Bomb*—amounts to a recognition that in a world universally subject to "terror from the air," our only response is a tragic or a satiric one.

Dr. Strangelove is the central and culminating expression of Kubrick's vision of civilization and war as equivalent—and equally transient. We have seen the movement from Moon-watcher's discovery of the first weapon and tool for social organization through its Roman, British, Prussian, French, and American manifestations, constantly increasing in scope and complexity. At the start of *Dr. Strangelove*, we see a B-52, loaded with nuclear bombs, being refueled. We see radar dishes scanning the atmosphere for signs of trespass. We see Air Force Base billboards, posters, and signs asserting that "Peace is our Profession." A vast web of surveillance, communication, and nuclear response has covered the earth, no part of which is removed from the theater of total war.

The Strategic Air Command (or SAC) operated from 1946 to 1992, from the beginning of the Cold War to the end, when it was dissolved and its mission reorganized and reassigned. Its original mission statement, as formulated in 1946 by General Carl Spaatz, Commanding General of the US Air Force, is a strikingly ambitious one:

> The Strategic Air Command will be prepared to conduct long-range offensive operations in any part of the world, either independently or in co-operation with land and naval forces; to conduct maximum-range reconnaissance over land or sea, either independently or in co-operation with land and naval forces; to provide combat units capable of intense and sustained combat operations

> employing the latest and most advanced weapons; to train units and personnel of the maintenance of the Strategic Forces in all parts of the world; to perform such special missions as the Commanding General Army Air forces may direct.[18]

This mission statement was reduced and widely distributed as a motto—"War is Our Profession—Peace is Our Product"—and an emblem: a mailed arm and fist gripping a lightning bolt. In order to accomplish this mission, SAC would have to become the most sophisticated and far-reaching technological interface in human history, joining world surveillance, communication, transportation, and destruction. The megalomaniacal ambition of nuclear war culture was fully in keeping with Sloterdijk's view of explication: It revealed life itself, the earth and its atmosphere as an enormous weapon—directed at itself. All of life was nothing more than a war machine, and the biosphere a thanato-sphere. The strategy of MAD made this official government policy.

Not everyone was happy with MAD. General Curtis Le May, especially in the early years of the Cold War, saw the benefits of Preemptive War (for some reason, this strategy was never granted the acronym PEW). Le May, the model for Generals Jack D. Ripper and Buck Turgidson, believed that a swift and unexpected attack on the Soviet Union would result in American victory and global hegemony, albeit at the cost of millions of civilian lives and global nuclear fallout, what would later be called Nuclear Winter—with darkened skies, lowered temperatures, and the poisoning of the earth.

Dr. Strangelove is a kind of thought-experiment meant to play out PEW. When General Ripper initiates Wing Attack Plan R, the vast, interlocking system of SAC becomes an entity of its own, resisting civilian and military communications of a counter order, forcing SAC to make war on itself by attacking its own bombers. Only one B-52, due to the "initiative" of its pilot Major Kong, manages to deliver its payload, and so trigger the Soviet Doomsday machine and the destruction of life on earth—with the exception, as we have seen, of a select core of elites and their descendants who will descend into mineshafts and wait out the 93-year half-life of the cobalt thorium G shrouding the earth.

While the men in the war room plan the accommodations of their mineshafts—Dr Strangelove observing that women would have to outnumber men in order to propagate a new race and would have to be chosen for their sexual attractiveness—Turgidson foresees a problem. If the Soviets stock more mineshafts than the Americans, they will, when the radiation poisoning has dissipated, be able to gain an advantage and assert world domination. "Gentlemen," he warns, recalling John Kennedy's bogus 1960 campaign claim that the Soviets had more missiles than the United States, "we cannot allow a Mineshaft Gap!" Like their hominid ancestors, the elite children of the mineshafts will emerge to wield weapons, once again, against their neighbors—and so build new, if not different, civilizations.

Archetypal war

The narrator of *Fear and Desire* places the story that is about to unfold beyond time:

> the enemies that struggle here do not exist unless we call them into being. For all of them, and all that happens now is outside history. Only the unchanging shapes of fear and doubt and death are from our world. These soldiers that you see keep our language and our time, but they have no country but the mind.

Despite its claims to universalism, the film derives from post-war existentialism and Freudian and Jungian psychology: War is a manifestation of deeply seated psychic demand. We war against projections of our own demand for violence and so commit a symbolic suicide.

Each of the four men in *Fear and Desire* thinks of the war in terms that reflect their own social position and psychology. The officer in charge, Lt. Corby, a lofty ironist who has done a lot of reading, treats their situation as if it does not affect him. He uses verbal formulations to repel the reality of their dangerous position behind enemy lines. The non-commissioned officer Mac mocks the Lieutenant's pretentious phrases and in his blunt way confronts their situation physically. The war for Corby is an existential epiphany; for Mac, it is a last chance to act significantly, to accomplish "something" before he returns to a civilian life of repairing washing machines. When Mac comments sarcastically about the privileges of the enemy General they plan to kill, Corby comments tartly, "This is no time to be a revolutionary." So, an element of this war outside of history is the conflict between officers and enlisted men—and the class allegiances across enemy lines. The other men, Fletcher and Sidney, represent poles of genuine detachment and frantic, neurotic engulfment. Where Corby aspires to philosophic remoteness from their situation, Fletcher is genuinely thoughtful, deliberate, and considerate. Most of the trouble in the world, he says, comes from people who need to be important. In this, he is the opposite of both Mac and Corby. Sidney aspires to a humanist engagement with the enemy, but it is he who assaults and murders the fisher girl they have captured. For the four of them, the war has no political or philosophical significance. It is nothing more than a particular manifestation of the dilemma of being-in-the-world.

Both sides are, in the end, presented sympathetically, but also as mirror images. Following the intense partisanship and enforced patriotism of the thirties and forties, and the incipient ideological pressures of the Cold War, *Fear and Desire* attempts to reconcile enemies—not from the vantage point of a proud and pacific brotherhood—but from the perspective of universal violence. When Lt. Corby and Fletcher shoot the enemy General and his Captain, they recognize each other as doubles. The wanderings of the General's dog Proteus underscore the links between the two sides. Early in the film, he has wandered off and tries to befriend the four soldiers, but they send him off with a thrown rock. He is welcomed back by the General whimsically, but when he is shot, the dog laps up his blood. These linkages across the immaterial enemy lines undermine whatever purposes the two States had in pursuing the war. When the film ends, Corby and Fletcher have to reconcile themselves with the fact that they and the enemy are locked into an embrace of mutual identification.

Although Kubrick never revisited the existential, archetypal allegory of *Fear and Desire*, his subsequent war films indicate that beneath the historical surfaces, from prehistory to imaginings of the future, an unchanging armature can be found. Time and again, the films are structured by a kind of a flip where the enemy changes identity and/or the premise of the action shifts. In *Paths of Glory*, the French assault on the German Ant Hill leads to the trial and execution of innocent French enlisted men. Cinematic space shifts from the battlefield to the courtroom. In *Barry Lyndon*, the young Irishman Redmond Barry enlists in the British army and then the Prussian Army. The cinematic space of the battlefield, where life and death are largely determined by chance, shifts to the card table and the gaming room. In *Full Metal Jacket*, the Marines are at war with the Viet Cong, the North Vietnamese Army, as well as themselves: On graduation day from boot camp, Private Pyle kills his Sergeant and himself. Later, the cinematic space of the Vietnamese jungle and rice paddies is supplanted by ruins of the City of Hue: Guerilla war becomes a battle between a sniper and the Lusthog Squad. Sergeant Joker kills the Viet Cong sniper and, with her, the last remnant of his own psychic complexity. In *Dr. Strangelove*, military culture and technology trigger the Doomsday machine: fail-safe devices and protocols trigger the destruction of the biosphere. These flips or switches indicate the elemental and ever-present play of polarity in war and civilization. Kubrick's anatomy never strays from this iron law.

5

Light

Modernist writers, painters, and composers created some of their characteristic effects by drawing attention to the media of language, image, and tonality and then reinventing them. Joyce, Picasso, and Stravinsky not only created works of art, they made critical interventions in their histories. Their contemporaries working in films had a quite different situation: They had first to invent the medium of their art. They had to find a way to transform staged reality into a dynamic medium of narrative and expressive photography. They had to find a way to make light—like the word, the image, tonality—into an objective medium. By mid-century, Hollywood pictures especially had firmly established a code and technology of affective realism that enjoyed worldwide admiration and loyalty. Like the modernists of an earlier generation, Kubrick set about to turn this medium into a subject for dramatic and esthetic reflection and expression. For Kubrick, like other great directors, light is not only the medium of photography, it is the medium of illumination.

A. R. Fulton provides a fundamental distinction between "arbitrary" and "natural" lighting. "Arbitrary" lighting schemes use light that is "not represented as originating in a natural source, such as a lamp, a fire, or the sun shining through a window, but [is] cast flatly for the purpose of obtaining a clear picture."[1] Arbitrary lighting is thus independent of the setting and its theme: It suggests, if only subliminally, that cinematic "reality" is likewise arbitrary, which is to say unmotivated. By contrast, "natural lighting" is motivated by its position within the frame, "originating or seeming to originate from a natural source."[2] Classic three-point lighting became so established by the mid-century that its reality effect became pervasive but also trite. The audience always knew, if only in a half-realized way, that it was watching events enacted in a studio or in a highly conditioned location. "Natural lighting" could not be an end in itself because any lighting regime that is consistent becomes increasingly artificial and finally "arbitrary." In his films, Kubrick strove neither for purely arbitrary nor natural lighting: It had always to be actually observed and felt, whether it appealed to the audience's sense of empirical reality or to its emotional appetite for beautiful, uncanny, or menacing atmospheres.

Windows

When Kubrick began directing in the fifties, most American films were extremely well-lit by artificial light sources that could not be justified by the scene being photographed. It was a convention that insured an attractive and glossy look but which was often lacking in mood, atmosphere, or realism. Film noir was the exception, using as it did chiaroscuro effects derived from Rembrandt, Caravaggio, and German expressionism. Limited to the underworld of the modern city, noir lighting scheme worked mainly as a marker of the genre and the fundamentals of moral choice.

Citizen Kane, which inspired some of the noir sensibility, was of course not a genre picture. And this was what Kubrick learned from Welles: Lighting, in order to be more than arbitrary or natural, has to be disassociated from genre. *Citizen Kane* is about a wealthy young man who takes up journalism for the fun of it, the question finally becoming, is Kane a crook who controls and deceives the masses—a fascist, a communist—or just an "American"?

This thematic quandary is established in Welles's lighting contrasts—especially the formal and thematic motif of light pouring through windows into darkened rooms. The most striking example is the scene at the Walter Thatcher Library where the reporter Mr Thompson is seated at a large table and presented with Thatcher's memoirs. Into the darkened room, two diagonal shafts of light fall from the high window on the library table. The light appears to be solid sculpture penetrating space, suggesting both the search for the truth about Kane, and also the Gothic and Manichaean aspects of his character and story, as well as his life-long conflict with Thatcher. The windows implicitly state that knowledge comes from outside, from a source beyond the scope of the memoir—and introduces an atmospheric sense of conflict between elemental forces.

The tactic seems natural in Gothic material—*Dracula*, *Jane Eyre*—but more disturbing and strange in such a contemporary setting. Starting with film noir subjects in *Killer's Kiss* and *The Killing*, Kubrick would later adapt its lighting esthetic to a range of settings: from the Pentagon to the US Moon base at Clavius. In Kubrick's lighting, both a kind of film verité authenticity and a destabilizing psychology are established. It is one thing to see shoot a meeting of underworld types in a chiaroscuro lighting scheme, it is quite another to put the President of the United Sates or a gathering of NASA scientists in one. The dialectic of room and window, darkness and light not only suggests age-old moral conflicts, but also fundamental conflicts between the unknowable and the supposedly known. It is a dialectic evident in photography itself between the camera (or room) and its aperture (or window) opening to the light.

The window is an objectification of the play of lens and film, curtain and shutter, a reminder of the authority, but also the partiality, of light. By contrast, scenes shot with conventional studio lighting are deprived of this cognitive cue, being illumined, it seems, by the light of natural and impartial truth—"the way things are." In order to break with the conventions of Hollywood "realism," windows or practical lighting within the scene can be employed and amplified. In Kubrick's four films from the fifties (*Fear and Desire*, *Killer's Kiss*, *The Killing*, and *Paths of Glory*), one can observe a deepening of the semiotic potentials of natural window light—from atmospherics, to dramatic contrasts and political irony. Shooting the scheming, murderous Generals in *Paths of Glory* in the window light of a French Chateau puts their actions into an uncanny and yet appropriate setting.

After exploring the possibilities of open windows as apertures for the admission of natural or artificial light into the scene, Kubrick would turn his attentions to windows that only appear to admit outside light. The conference scene in *2001* introduces this uncanny effect, which Kubrick would expand while building the set for the Overlook Hotel in *The Shining*: Here "windows" become lighting sources for interior photography but reveal little or nothing of the "outside" world. The claustrophobia and psychotic contagion in the films are thus illustrated in a low-key, nearly unconscious way.

Ceilings and floors

In order to allow these studio lights to illumine the scene, ceilings were all but nonexistent in most conventional films. A visible ceiling not only requires interior scenes to be lit naturally, it also introduces a sense of confinement and menace, even if it is unwanted. Vincent LoBrutto describes how Kubrick insisted on ceilings on all the sets of *Dr. Strangelove*: "I don't want the camera to light from the top. I want to use source lighting," Kubrick told his set designer Ken

Adam. As LoBrutto explains, the sets then required low camera angles, inspiring Adam to "creat[e] dramatic architectural structures for the basis of the design."[3]

Such structures redefine the characters. If the hero is actually confined in a room, the ceiling and practical lighting are easily assimilated in the interests of expressive realism. But Kubrick likes to work with ceilings and practical lighting in banal scenes: a job interview, a bureaucratic briefing, a married couple talking. The ceiling in such scenes indicate not only menace and confinement—things that can be escaped—but an existential realization of pervasive and insuperable human limitations.

If the use of ceiling and window light sources can operate to undermine an implicit sense that appearances are to be trusted or at least to be perceived uncritically, lit floors appear to heighten anticipation and wonder. We first encounter Group Commander Lionel Mandrake in a computer room at Burpelson Air Force Base. He fumbles with the sixties-era computers as they print out information into ungainly loops of paper. Beneath man and machine, the floor is opaque white and ironically reassures the audience that technology is immaculate, clinical, and reliable. The floor of the rotating *Space Station V* in *2001* is even whiter, and the floor in the strange room that David Bowman finds himself—at the end of his journey through time and space—is whitest of all. Although all these lighting schemes are in one sense simply solutions to the problem of establishing illumination for photography, they inevitably establish an atmosphere of containment and radiance, a clinical, futuristic ambience where fear and hope are suggested in equal measure. In an odd way, then, the search for practical solutions to camera lighting can drive the discovery of startling settings and designs.

Black and white

The journey of these modulations of mood and luminosity is a long one. The light in *Fear and Desire* is both studied and naïve. Drawing upon the recently released *Rashomon* (1950) and the classic Soviet cinema of Dovzhenko and shot in the San Gabriel Mountains with a minimum of expense (Kubrick was the camera man), the film complements its archetypal temporality and its existentialist theme with the natural and the inexpensive moodiness of dappled light and lingering close-ups. The dappled light in forest and hillside illustrates the film's concerns with dualism, doubles, and the shadowy and luminous aspect of instinct of civilization and character. Together with Gerald Fried's musical score and the often lofty narration and dialog, the lighting emphasizes the film's high-art aspirations and seriousness, sometimes with mixed results. As the maddened Sidney improvises a pantomime of the enemy General for the captive girl belted to a tree, the dappled light lends an arty lyricism to a grotesque scene of failed seduction, soon followed by murder. Light in *Fear and Desire*, despite its being natural, has an artificial expressive theatricality that stresses the same qualities in the script.

The first scene in *Killer's Kiss* in the original Penn Station (destroyed in 1963) is lit by natural light falling from high, distant windows into the drafty and airy space. As he begins his voice-over narrative, Davy stands tentatively in this diffuse light. The light in the station has such a softly luminous texture that it is difficult to pay attention to his narrative: The light is absorbing, his words are trite. Here the natural light suggests Davy's innocence—and the contrast between the sinister tale he will tell: His escape with his girl Gloria from a corrupting city where men and women are reduced to the status of bodies paid to box and dance. This city is lit by Kubrick in strong contrasts by which light is surrounded and dominated by darkness. Davy and Gloria's dimly lit apartments, subway cars, dressing rooms, offices, the boxing ring, dance club, Times Square, the night-time skyline of New York: each photographically deepens the theme of light threatened to extinction by darkness.

In this labyrinth, the voracious Vince Rapallo like the Minotaur (the film was a "Minotaur Production") threatens Gloria (Ariadne) and Davy, the Theseus of the tale. As if to reverse this lighting scheme and perhaps indicate his awareness of its elemental triteness, Kubrick presents Davy's dream after his defeat in the ring in negative processing. To a large extent, *Killer's Kiss* indicates a deeper interest in exploring the ways in which source lighting can deepen the complexity and menace of inexpensive sets. The scenes again and again present the source of light as threatened or inadequate to the immense obscurity around it. The only exception is the climactic battle between Vince and Davy in the manikin warehouse: Here the lighting on the ghostly dummies appears to be without source. They crowd out of the darkness of the warehouse into the light of the scene as if they were the unconcealment of the city Davy and Gloria hope to escape.

In *The Killing*, there is a remarkable scene in the stable of the racetrack: A large window channels white light onto thoroughbreds trotting over the straw toward the paddocks. In these black and white scenes, apparently filmed on location by

Kubrick's friend and collaborator Alexander Singer, the window shapes light into eye-seizing forms that throw more than illumination on the scene: They recall the dialectical nature of experience—we can see only with light—and so arouse consciousness, if not knowledge, about what we cannot see. While *The Killing* is a film about a crime meant to elude chance through perfect organization and timing, it ends by showing explosive consequences of the slightest interventions of chance. Throughout the film, Kubrick places source lighting clearly in view, usually with lamps in dingy and confined rooms: The atmosphere is of course characteristic film noir. In these settings, Johnny Clay and his gang attempt to control chance and enforce their will upon the contingencies of existence. The opening scene in the stable has a luminosity, a portentousness, and a beauty that is more difficult to interpret. It is as if the thoroughbred horses, agents of pure energy and chance in the gambling industry, are revealed as the antithesis of all attempts to eliminate contingency. They move out of this elemental and sacral light through the darkened frame of the stable into the general daylight.

In *Paths of Glory*, the scenes in the chateau—where the Generals chat, drink, dine, and conspire against their own men—are also naturally lit. The ornate windows in the eighteenth-century chateau provide enough light, but it is an impotent, or perhaps an ironic light that falls on their hypocritical and criminal affairs. *La siècle des lumiéres* and the Revolution have come to this: The soldiers of France are to be sacrificed for the promotion of General Mireau and to suit an arbitrarily planned schedule. The trenches are lit from above and always partially in darkness. The officer's rooms are lit by hanging lights or candles. And the brig where the condemned men are confined is lit through barred cellar-windows. The sunlight pours through, brightly or dimly, in ways that recall the stables in *The Killing*. Although it is clear that in both instances Kubrick is indulging himself in the pure esthetic pleasure of exhibiting light as light, one can also see that both scenes have a sacral and sacrificial aspect: In each confined space, we witness the agents and victims of chance.

Lolita is less mannered than these films, but it accomplishes an even more remarkable result. In the scene beneath the opening credits of Humbert painting Lolita's toenails, the light seems to emerge from hand and foot, as if we witnessed a true epiphany or showing forth of the sacred. Light does not appear to be cast or channeled but to be released from Lolita's flesh, as a manifestation of Humbert's veneration or abjection before the beloved body. Something of the same effect is achieved in the scene when Humbert first beholds Lolita sunbathing: Both accomplish something like a photographic equivalent of sacred painting and witnessing—the pedophile's vision and recovery of the lost child of his youth is granted externalization and, in a sense, a kind of cinematic reality. The epiphanic nature of this scene is retroactively heightened by the cut: It is Humbert driving through a heavy mist to Quilty's mansion.

In his last black and white film, Kubrick applied the expressionist power of his noir films to the theme of national security and nuclear holocaust. This style is so thoroughly associated with the underworld that its use in a film about the highest levels of the US government and the US Air Force achieves an immediate sense of moral disorientation. Where Anthony Mann's *Strategic Air Command* (1955), celebrating the mission of Air Force and the duty of Americans to serve, is filmed in brilliant color, Kubrick's film manages to ironize light as a force of moral clarity. He exhibits light in a condition that he would exploit in many subsequent films—as glare. The opening scenes establish this pattern of objects illuminated by glaring lights clearly in the frame: the opening scene of a B-52 on the flight-line, General Ripper sitting at his desk, the crew of the B-52, Miss Scott in a bikini sprawled out under a sunlamp, and the great round table in the "War Room." Human beings and machines are similarly illuminated by the ironic glare of lights that do not reveal so much as they flatten out differences and identities. In a film without daylight (other than the shots of the B-52 in flight), these reiterations enforce a sense that enlightenment has been transformed into obscurity. That instrument of American nuclear might, the B-52, appears under its glare as weirdly sinister and sacral—more like a cult object than a war place. The public and the manifest become the secret and the subversive. Sterling Hayden's General Ripper may wear the same uniform as James Stewart in *Strategic Air Command* but he looks like a mobster—while Stewart looks like an Eagle Scout. Meanwhile, in the war room, the table where the fate of the planet is being determined is lit like a titanic poker table—from a point of view that keeps the circular lighting above clearly in view. As in all these instances where the source lighting is in the frame, the viewer is constantly made aware of the conditions and limitations of seeing and knowing: There is no reliable "studio" light beyond the scene. Burpelson Air Force Base and Washington, DC, are benighted throughout the film: Only the sky and snowy wastes of Siberia have any share of "natural" light.

The spectrum of possibility

In *2001*, light and its spectrum are nearly the whole story. From the opening scenes of the "Dawn of Man" to "Jupiter and Beyond the Infinite," "mankind" is translated from animal unconsciousness beneath a bright sky to an enlightened consciousness mediated by light itself. The light schemes range from the banal to the sublime. The meeting where Dr Heywood Floyd is briefed about the discovery of the monolith on the moon takes place in a low-ceilinged room with projection screens on three sides and a "U"-shaped table. After his sublime journey from the earth, to the Space Station, to the base at Clavius, Floyd finds a room that adequately expresses the limitations of his imagination. Having slept most of the way to the moon, he is now safely ensconced in the banalities of human space and language. His main job is to explain why the discovery cannot be made public and the cover story is necessary—and to insist on signed security oaths from all those in the know.

In this context of conspiracy and deceit, the low ceiling expresses the repression of truth and of wonder, a human response to the limitlessness of space. Ordinary human beings are thought by the experts to be incapable of wonder, capable only of "cultural shock and social disorientation" if they learned the truth of extraterrestrial life. The light in the scene is provided by the projection screens so that the meeting can proceed and so that the cameras can film—but it is nothing like the light of truth or realization. It is an opaque glare that expresses conspiratorial dissimulation and fear that, at the same time, is being dramatized for all to see. The screens are, in other words, an inversion of the monoliths: They reveal all that they are, but that is nothing at all.

This setting is recapitulated at Tycho Magnetic Anomaly 1: The monolith stands excavated, exposed, and lit by floodlights. Like the conference scene and the exhibition of the B-52 and Miss Scott, the lighting is accomplished within the scene and not outside of it. Again and again, Kubrick wants to illuminate objects and people within the terms of his film world, not within the terms of its production. The audience is integrated within the illumination of reality, becoming a participant and not merely a witness of cognition.

What is distinctive about lighting in *2001* is its creation of a spectrum of reds that connects black and white. Black is the color of space, the monolith, and the mystery of existence; white is the color of the moon, space craft, satellites, space station, and technology. Kubrick's reds are found inside of technology: the flight bays in the space station, the landing station on Clavius, the interior of the HAL 9000 computer, and his/its hypnotic, glossy, mysterious "iris." The anthropomorphic aspects of technology are enhanced by these diluted, blood-like washes of light, visually suggesting that human interiors have been transferred to technological interiors. The diluted, blood-like washes lighting the landing bay at Clavius have a womb-like vibrancy and vulnerability. The interior of HAL's brain, lit in a slightly darker tone, likewise balances superiority and weakness, domination and exposure. These tonalities prepare for the final manifestation of the astral fetus.

With Bowman's cosmic journey, the full spectrum of colors is revealed: His enlightenment is manifested via an immersion in light and color alien to mundane existence. More significantly, they emerge from the blackness of space, as if concealed within the lightless absence of space were another world with another light and other colors—an alien light scheme, the ultimate natural lighting. The *fiat lux* of Judeo-Christian mythology is reimagined here as the revelation of light within darkness. Bowman's odyssey back to earth and rebirth is largely accomplished through the use of color negatives of the human eye and a range of deserted terrestrial locations: mountainous wastes, vacant oceans, canyons, attenuated clouds. The palette and imagery of the trip is impossible to describe simply because it does not resemble anything—other than a kind of inverted or reversed vision of the earth. The transitional image between the trip and the room where he lives out the remainder of his identity as David Bowman is his eye seen in various color negatives concluding with its natural color. The room is lit from whitened floor panels, its wall sconces remaining unlit. Like the space station and the computer room in *Dr. Strangelove*, the effect is indeterminate: Things are upside down, as if one were walking on the ceiling. Having cycled through life, death, and rebirth, Bowman finally appears as the astral fetus, a self-illuminating, human planetoid born of the void itself—an enlightened being.

Bulb-light and candlelight

After this sublime scheme of enlightening luminosity, *A Clockwork Orange* looks like a sardonic, bitter rebuke to human hopes. The title and credits appear on an orange and then a blue screen: We have gone from the depths of space to the flatland of Pop Art. Light is mocked in this film, as are notions of human transcendence, since it can reveal nothing but surfaces. To this end, the lighting is nearly always evident in the scene, most often in the form of actual and stylized light bulbs. The Korova Milk Bar is so lit, as are the Alexander "Home," Alex's bedroom, the Cat Woman's house, the police interrogation room, and the changing room at the prison. Kubrick supplements this satirical exhibition of light with glare—in the scene where the droogs beat the old man in an underpass near the Thames embankment and in Alex's home, where the windows opening onto the outer world reveal little more than an opaque, banal, remote brightness.

These lighting schemes, together with the theatrical settings—the abandoned rape of a girl in an old theater and the stage at the Ludovico Center where Alex's new corrected "nature" is demonstrated to the press—suggest the barrenness and the triviality, the brightness and emptiness of this alternative future. There is no natural light to speak of—no sun, moon, or stars—in this urbanized world in which human nature can be altered through conditioning by drugs and celluloid.

Nothing could be further from the rich array of luminosities to be found in *Barry Lyndon*: here are cloud-light and moonlight, sunlight and candlelight. But is it, one wonders, any less an empty or a vain world than that of *A Clockwork Orange*? Perhaps not, but one can more easily recognize what a contrast there is between the potentials of beauty to be found in nature and what human beings have made of them. It is like the contrast between candlelight and bulb-light. The first is dynamic, fluxional, and responsive to air and breath; the second is flat, immediate, and without human relation.

The eighteenth was the last century to escape photographic scrutiny, representation, and banality—it is perhaps for this reason that Kubrick was attracted to it as the subject of his most expansive and complex picture. Dissatisfied with film representations of the past, Kubrick set out to discover the lost world of the eighteenth century by dispensing with film conventions. Instead of using the theatrical frame—a sound stage with lighting that illuminated the smallest thing, as if to account for the costume budget—Kubrick turned to period painting and its reliance on natural light and tried to reinvent it in natural settings, country houses and their rooms. In order to capture natural light, Kubrick used lenses developed by the Zeiss Company for the Apollo program. Such a linkage between Kubrick and NASA was a natural publicity coup but it also led to an unprecedented naturalism. Gone were the stagey looks of traditional costume dramas: Kubrick had managed to transform one of the most conservative film genres into an avant-garde exploration of the nature of light.

The first scene in *Barry Lyndon* is the duel in which Barry's father is killed. We watch the killing, distant in time and space, from behind a rock wall and a tree. The sky is darkly clouded above the men, but beyond the light falls above a sloping hillside. It is an extraordinarily evocative scene, and a complex one, placing the death in a narrow aperture between foreground and background. Light in this framed scene is evidently subject to rapid transformations, from obscurity to clarity, a distracting foreground and a beckoning background: between them the chancy events of a duel transpire—one of many to follow in the picture. Kubrick introduces us to the complexity of natural light's metamorphic powers in the context of weather and its distance and intimacy with human affairs. Other outdoor scenes discover the constant dynamism of natural light in a frame of clouds, shadows, birds, building, and men. After the brittle clarities of *A Clockwork Orange*, this light falls as if on another world.

When Kubrick moves the scene indoors, the effect is to structure and organize light, to channel and sculpt it for dramatic and atmospheric purposes. Windows allow us to see light as light, and so in this picture of eighteenth-century life, it shows us a world that is old and weathered, and clinging to political and class prerogatives soon to be demolished. In dining and club scenes, Kubrick uses windows—their panes and muntins—not only to cast light but also to throw confining shadows on interior walls, tapestries, and paintings. This optical play in the background puts action and dialog into a subliminal context of illumination and obscurity, escape and confinement. The effect is to imply optically a sense of perpetual limitations. (Weather and the passage and the play of outdoor light in *Barry Lyndon* cast the apparent freedom of movement in space into a similar context.) At the dinner scene when Barry challenges Quin to a duel, light pours through the window, throwing a grid of shadows on walls and tapestry: There is no freedom to be had, however. His aim is to show Nora that he is a man and deserving of her hand, but the subsequent duel has been rigged by Nora's kin to spare the Englishman and gain his fortune for their family. Instead of winning her hand, he will begin an aimless life. And later when his stepson Lord Bullingdon comes to challenge Barry to a duel, his rich wife estranged and his fortune nearly spent, he discovers the man asleep in a chair at his club. The late afternoon light cast on the scene tells the whole story of his rise and fall.

If outdoor and indoor sunlight creates an atmosphere of flux and dilemma, moonlight appears as beautiful illusion. The scene in which Barry wins Lady Lyndon shines with moonlight—whether it is simulated or not, it appears real enough. The illusory nature of his motives is as secondary—or as tertiary—as the moonlight. Candlelight, on the other hand, offers a partial and wavering kind of illumination that allows for intimacy and confession (Barry with Grogan), intimacy and deceit (Barry and Col. Potzdorf), and intimacy and adultery (Barry and Lischen). These candlelit scenes, which Kubrick and John Alcott went to such lengths to film, also include gaming and whoring. But to read these scenes, and the others, purely in terms of thematic correspondences is to miss something more intangible and striking. We are being shown a world in which light has yet to be domesticated and conserved. It is a wavering and partial light, distant indeed from the bright floors of the space station or circular lighting in the war room, far from the fictive futures of the previous three films.

Three visions of color

Given the haunted house premise of *The Shining*, one would expect—from any other director—a lighting scheme that emphasizes the Gothic tradition of chiaroscuro. But there is no darkness at the Overlook, no mysterious shadows, no sudden loss of power and light, and no wavering candlelight. The hotel's abysses are concealed not by darkness but by light. Using very powerful lamps, Kubrick arranged that the hotel be illuminated via windows that nearly always are opaque (or white with glare) and with ceiling lights and room lamps. The claustrophobic, labyrinthine world of *The Shining* is thus lit as if for a laboratory experiment or for yet another repetition of a mythological archetype. Kubrick is trying to penetrate light and find a different, an invisible, darkness within it.

Consider Jack Torrance's interview for the caretaker's job, which is a variation on Heywood Floyd's briefing on Clavius. Mr Ullman sits at a desk beneath a window that lights the scene with a cloudy, formless light that is reflected on the ceiling. Across the desk, Torrance and a subordinate sit in well chairs; the walls are covered with plaques, diplomas, and a clock; the desk is cluttered. The conversation and atmosphere is both too cheerful and too casual, as if to stress suppressed thoughts – Ullman's awareness of the hotel's violent past and Jack's fear that he would not get hired. When the predictable banter is concluded, Ullman carefully broaches the matter of the caretaker Delbert Grady who had murdered his family and then killed himself. It is the light source and glare on the looming ceiling that communicate an unstated malaise within the chipper banter that follows the revelation.

The sadness at the heart of *The Shining* finds its objective correlative, not in romantic shadows and pitch darkness, but in the empty ubiquity of artificial light. Indeed, as far as one can judge, the lights never go out at the Overlook. The abyssal and labyrinthine hotel does not require darkness as a medium for the evil and the grotesque: the seventies' décor, the yellows, oranges, and tans transform brightness and cheerfulness into the uncanny, the expression of a mind reverting to primal instincts, fears, and hopes. Thus, the bathroom in room

237, the navel of this dream-house, is coolly but thoroughly lit, immaculate, and yet frighteningly explicit, seemingly incapable of concealment. Kubrick realized that in making a film with such a title, light itself would have to be mined for its fully evident horror value—in a place that never goes dark, an eternity of pastels and tans, only occasionally refreshed by visions of deep-red blood.

In *Full Metal Jacket*, Kubrick turns away from this palette of soulless angst toward an impassioned polarity of blues and reds. Blues and shades of blue dominate the opening panel devoted to the instruction and transformation of young men into Marines. Violent as this instruction is, it has a theoretical and verbal remoteness from what is to follow. The war scenes in Vietnam are illumined often by the reds and oranges of bursting shells, bombs, fireballs, and burning buildings. The chromatic dynamism in *Full Metal Jacket* is simply stated: The cool blue of violent instruction flips to its opposite on the color wheel to violent, fiery practice.

The scenes of instruction dominated by Sergeant Hartman have a lyric understatedness. The light often has a sedate and withdrawn aspect, a suppleness and a fragility, especially in the barrack scenes, where the windows are the opaque source of illumination. With the fluorescent ceiling lights off, the lateral light leaves the barrack in a complex play of reflected light on the polished floors. The muntins in the windows, like the arrangement of bunk beds, emphasize the domination of particulars by laws of symmetry, the domination of men by the codes of Marine Corps instruction. The outdoor light has no particular weight or heft, leaving the barrack entirely to Hartman's enforcement of new rules of reality. At night, illumination is provided by fluorescent ceiling lights, and they too provide no sort of opposition or alternative to Hartman's rule. Deepening these scenes of instruction, scenes of revenge are lit with blue-filtered moonlight or outdoor lamplight. When Private Gomer Pyle is punished by his squad, the bluish light suggests a distinct kind of emotional reality, a surreal atmosphere somewhere between outdoor and indoor illumination. The same kind of light fills the head when Pyle shoots Hartman and then himself. The domination of blues establishes a psychic coldness and frustration, a violence that is contained and in effect *theoretical*.

With the shift to Vietnam, this kind of mental anguish is transformed into a violent actuality represented and photographed by the light of fiery explosions. In a sense, the practice, as opposed to the theory of war, is liberating: The men no longer labor under the oppressive presence of authority. They practice violence, killing and being killed. In contrast to the cool lights of Parris Island, the film is now illuminated by the scattered fires of bombing and artillery. Kubrick turns to fire itself to provide an atmospheric equivalent of combat. In the final scenes of the film, as darkness falls, the dialectic of night and fire intensifies. When Joker executes the wounded female sniper, his face and those of his platoon are lit by fire, as they are when they march from Hue to the Perfume River. Concealed in the blues and shades of Hartman's barracks, where the violence is mainly psychological, the potentials for violence are now fully realized.

Although an exploration of dream, *Eyes Wide Shut* has no precise boundaries with waking life. Instead, it ranges in depth and strangeness between the night and daylight scenes, nighttime interiors and exteriors, the concealed and the revealed, desire and consequence. Kubrick is demonstrating once again what happens when the ends of the spectrum meet, as desire and danger do. In this regard, the dialectical chromatics in *Eyes Wide Shut* are a variation on the dialectic of reds and blues of *Full Metal Jacket*. The reds speak of desires and potential pleasures; the blues of the cold world of fact, where desires and pleasures are called to account. Thus, we see Alice in the first scene dressing for a party and then disrobing before a scarlet curtain, doubled by a mirror. Her russet hair and warm flesh, which she reveals by letting her dark gown fall to her feet, echo this light. In contrast, the blues beyond the blinds in the window imply the cold reality beyond this intimate and secure room. We see her alone in a kind of theoretical space of confident self-disclosure. In one of the last scenes, she and her husband Bill confess their erotic secrets in a room suffused with blues, her eyes wet with tears. In this polarity, there is an age-old drama at work, purely visible as light.

6

Eros

The cinema has always dealt with sex, but too often in euphemistic, idealized, cute, or merely callow ways. Few directors have explored and exploited its mystery and power like Kubrick—most often with respect to the erotic power of the female body. This is so much the case that some have suspected his films of having a "misogynist" motive and a pornographic appeal. There is no doubt that Kubrick's conception of eros is heavily weighted on the male and heterosexual side: and his observations of homosexuality are often dated and shallow. He is a mid-century male artist for whom eros is a matter of female flesh, preferably nude and preferably beautiful. There is nothing of Fellini's comic carnality, for instance. He has no interest in light comedic sex dramas. Nothing could be further from his sensibility than the "screwball" comedy. Although he sees the comic aspect of erotic capture (in *Lolita*, certainly), it is essentially a serious affair. His cinematic analysis may begin with what may appear to be a bald and perhaps crass exhibitionism, but it concludes by framing and distancing the (female) flesh, moving the (male heterosexual and perhaps the female homosexual) viewer from a reactive to a contemplative stance.

Kubrick's cinematic vision of eros or lust is distinctive because he does not see it as the wicked alternative to love or *Amor* but as its origin. Eros for the Greeks was the indiscriminate energy or libido represented by Aphrodite. Agape for the early Christians was the indiscriminate asexual love represented by Christ. Amor for the troubadours and medieval romances is the ideal love for a particular human being: Isolde is everything to Tristan. In the East, this energy or *Shakti* was to be translated by meditation into spiritual enlightenment. In the nineteenth century, this last notion began to penetrate European thought, finding its expression, for instance, in Schopenhauer's philosophy and Wagner's music dramas. Strange as it may at first seem, something of this last redress to the libido can be found in Kubrick's films.

An exemplary expression can be seen in the last scene of *Paths of Glory*. Following the harrowing depiction of the trench warfare of World War I and the bogus Court Martial and execution of innocent enlisted men, Kubrick introduces the film's first and only woman. A young German girl is forced onto the stage of a bistro to sing to a crowd of unruly French soldiers who hoot and mock her. The host's gestures and remarks are sarcastic and demeaning: She is beautiful, but she is also the enemy. She struggles hesitantly and erratically through stanzas from the well-known folk song "Der Treuer Husar," which tells of a hussar who is faithful to his lover, but not to his soldier's code. When she falls ill, he deserts and returns home to bury her. Abandoning the soldier's life, he assumes the burden of endless grief:

Es war einmal ein treuer Husar,
Der liebt' sein Mädchen ein ganzes Jahr,
Ein ganzes Jahr und noch viel mehr,
Die Liebe nahm kein Ende mehr.

Der Knab' der fuhr ins fremde Land,
Derweil ward ihm sein Mädchen krank,
Sie ward so krank bis auf den Tod,
Drei Tag, drei Nacht sprach sie kein Wort.

Und als der Knab' die Botschaft kriegt,
Daß sein Herzlieb am Sterben liegt,
Verließ er gleich sein Hab und Gut,
Wollt seh'n, was sein Herzliebchen tut.
. . .
Und als das Mägdlein gestorben war,
Da legt er's auf die Totenbahr.
Wo krieg ich nun sechs junge Knab'n,
Die mein Herzlieb zu Grabe trag'n?

Wo kriegen wir sechs Träger her?
Sechs Bauernbuben die sind so schwer.
Sechs brave Husaren müssen es sein,
Die tragen mein Herzliebchen heim.

Jetzt muß ich tragen ein schwarzes Kleid,
Das ist für mich ein großes Leid,
Ein großes Leid und noch viel mehr,
Die Trauer nimmt kein Ende mehr.

The girl's song moves the men from lust and derision to sympathy. Her fumbling performance is joined and then dominated by their humming chorus.

The song transforms the girl from anonymous flesh and eros into an expressive being, a Mädchen, a maiden, a *jeune fille*, and a champion of romantic love. Joining her fumbling rendition with their soulful but wordless chorus, something like a union of sentiment is achieved. If they understand the song or know its story, they will have been moved as much by its pathos as its rejection of martial duty. More importantly, for our purposes, the abstract and anonymous eros is transformed by the invocation of love.

In *Eyes Wide Shut*, the young doctor Bill Harford, after a frank discussion with his wife about her overwhelming sexual desire for a stranger, crashes an orgy in a mansion and, assuming a carnival mask, discovers that a bizarre masque is in progress. A ring of women cast aside their capes and stand all but naked in carnival masks, g-strings, and high heels, greeting one another formally to the strains of a postmodern, hieratic hymn. Discovered as an interloper and threatened in a vaguely menacing way, Harford is saved by a woman who comes forward to accept whatever his punishment will be: Anonymous flesh is transformed into human subjectivity by a gesture worthy of a Romantic Opera or Tale.

In both scenes, the power and the mystery of the flesh is staged—in bistro and mansion—and a ritual of transformation is accomplished. The ancient physiology of sexual attraction is inescapable and nameless, and yet disturbing. It seems to come from nowhere and to appeal to something within that is itself beyond choice or motive. The masking of this flesh by human sentiment or romantic gesture comes as a relief, as if to spare the soldiers and Bill Harford the full force of the flesh. The rowdy men engaged in a pointless exhibition of sexual desire are happily quelled by feelings of common humanity and love. Likewise, Harford's masked face can only exhibit his own generic sexuality as he watches the masque of the flesh. Once his mask is removed and he is "saved" by the mysterious woman, he leaves the mansion in a new situation. He had entered as a man eager for sexual experience, and he leaves as a man mystified and redeemed by romance—and eager to discover who the woman is. In this way, the seizure of pure sexuality is modulated into a romantic quest and the alienating effects attendant on a radical experience of the flesh are overcome. What some saw as something a little too close to pornography, others may see as an unembarrassed assessment of the ruses consciousness devices in order to manage the witnessing of a power the ancients understood as a goddess.

Kubrick's cinema itself responds to the flesh with a similar transformative gesture. The importance of female nudity in Kubrick's subsequent films can hardly be exaggerated—both as an example of the breakdown of censorship in the 1960s and in the development of his own imaginary film language. Kubrick's use of the female nude is never coy or sentimental, the usual ways in which the illicit and the sexual are domesticated in popular representations. Instead, it is unembarrassed and, risking the charge of depersonalization, detached and objective. As an instance of the typically coy and sentimental use of seminudity, we can recall the scene in *Spartacus* where Lavinia bathes in a pond. Her nudity is evident, but it is veiled expertly by a single frond. Typical as this kind of thing was in the days before the end of the Code, it seems to have embarrassed Kubrick so much that his subsequent treatment of nudity is always direct and clearly lit. Even the scene in *Barry Lyndon* of a brothel with two seminude women, lit by a single candelabrum, is neither coy nor erotic, placed as it is between two domestic scenes that stress Barry's caddishness. Thus, candlelight, which became a virtual symbol of the romantic encounter, is stripped of its connotative freight and is exhibited objectively as a form of illumination that was superseded by the lightbulb. Rather than sentimentalize the body, Kubrick wants to exhibit its native force and palpability, not revel in its sensational potentials. Even so, there is also no doubt that he was not devoted to documentary "realism": The female bodies he chooses to reveal are nearly always beautiful. Where Fellini, for instance, satirized the erotic impulse by his compulsive exhibition of fat and grotesque bodies, Kubrick has a proper respect and veneration for its dire powers.

The World as Will and Representation

Arthur Schopenhauer's philosophy provides an excellent framework for a critical analysis of Kubrick's cinema of the flesh. This is not an arbitrary point of comparison. Michael Herr recalls that Kubrick was intrigued by Schopenhauer and saw past the cliché of his "pessimism": "Frankly, I've never understood why Schopenhauer is considered so pessimistic."[1]

Schopenhauer's masterpiece *The World as Will and Representation* (1819, 1844) maintains that the world is characterized by a nameless force (the "will") that moves through all organic forms which are, in effect, representations of it. Schopenhauer argued for an utterly natural conception of life without reference to supernatural or spiritual forces. The "will" is nothing more than a minimalist characterization of the "life force" that passes from species to species and from generation to generation in constantly changing formations or representations:

> It [the will] is the innermost essence, the kernel, of every particular thing and also of the whole. It appears in every blindly acting force of nature, and also in the deliberate conduct of man, and the great difference between the two concerns only the degree of the manifestation, not the inner nature of what is manifested.[2]

Anticipating both psychoanalytical understandings of the unconscious and biological fundamentalism of the sort championed by Richard Dawkins, Schopenhauer essentially relegates human volition and "free will" to a subsidiary role when it addresses the overwhelming and nameless drive of the flesh. In Kubrick's films, we see that human being is an experience of inhabitation and self-alienation, a recognition that one's choices are not free, but determined by appetites and drives that are alien to conscious choice and will.

> So long as we are given up to the throng of desires, with its constant hopes and fears, so long as we are the subject of willing, we never obtain lasting happiness or peace . . . [T]he subject of willing is constantly lying on the revolving wheel of Ixion . . . When, however, an external cause or inward disposition suddenly raises us out of this endless stream of willing, and snatches knowledge from the thraldom of the will, the attention is now no longer directed to the motives of the will, but comprehends things free from their relation to the will.[3]

For Schopenhauer art can play such a role: A well-executed painting can bring about this transformation:

> This is shown by those admirable Dutchmen who directed such purely objective perception to the most insignificant objects, and set up a lasting monument of their objectivity and spiritual peace in paintings of *still life*.[4]

Art, in other words, pleases, engages, and even enlightens insofar as it removes us from the hectoring demands of the purely irrational and kinetic urgings of the will.

For Schopenhauer, the naïve and unself-conscious representations that the individual mind ordinarily makes out of the force and flux of the will are quite different from the esthetic contemplation stimulated by true works of art. He argues that the individual, following the experience of art, can renounce the will and be released from its unconscious and anonymous forces. Schopenhauer characterizes this specifically with reference to the Buddhist conception of Nirvana—the release from desire which effects a release from suffering.[5] Kubrick's films likewise show the fading of illusions of independent human agency and choice before the mystery of flesh—the world as will breaks through the screen of representation. But his films, insofar as they strive to realize their fullest esthetic potentials, create, even when satirical, the conditions for esthetic contemplation and sometimes the renunciation of the will that is Schopenhauer's ultimate concern.

In a sense, Schopenhauer's conception of individual mental representation is evident and concrete in the terms of social fictions, customs, masks, conventions, and so forth. All these cultural forms serve to mask the "thing in itself," the nameless force of "life." In other words, Schopenhauer's initial assessment of the human condition is evident in the dialect of concealment and unconcealment, the interplay of cultural pretense and nature's will. At this preliminary and widespread stage, the will can be dramatized by the flesh and representation by the gaze. A naked body and a violent body, as expressions of the anonymous, unconcealed power of the will, demand the gaze of desire and fear. When these same bodies are represented in a "true" work of art, they will be inflected with beauty and will encourage esthetic contemplation, not kinetic emotions.

Das Mädchen und der Treuer Husar

The first manifestation of this dialectic of desire and idealization appears in *Fear and Desire*—but in reversed order. Once the fisher-girl has been captured, Sidney speaks up for her, argues that she is not dangerous, and should not be tied to the tree. Denying his own desire before the others, he appears to his comrades as the soldier who defends the maiden from their suspicions and lusts. Once he is left to protect her as the others scout the river, he tries to seduce her by telling her the story of *The Tempest*, doing a comic impression of the enemy General, and making a plea that even if she hates him, please like him. When his dramatic efforts have failed, he embraces her as she pretends interest. Once she has freed herself from her bondage, she runs to the forest—and Sidney shoots her dead. The sacrifice is complete, but no one is redeemed.

The exhibition of the flesh and the practice of looking become mutual in the next film. The scenario of *Killer's Kiss* has the rigor and some of the artifice of a philosophical essay on male and female flesh, violence and sexuality, staged and framed through apartment windows, boxing ring and dance-hall. Both young and attractive, Davy and Gloria are trapped in their professions, their apartments, and New York City. The opening scenes show the two covertly gazing at one another through theatrically open windows across the air shaft of their apartment building and then meeting briefly as they descend to the street: The imaginary realm yields to the real. Kubrick meticulously exhibits them as male and female doubles, each forced to trade on their physicality to make a living. When Davy saves her from Vince, her lecherous boss, after his own defeat in the ring, they—"fall in love." When they try to escape from New York City, Vince's thugs mistakenly kill Davy's manager, Albert. Gloria is captured by his thugs and Davy once again rescues her. In a scene that anticipates the masked orgy 40 years later in *Eyes Wide Shut*, the final battle between Vince and Davy takes place in a storage loft filled with female manikins. Throwing manikins at each other, occasionally impaling them with an iron rod, and beheading them with an axe, the two fight until Davy finally kills Vince. Waiting at Penn Station and wondering whether she will join him, the boxer wonders whether "love" can happen so quickly—in only 2 days. At the last minute, she appears and they are ready to escape from New York City.

What makes this early genre film significant is the way in which Kubrick stakes out a dominant theme in his future films, the purely anonymous mystery of the flesh and its instinctual engagement by the gaze. Kubrick develops this point imagistically by comparing and contrasting the staging of the prize-fights and the dance-halls, but also by the high art anonymity of Gloria's sister Iris, a ballet dancer and the manikins used to exhibit and stage clothing in department stores. In this way, violence, sexuality, "high" art, and commerce are linked. While Davy and Gloria wonder if love, rather than passion, can be real, the film's imagery suggests its illusory nature. If Davy and Gloria imagine they may be particular or unique beings, instead of mere denizens of the city, the film suggests otherwise: other pairs, identical pairs, are on view, the two Shriners who run off with Davy's scarf and cause him to miss his appointment with his manager. Once Davy leaves, his manager arrives and takes his place outside the dance-hall: Everyone is substitutable. So Rapallo's two thugs, equally anonymous and without particularity, take him away, instead of Davy, and decide to rob and murder him instead of beating him, as they were charged by Vince, to scare him away from Gloria. Likewise, the boxer and the dance-hall girl, the faithful Hussar and the Beautiful Maiden, exist in a world of polarity, of pure flesh and uninflected archetype. They are joined not by understanding or knowledge but by the reflexive and instinctual force of the gaze—and its motive and content in the will. Still, they wonder if it could be "love" that they have discovered.

We have seen how In *Paths of Glory* Kubrick has the German girl staged and positioned before the raucous crowd of enlisted men and how her mere physical presence at first stimulates violent, derisive, and erotic gazes and then, as she sings, their gaze is transformed into an idealized witnessing, art come to life, the screen of the romance of home and devotion falls across the previously reviled and desired flesh. *Spartacus* develops this theme in its own way. As in *Killer's Kiss*, the film focuses on two performers, two slaves of the gaze, one a gladiator and the other the beautiful slave girl Varinia who works in the kitchen and is deployed for the sexual gratification of the gladiator trainees. The two are drawn to one another almost by a law of paired affinities. When Lavinia is sent into Spartacus's subterranean cell to sleep with him, he gazes at her with awe and respect, touching her cheek, throat, and shoulder with great tenderness. But all the while Batiatus and Marcellus are leering down at the scene, and once she has disrobed, they urge Spartacus onward. "I'm not an animal," Spartacus savagely screams at his tormentors, to which Lavinia whispers with distinct dignity, "Neither am I." At this point, Spartacus lets Lavinia leave the cell, untouched. In this moment of opposing gazes—Spartacus at Lavinia, Batiatus and Marcellus at both of them—humanity, agency, sexual modesty, and other family values are discovered at the same instant. The motive of the slave rebellion has been realized.

Born to slavery, the "Thracian dog" Spartacus is deprived of all agency, but by the middle of the film, he is a warring chieftain, the leader of a people, and a rival to the rulers of Rome. He rampages throughout Italy and forms a kind of anti-Rome in the countryside, complete with virtuous women, valiant men, laughing children, smiling seniors—and all with American accents. In this idyllic retreat from pagan Rome, a proto-American Communism is established with Spartacus as a jovial and smiling dictator. The children in this idyll are seen as the hope of the future, a new society raised with communal values.

In other words, Spartacus represents the full-fledged example of the Hollywood ideal of the power of the individual against the forces of history, social order, and State violence. Against all odds, the historical rarity Spartacus becomes, through film's ability to elicit identification, a representative of the human hero, someone who can inspire twentieth-century workers to throw off their chains and realize and recover their alienated humanity. All of this derives from the scene in the cell when Spartacus gazes at a beautiful woman and renounces his sexual pleasure for the more mysterious pleasures or demands of manhood.

What makes *Spartacus* a less than satisfactory expression of Kubrick's vision is that both characters, despite their degraded positions in life, are magnificent expressions of middle-class virtue. In contrast to their corrupt Roman masters, they transcend their flesh to embody all the humanist virtues—freedom, community, family, modesty, and self-sacrifice. The rebellious slaves led by Spartacus are in equal parts stand-ins for the Christians to appear in the next century and the labor movements to appear 2,000 years hence. Struggling under the weight of these twin burdens, Howard Fast's and Kirk Douglas's allegory collapses into sentimental and irritating kitsch. In this light, it is easy to see why Kubrick would turn to Vladimir Nabokov's *Lolita* for his next, independent film.

Lolita is Kubrick's central romantic work, but only with respect to the private rubrics of Humbert Humbert's arcane science of the nymphet. If "Romance" in the most general sense is the representation of the will by a human institution or fiction, Humbert's love for Lolita is no less romantic than any of those eagerly consumed by readers and moviegoers. The will that runs through Humbert's body and those he admires and desires, in other words, has been represented by a code that is perverse and illegal, but also observant of the high and remote code of romance invented in medieval Europe, *Amor*. The Ladies of Romance were more properly, from contemporary standards, girls—and the love they inspired pedophilic.

Professor Humbert is an able exponent of such a thesis, having come to the United States steeped in French poetry and the cloying rhythms of Poe's poetry in celebration of a dead child bride. He also comes complete with his own private theory and practice of romance—the amorous cult of the nymphet derived from the lost love of his European adolescence. He is thus well-provided with a representation when the will manifests itself in the form of young Dolores Haze. Nabokov's Humbert writes:

> Between the age limits of nine and fourteen there occur maidens who, to certain bewitched travelers, twice or many times older than they, reveal their true nature which is not human, but nymphic (that is demoniac); and these chosen creatures I propose to designate as "nymphets."[6]

Kubrick's film can include only a fraction of Humbert's Nymphology, relying instead on the cinematic account of the meeting of the flesh and the gaze as compensation.

Alone among the "normal" and "healthy" denizens of the decidedly goatish town of Ramsdale, New Hampshire, Humbert Humbert is a man with an imagination and a wide repertoire of its representations. Charlotte Haze, her friends Diana and Jerry, Clare Quilty, and Lolita all approach the fact of flesh with an unrelenting shallowness and crudeness. Jerry and Diana are eager to swap partners with Humbert and Charlotte; Quilty and Lolita are promiscuous and vulgar. Only Humbert knows that Love—the Amor of the troubadours—is a matter of life and death, a witnessing in the Lady of the transcendent in the form of flesh. In Wagner's music drama, the mutual gaze of Tristan and Isolde, after they have unknowingly drunk the potion, is a fatal epiphany, an acceptance of love as death, an inescapable annunciation. The realization can likewise be seen in Humbert's stunned gaze—when the timeless nymphet of his memories and imagination becomes manifest in a young American girl. James Mason's crushed and transfigured expression says it as powerfully Wagner's Tristan chord.

Disciplining the gaze

Where Humbert's gaze connects Lolita's flesh to a personal mythology of nymphets, Alex in *A Clockwork Orange* has only the barren and anonymous premises of the "old ultra-violence" and the "old in-out, in-out" with which to adorn the will. He has no other element in his representational repertoire to mediate or inflect his impersonal appetites for sex and violence: An old man is to be beaten, a young woman is to be raped, and a middle-aged woman is to be taunted and murdered. As the society of a "near future" (as imagined circa 1970) falls to pieces, crime has become nearly the norm. Young Alex and his droogs are simply uninflected manifestations of the will.

The first assault on a woman takes place in the ornately framed stage of an abandoned theater. The film audience is thus doubly situated and doubly framed—and the violence, to those paying attention to such things, made doubly artificial. The nude girl whom Billy Boy's droogs are dragging off to rape is groped, picked up, and twisted. Her breasts swing and her arms flail. Just as the rape would have seemed inevitable, Alex and his droogs appear, and Billy Boy's gang discards the woman, who manages to escape, for the perhaps headier instinctual pleasures of a brawl. The artifice has made the scene less disturbing but not less involving, and perhaps easier for some to watch. It is this threshold of pornography and art that leaves some viewers with an uneasy sense of kinship with the would-be rapists as they gaze on the unfolding scene. Who is degraded in this scene other than a self-conscious viewer?

Following his cinematic conditioning, Alex is brought onto a stage by Dr Ludovico to show the success of the violence-aversion treatment. An inoffensive and grinning Alex is confronted by a comic who insults, provokes, and having mastered him, makes the prostrate boy lick the sole of his shoe. He then confronts a beautiful woman, nearly nude, before whom he ends cowering as his impulse to seize her prompts a gag and vomit reflex. Here, it is Alex who is degraded, and the exposed woman, having vanquished the rapist, takes a series of flamboyant bows as she leaves the stage. Once again the scene is doubly framed and staged, and the audience in the theater sits in judgment with the audience of politicians. Yet those who felt an unwelcome identification with Alex in the earlier scenes will now suffer a similar degradation. By abandoning a morally superior stance, Kubrick's film inevitably gains pornographic as well as moral energies that threaten to go off in unpredictable directions.

After his conditioning is undone by hypnopedia, Alex is once more staged, this time at a press conference arranged by the Minister of the Interior. Alex has become celebrated in the tabloids as the "poor boy" driven to suicide by the government. Lying in a hospital bed, his body is covered by plaster casts. A massive stereo is wheeled into the ward and Alex listens to the coda of Beethoven's "Glorious *Ninth*." With this paean to Brotherhood as a score, Alex's fantasies of sexual domination and potency are dramatized. Kubrick shows something different from the two earlier scenes of degradation: in a snowy scene, witnessed by an audience in Regency attire, a well-arranged world quite alien to the London of the 1970s, a naked Alex writhes beneath a naked young woman who seems to be enjoying herself. Alex is once again an agent of the will, but he is no rapist. Although this is only Alex's fantastic inward gaze into rekindled desire, it suggests a promising change in his fantasy life—one that Burgess made explicit in the final chapter of his novel, cut from the American edition on which Kubrick based his screenplay.

Barry Lyndon, *The Shining*, and *Full Metal Jacket* are rich with scenes that further develop these themes and images in different ways. In all three, the male gaze at the female body, as an expression of Schopenhauer's will, is interdicted and disciplined by fear, impotence, or terror. Redmond Barry and Nora Brady, in the first scene of *Barry Lyndon*, play out the immemorial confrontation between the flesh and the gaze. Barry is playing a game with Nora suffused with sexual tension: She hides a ribbon in her low-cut gown and asks the blindfolded youth to find it. Unmasked, he looks always away from her bosom and finally retrieves it, without looking at her rising and falling breasts. In his case, romantic infatuation, nobility, and devotion are all evident in a "veneration" of the flesh and his inability to meet Nora with his eyes. When his eyes are opened, all flesh—the body of his Lady at bath and the whores in the gaming room—become defiled and emptied of power. Betrayed by a woman of Ireland to whom he subjected himself, Barry sets out to acquire a Lady of England, and assumes all the vices attendant on a fortune hunter: He becomes a gambler and practiced libertine whose casual appraisal of women's naked bodies is perfunctory and shallow. Barry Lyndon's downfall is expressed by, and perhaps turns on, his response to eros. In Nora, he sees a goddess worthy of his abject submission; in Lady Lyndon, he sees property to be possessed by expertly performing the role of a smitten lover.

In *The Shining*, the unspoken premise of Jack Torrance's descent into madness is the failure of the flesh to engage his imagination and his consequent fascination with the dead and the past—figured forth by his unconscious mind. Kubrick takes great pains to make the lovely Shelley Duval into a sexless and poorly dressed housewife. The emptiness of their marriage is dramatized by the emptiness of the Overlook Hotel (the name ironically suggests not the intended sense of scenery, but of a failure to see, to gaze, and to engage the living world around). His visions populate the emptiness with spectral illustrations of the story of the caretaker Delbert Grady. Relevant to our theme is his vision in room 237 of a beautiful young woman emerging from the bath. Here, we see his unconscious mind staging an encounter with the flesh: His gaze is absolute and undeflected. As the scene slowly develops, the young woman's body becomes suddenly that of an old woman, her flesh saggy, wrinkled, and ulcerous. Like an allegory from a medieval morality tale, the scene dramatizes Torrance's farewell to the flesh and his irreversible commitment to the dead—the phantoms who populated the Overlook of his mind. Like Barry, Jack's turning point is an inability to address eros on terms adequate to its challenges. Both turn from eros to the possession of a vast and storied house.

Stripped of their identities, their hair, and their privacy, the Marine trainees in *Full Metal Jacket* are treated as little more than unformed flesh. The premise of Sergeant Hartman's training is that unless a trainee can make himself an image of his "Beloved Corps" sheathed in a "full metal jacket" of Marine rectitude, he retains his unformed, female nature. Sergeant Hartman's men are in fact "pussies" and "ladies" until they can remake themselves according to the representational norm of the Corps. It is as this form of female flesh that they are subject to the fierce gaze of their drill instructor and the sexualized humiliation that is directed their way. This fiction that civilian men are in effect female flesh guides the strategy and tactics of the training section of the film, but it is reversed by the action in Vietnam. So as to foreshadow this shift, the first scene in Da Nang is a tracking shot of an apparent Vietnamese prostitute as she approaches Private Joker and his green buddy Rafter Man. After flirting and prancing before them ("Me love you long time"), her accomplices walk and drive by, snatching Rafter Man's camera. It turns out that women are more than Sergeant Hartman prepared them for. Even so, when Joker and Rafter Man join Private Cowboy's platoon during their assault on Hue, they cannot suspect who their deadliest opponent will be. The sniper who is decimating their platoon from her vantage point inside a gutted building is a young Viet Cong woman, fierce, plain, pig-tailed. After Rafter Man cuts her down, the "men" circle and gaze down at the mortally wounded girl. Where the innocent *Mädchen* in *Paths of Glory* transforms the French soldiers with her naïve song, this young woman pleads with the American soldiers to put her out of her misery. Given the Lusthogs' insulted masculinity and their eagerness for "payback" ("let[ing] her rot"), Joker's "hardcore" mercy killing appears as an act of gallantry.

The masque of the will

In adapting Arthur Schnitzler's *Traumnovelle* into the screenplay for *Eyes Wide Shut*, Kubrick and Raphael had to find a way to cinematically represent the dream-like atmosphere of Schnitzler's Viennese story without resorting to a clear-cut distinction between "reality" and "dream." Kubrick told Raphael, "It can't *all* be a dream . . . If there's no reality, there's no movie."[7] It appears that Kubrick wanted the dream and the waking world to encroach on each other. Michel Chion has carefully described various aspects of what he calls "cinematographic irony," the way in which the film seems to intend something other than what it depicts.[8] A scene seems badly acted, the dialog seems redundant and fails to advance the story, and characters repeat each other's words. To Chion's account, I would add my own sense that the colors are too beautiful and deep to be "real," that the sexual opportunities presented to Harford are excessive, and that the women have a dream-like intensity. All these ingredients of "de-realization" are manifestations of dream: a strange richness, deeply suffused colors (especially red and blue), brilliant lights, plenty of darkness, repeating phrases, slowly advancing action, stagnant scenes (the explanation scene with Ziegler in the billiard room), unfulfilled dramatic possibilities, feelings of paralysis, terrifying dangers, shame, fear, and desire. But this is not dream as opposed to reality. It is *life*, as Schopenhauer describes it—the anonymous force of the will draped in human representations—the dream from which ultimately Schopenhauer thought we must awaken.

Kubrick not only sets out to dramatize the ways in which Bill and Alice Harford confront the veiling and unveiling of the will, he also wants to implicate the viewer in a parallel drama. Thus, the advertising campaign and publicity mounted in the summer of 1999, organized by Kubrick before his death in March 1999, quite crudely implied that the film would be a "sexy" drama about a man and his wife (both psychiatrists, according to one report) played by a man and his wife. This campaign may have contributed to the bad reviews and the lackluster box office receipts, but it operated successfully in another way. Any audience responding to the desire to see, for instance, Nicole Kidman naked, did not even have to wait long: Spliced between the cards "A Film by Stanley Kubrick" and "Eyes Wide Shut," we see Alice Harford let her evening gown fall to her feet. Naked in high heels, she stands, as Chion comments, "turned into a statue and magnified."[9] Is this photographed flesh pornographic or esthetic? Does it prompt desire or disinterested contemplation? One thing is certain, Kubrick puts the viewer into a situation of feeling or thinking about desire and contemplation, sex and beauty. The scene is in no way vulgar, but because it interrupts the credits, it seems illicit—the film's first violation of propriety.

The first scenes in the film contrast the staged and unstaged aspects of social life. Before going to the formal and posh party thrown by Ziegler, Alice and Bill are getting dressed and masked for the performance. Alice is now exposed in a different way as she rises from the toilet and wipes herself, wondering if her hair is alright. Bill, with the ordinary blindness of a husband, says her hair looks "perfect." She responds, "You're not even looking at it." His eyes are wide but shut: He does not see his wife, either with sexual interest or with esthetic appreciation. Thus, even before the masks of social performance descend at the party, his familiarity with the domestic scene blinds him: The film begins with him looking for his wallet.

When they arrive at the Ziegler mansion, a different kind of blindness and masking ensues: They are greeted fulsomely by Ziegler and his wife in a scene that is "badly acted"—as such scenes often are in life. The "cinematographic irony" that Chion discusses puts a gap between the viewer and the film that leads to an uncomfortable feeling of being inside and outside of the drama on the screen. As Bill and Alice separate and mingle, each is tempted: Bill by two beautiful models,

Nuala and Gayle, and Alice by the egregious Hungarian Sandor Szavost. These scenes go on "too long" and are "badly acted": The feeling of discomfort, the dream-like sensation of fascination, desire, and delay deepens. The "dream" of social life is characterized by unreality without revelation: It drags on without climax.

It is at this point that Bill is "rescued" from the temptresses by Ziegler's man Harris and crosses the threshold from the dream of social life to a vision of the flesh and a glimpse of the will. Ziegler asks Bill to examine a woman who has overdosed in his palatial bathroom on a combination of heroin and cocaine. Where earlier Bill had not "really looked" at Alice rising from the toilet, here he cannot help but gaze, at least with his doctor's eye, on a beautiful, utterly naked woman. Although Bill maintains his professional detachment, the viewer must once again deal with a powerful digression from performance and representation to the flesh and the will. The scene is prolonged and the uneasiness it creates is a result of the contrast between the banality of the dialog and the opulence of the scene: There is something here that simply cannot be stated. Ziegler's approach had been directed by his appetites, while Bill, fortunately, has his professional discipline to direct his actions. Now Ziegler simply wants to get the woman out of his house, while Bill, following the flirtatious girls, is again facing the blunt, uncomfortable fact of eros. All the while (as we see through a series of crosscuts between ballroom and bathroom), the egregious Hungarian lover carries on his worldly wooing of Alice, complete with allusions to Ovid's *Art of Love* and the "necessity" of deception in marriage.

Significantly, however, it is she who initiates Bill's and her own journeys toward the will. When the couple later discusses the flirtations at the Ziegler party, Bill smugly assumes that women are less driven by eros than men and more concerned with preservation of the family. The evolutionary perspective offered by her physician husband nicely endorses family values (women are more interested in children than lovers), insulating Bill from any suspicions of his wife's faithfulness. Rejecting her husband's claim that women are more nurturing and family oriented, she tells him that when she saw a naval officer during their vacation the previous summer, she "was ready to give up everything" to be his lover. To her husband's self-serving "Darwinism," Alice answers with an endorsement of the anarchic force of the will. The whole social dream—her "whole fucking life"—is nothing compared with this anonymous force. Their marriage, founded on words, pledges, conventions of romance and family, rests on impersonal energy.

After her confession, Bill's security is gone. The scenario is now directed by jealousy. It is jealousy that drives Bill into the night, initially to confront the fact of death (one of his patients has just died), but then to engage the will, as a means of revenge against Alice's confession. Jealousy enrages, we can see, because it is a revelation, a catastrophic recognition—often the trigger of tragic action—that human words, bonds, and customs are less than nothing in the face of eros. It is a humiliation of every wish that ideas can master or bind the mindless will. As Bill travels in a taxi to the deathbed, we see its dehumanizing effects on his face and its compulsive manifestation in his imagination: He imagines his wife *in flagrante* with a handsome naval officer in dress whites. Jealousy seems to take erotic energy and turn it into a masochistic energy: He realizes in the imagination what never happened in reality and then experiences it over and over again. The compulsiveness of this self-torment is striking, making one wonder if it is not the fulfilment of a wish.

To escape this torment, he must either kill someone (his wife or the innocent and fugitive officer) or he must mimic and perhaps realize his wife's passion. At large in the city, Bill's jealousy is transformed into a dream-like sequence of sexual encounters: following Nuala, Gayle, and Mandy the overdosed prostitute, he will be "tempted" by Marion Nathanson, Domino, another prostitute, Milich's daughter, and then, at the orgy, by the "mysterious woman." Afterward, he is tempted by Sally, Domino's roommate, and Mandy once again, this time as she lies dead in the morgue. He is also the subject of interest for a number of men, including Nick Nightingale, some rowdy college students, a desk clerk, and a stalker who tracks him for a few blocks. Once he has experienced the will, he sees it everywhere. And yet Bill never acts on his opportunities. Their very plenitude seems to have drained them of urgency, since each failed chance simply leads to another. Thus, the tragic recognition is to some extent only realized fully by comic exaggeration. Bill's dream journey, in all its luridness, curiously preserves his fidelity.

While Bill's journey is through a kind of unreal, dream-like city, Alice's journey is private, domestic, and a literal dream. While Bill witnesses the orgy, she dreams of an orgy where she is passed from man to man. The orgy at Somerton is thus an exterior manifestation of the will which Alice experiences asleep. Both are equally "real" and "unreal." Each character has made a profound descent into the realm of the will—and it is this that puts their marriage on a new, dangerous, and yet, potentially, more vital footing.

The orgy at Somerton, as originally shot and edited, one of Kubrick's most impressive inventions, proved too much for the censors who threatened the film with an X rating. In other words, the Board considered these scenes—among the most beautiful and mysterious scenes in his canon—to be pornographic. Kubrick was forced to reedit and modify the scenes through computer graphic imaging, to veil the act of coitus, in order to gain an R rating. This is quite interesting, since the orgy struck many overnight newspaper and magazine critics as not only *not* "sexy," but dull. But Kubrick is interested in something a good deal more profound than providing a "sexy" orgy: He wants to stage a masque of the will—a ritual of the flesh. Since cinematic orgies, whether Roman or from the Age of Aquarius, tend to be comic, even when unintended, Kubrick was looking for something somber and forbidding, something transhuman.

Upon entering the mansion and offering up the password "Fidelio," Bill dons his Venetian carnival mask. Like Bill, the audience is admitted to a mystery and initiated into a cult—something like a fusion of a Roman Catholic ritual, a pagan fertility ritual, and a high-class men's club. With his mask and hooded cloak, Bill joins a crowd of similarly attired men and women as they look at a circle of women also masked and cloaked. The "orgy" at Somerton is enacted not as comical revel of lust but as a somber ritual in which bodies are revealed and faces are covered. The masked participants disappear into the language of the flesh, and the viewer has to keep his or her eyes on pubic hair and breasts in order to keep the women that Bill encounters distinct. ("The genitals," as Schopenhauer reminds us, "are the focus of the will."[10]) Once again Bill, the audience in the film, and the audience of the film are all forced to establish a kind of gaze, embarrassed, erotic, esthetic, or disturbed. Masked as the participants, both the nature of their observations and the quality of their voices are unknown. The beautiful carnival masks add a melancholy remoteness, a perennial and futile aspect to the ritual and the sex that follows. Bill walks through room after room of joyless couplings. As in Schopenhauer's view, sexuality is a dynamic driven by pleasure but cares nothing for the "individual," nothing for "love" or "sacrifice." Yet it is precisely these qualities that Bill has resorted to when "the mysterious woman" intervenes on his behalf once he is shown to be an interloper.

Having tripped from one sexual temptation to another since leaving Alice earlier in the evening, Bill has now come into the cavernous mystery of the flesh—and is once more "saved." Finding his way home and then setting out the next day on a quest to find out what has happened to "the mysterious woman," Bill must finally be disabused of her story. When Ziegler explains, in the prolonged, dreamy dialog around the billiard table, that the whole setup was a "charade" and his redeemer a "hooker" who later "got her brains fucked out" and then "OD'd," Bill must find a way between the will and the "charade." He must, in other words, find a human path between the extremes of the naked will and the fantasy of romance. Alice and Bill can find that middle way only by the tried and true method of conjugal sex. "The important thing," Alice tells Bill in the last scene in the toy store, "is we're awake now and hopefully for a long time to come."

Traditionally, it has been these "representations"—the law and romance—that have been employed to veil the unspeakable and unrelenting drive of the will. But these are essentially attempts to look away from the will's inhuman power, the first by legal force of marriage, the second by the liberating promise of love. By contrast, art can, according to Schopenhauer, take us from instinctual desire to an *esthetic* contemplation of the world which would be, at the same time, an intimation of enlightenment and release. We can scarcely claim that Kubrick—or indeed any artist—can realize such exalted ends. Still, it is in this context that Kubrick's ultimate concerns can be found. The esthetic act—the lighting, posing, framing, and filming—is inevitably a kind of transcendence of the will, a subduing of its transhuman insistence and stupidity.

7

Music

Kubrick revolutionized the use of the score in cinema by breaking its links to the theatrical tradition as program music and replacing it with what could be called a repertoire of musical citation. Program music, as it was practiced in nineteenth-century theater and ballet, offers a parallel sonic realm: an illustration and deepening of affect generated by the drama. It was provided by a single composer and was committed to a consistent musical style. The silent era carried on this tradition by having live or recorded music accompany the exhibition of the film in the theater. With the advent of sound films, program music was mixed with the sound track and synchronized with the film imagery thus to form a synthetic aural and visual experience. The musical score was so steeped in the drama that it was not meant to be "heard" as such, but felt as a kind of musical manifestation of the plot. It was, as Claudia Gorbman observes, used "to reinforce, intensify, and clarify narrative and emotive aspects of the film."[1]

Before 1968, like most directors of the time, Kubrick used film scores and folk or pop standards that could be inserted to amplify the dramatic situation. Gerald Fried, Alex North, Nelson Riddle, and Laurie Johnson were credited with the music of the films up through *Dr. Strangelove* and worked very much within this tradition. Yet even in their somewhat typical use of music to underscore the drama, signal themes, and deepen emotion, there is some anticipation of later developments.

The conclusion of *Paths of Glory* provides some relief from the horrors of trench warfare and murderous Generals when a German girl sings a traditional song about a lover's devotion, "Der Treuer Husar"—and transforms a crowd of loutish soldiers from jeering to quiet empathy. During the closing credits, the girl's faltering song is taken up pompously in a march. Thus, a film that had begun with a *La Marseillaise*—which even by the standards of national anthems is quite violent and xenophobic—ends with a love song about a dead enemy soldier.

Consider other examples. In *Lolita*, Nelson Riddle's Rachmaninoff-like theme, signaling Humbert's ardor, is played off against Bob Harris's "Lolita Theme," a wordless—ya-ya, ya-ya-ya-ya-ya—anthem of mindless suggestiveness that evokes Lolita's eroticism. *Dr. Strangelove* begins with fifties' lounge music ("Try a Little Tenderness") and ends with the World War II hit "We'll Meet Again"—and in between relentlessly exploits a sketchy rendition of the American folk classic "When Johnny Comes Marching Home Again" as an ironic counterpoint to Major Kong's prosecution of Wing Attack Plan R.

Music in these instances does not simply illustrate or amplify the dramatic situation; it assumes a nearly independent role in the film. It can act to undermine, underscore, mock, or comment on the explicit action. In doing this, the musical score gradually detaches itself from the action and assumes a denaturalized status. The way to pure collage is open.

At the last moment, Kubrick discarded the score he had commissioned for *2001* from Alex North (who had done the score for *Spartacus*) and replaced it with a collection of existing classical recordings of Richard Strauss, Johann Strauss, Györgi Ligeti, and Avram Khachaturian that he had used during rehearsals and filming. Kubrick's view of the matter was characteristically blunt: "There doesn't seem to be much point in hiring a composer who, however good he may be, is not a Mozart or a Beethoven, when you have such a vast choice of existing orchestral music."[2] While North's original score would have served the film's themes and drama, the classical pieces acted in counterpoint with the imagined future by evoking the past and, for some in the audience, distinct and different musical contexts. Chief among these was Richard Strauss's tone poem honoring Nietzsche's *Also Sprach Zarathustra*. With Nietzsche's text came associated ideas—the development of human consciousness beyond resentment against time to the acceptance of eternal recurrence, which Nietzsche's Zarathustra regarded as the ultimate test of one's ability to affirm life.

Strauss not only suggests the Nietzschean subtext in the *2001*, it also provides support for Kubrick's reliance on music in the film to express and inspire the emotional continuity of its drama, even as locations and characters change. According to Arthur Schopenhauer, Nietzsche's early influence, music is different from the other arts in that it is able to channel without undue modification the "will"—the impersonal force that works its way through life forms:

> music is by no means like the other arts, namely a copy of the Ideas, but a copy of the will itself . . . For this reason the effect of music is so very much more powerful and penetrating than is that of the other arts.[3]

Kubrick felt that Strauss's music was the perfect expression of the alignment of earth, the sun, and the moon—the voice of the universe itself, the will that moves through all forms toward a final realization of transcendence.

Despite this exalted understanding of music, Kubrick's use of the classics has been severely criticized by some. The prolific film composer Jerry Goldsmith, defending Alex North's discarded score, claims that Kubrick's "abominable misuse of music" was "distracting" and "unrelated" to the film.[4] Speaking as a master of film music, Goldsmith could see no good in this exploitation of the classics (that film composers so often imitated) because it was, in effect, not organic. But Kubrick's use of musical collage is directed against the homogenizing effect of program music, which is essentially what Goldsmith is championing. Goldsmith, steeped in classic film narrative and program music, failed to see that it can have other purposes. As Jerrold Levinson points out, "music composed *for* a film . . . is more likely to be purely narrative in function than pre-existing music appropriated by a film maker."[5] In fact, Kubrick's bold use of temporal juxtaposition in *2001* and other films virtually requires a break with the uniformity and homogeneity of the traditional film score.

The first audiences of *2001* sat before the curtained screen and heard or listened to the unfamiliar and otherworldly *Atmosphères* (1961) of György Ligeti—operating as a kind of musical portal to Kubrick's vision. Before the film had even started, one knew that something unusual was going to happen. *Atmosphères*, *Requiem*, and *Lux Aeterna* each conveys an ungraspable sense of primacy, the uncanny, and the sacred associated with the monolith and the journey through the star-gate. In all but one of these instances, it is clear that the Ligeti is extra-diegetic, exterior to the dramatic scene. But when the hominids first approach the monolith, their fascination and attraction to it would appear to be motivated by the *Kyrie* from the *Requiem*. The nature and urgency of this initiation into the mysteries of the monolith are difficult to imagine without the accompanying music—a frenzy of voices—that seems to emerge from it. In the Mass, of course, the *Kyrie* is a plea to the Lord for mercy; here it seems to be an ecstatic communication from a superior being. Hominids and the audience and later the astronauts and the audience are all joined in this participation mystique accomplished by music.

If Ligeti's music suggests and represents psychic energy and potential, Richard Strauss's *Also Sprach Zarathustra* dramatizes transformation and realization of the monolith's potentials—a kind of Jungian individuation in which the individual consciousness is exposed to a vast reserve of unconscious energy and potential and then internalizes it.[6] The heroic nature of this initiation and individuation is musically represented by Strauss's prelude. Following realization and individuation, Johann Strauss's waltz conveys a sense of bourgeois comfort and imperial security, the formalism of a technological utopia. Space travel in the year 2001 is a distant development of the hominids' encounter with the monolith, but that encounter has been buried and forgotten. Strauss's waltz suits the uniformed elegance and formal joviality of the Pan American crews, just as Khachaturian's mournful dance suits a massive interplanetary craft—piloted by a machine, carrying four astronauts in hibernation, and monitored by two laconic and depressed astronauts.

Where ordinarily music is used to accent or enhance verbal and musical motives in a film, in *2001*, it works with imagery to tell the whole story. The four composers and their music, in fact, form a kind of map of the psyche (and Schopenhauer's Will) that the film actualizes:

Ligeti:	energy
J. Strauss:	convention
Khatchaturian:	exhaustion
R. Strauss:	realization

Music and image are primary in *2001*, acting on the viewer's deeper, inchoate levels of response, leaving language as a kind of limping commentary on the psychic action. Where ordinary film or program music serves the word; here it is the word that serves the music.

If music in *2001* works out Schopenhauer's belief in its proximity to or identity with the will and the sublime, *A Clockwork Orange* is largely *about* music. But it takes an ironic stance: music is both an ideally esthetic and a fully corporeal expression of human beings. This irony is established by a story about a young hood like Alex who listens to Beethoven—not the Rolling Stones or the Who. The irony is deepened by an apparent contrast of Walter (later Wendy) Carlos's synthesized versions of Beethoven, Purcell, and Rossini, and their "natural" musical expression by a symphony orchestra. It is not that Carlos's versions are a debasement of the classics in the way that Alex's understanding of Beethoven is. Carlos's versions are witty paraphrases that uncover something sketchy and comic beneath the layers of orchestration—something sardonic and human. His banal electronic renderings—Carlos would certainly not see them that way—have their own weird sublimity and act to regenerate a sense of the "gorgeosity" of Beethoven's music—grown too familiar through mechanical reproductions.

This apparent conflict or contrast of the synthetic and the natural is of course central to the film, but it can only come to an ironic conclusion. The natural Alex is violent, unconscionable, but also witty and vital; the synthetic or conditioned Alex is tame, hypocritical, dull, and self-pitying. (The same contrast is evident in the contrast between the stodgy King's English as spoken by politician, priest, warden, and writer and the crazed, violent, private Nadsat dialect spoken by Alex and his droogs.) And yet even if the plot did not make this theme explicit, a listener would understand it in another way through the contrast of synthesized and natural music-making, of machine music and instrumental music.

The film begins—with the credits against a field of orange and then blue—with Carlos's synthesized interpretation of Purcell's "Music for the Funeral of Queen Mary." Carlos explained later: "The Purcell is transmogrified into something more spacey, electronic, weird."[7] Stripped of its distant pomp and its mournful strings, Purcell's funeral music becomes associated with Alex, his droogs, and the menace of "the old ultra-violence." The irony of its musical provenance remains, as the sounds of royal obsequies from the seventeenth century are "transmogrified" into a leitmotif of Alex's postmodern, violent chic.

A similar kind of transformation occurs with the Rossini overtures: a conventional recording of *The Thieving Magpie* scores the choreographed battle between Alex's and Billy Boy's droogs in the ruined theater; a synthesized version of the *William Tell* overture scores Alex's sex with the two girls picked up at the record shop. In the first instance, the theatrical, balletic enactment of the brawl is underscored by Rossini's light-hearted *Magpie*; in the second instance, the familiar *William Tell*, a favorite of the classic *Looney Tunes* cartoons and the theme of *The Lone Ranger*, casts a high–low cultural musical tonality on the speeded-up footage of Alex's repeated and comic copulations with the girls. And yet, it is Rossini's music, heard from an apartment window, that makes him realize what he must do after his droogs have challenged his authority: He beats and bloodies them into submission. Where Rossini's music, synthesized or not, suggests a careless expression of vitality (however violent), Beethoven's *Symphony* has a more complex tonality. For Alex, it is at first suffused with erotic violence, later he recognizes that Beethoven is an artist. While listening to the Scherzo, Alex fantasizes about Dracula drinking blood, a girl in bloomers falling through the trapdoor of a gallows, and so forth. And yet when the choral movement—in a synthesized version—is inadvertently used as the score of the conditioning film used at the Ludovico Center, Alex objects: "It's a sin! . . . Using Ludwig van like that. He did no harm to anyone. Beethoven just wrote music."

If Rossini's music is predominantly operatic "fun," Beethoven's *Ninth Symphony* delves deeper. But Alex's "Ode to Joy" is not about "Brotherhood" as Schiller and Beethoven understood it; it is as he and his "brothers" do. The *Ninth Symphony* is about "joy" as sexual pleasure—*jouissance*—and violent exertion. Only when Alex is conditioned—when he becomes "a clockwork orange"—is he repelled by Beethoven: not only because of his inadvertent conditioning against the *Ninth Symphony*, but by a recognition that violence has always been an aspect of his kind of music appreciation. Forced by the conspirators to listen to the synthesized *Ninth*, Alex attempts suicide. But when he is deconditioned, he can listen to a conventional performance of the coda without the slightest qualms, imaging a joyful copulation with a willing young woman in the snow, as an appreciative audience politely applauds.

Kubrick's treatment of classical and popular music stresses this hidden aspect of the art of music: beneath the superhuman musical dynamism of Beethoven's *Ninth Symphony* lies one man's tortured and repressed psyche. Music is the sublimation of violence and eroticism, a synthesized transformation of drives and instincts in the terms of a socially approved esthetic form.

But there is no clear distinction between synthesized and natural, violent and harmless uses of the classics—whether it is Beethoven or of Gene Kelly's "Singin' in the Rain." When Alex first sings the song while assaulting Mrs Alexander, both he and Kubrick are "having a go" at a feel-good standard about an idealized or impossible transcendence of sorrow. Alex "reads" out the violence, rage, sadness concealed within. When he later sings it in Mr Alexander's bathtub, after being conditioned, it is a recollection of his assault, but it is now drained of vitality: It hardly suggests a victory over sorrow so much as a plaintive recollection of the lost pleasures of violence. And when Kubrick uses Kelly's own performance with the closing credits—having bought the rights to it—the song sounds sinister and irrecoverable. As James Naremore observes, the song can never sound quite the same again (this is something that Kelly himself seems to have recognized).

While Kubrick altered—well, let us say ruined—"Singin' in the Rain," he performed a different service for classical music in general. Many in Kubrick's audience were introduced to classical and avant-garde music by *A Clockwork Orange*, *2001*, and later films. But this came at a price, for to some extent, Kubrick left his own mark on the music of Richard Strauss, Beethoven, Ligeti, Rossini, and others. If Elgar's "Pomp and Circumstance" march has been undone by countless commencement exercises, Kubrick uses it at least in a new, if not an entirely different, spirit: as the theme music for the Ludovico

(Conditioning) Center. And Rimsky-Korsakov's *Scheherazade*, a romantic exercise in Orientalism, is used—in Alex's fantasy—as the sound-track for the passion of Christ as well as a soft porn idyll of grapes and odalisques. In all of these instances, Kubrick uses classical music—at a time when it was popularly conceived as "square"—to accent its erotic, violent, and countercultural aspects. Kubrick turned back Hollywood associations of classical music with high society and high romantic drama.

Kubrick's use of music in *Barry Lyndon* is more traditionally consistent and focused; the only infraction Kubrick could be charged with is using Schubert's Piano Trio (Op. 99; 1827), when the film was ostensibly dedicated to an authentic recreation of eighteenth-century painting, fashion, and music. Both the classical repertoire and the traditional songs and melodies, like the film's painterly style, present a unified complement to the dramatic action of a bygone era. These musical selections remain firmly on the surface and engender generic and general response. They do not explore motives or complexities or make ironic contrasts and inferences; rather they integrate the individual with the social and esthetic fabric of the period. Thus, Barry's courtship of Nora Brady, dramatized through card-playing and a game of hide and seek with a ribbon, is accompanied by the traditional *Mna na h'eirann* (*Women of Ireland*); the review of the troops and Barry's reunion with Grogan are accompanied by the traditional *British Grenadiers* and *Lillibulero*. Likewise, Handel, Mozart, and Vivaldi are deployed to formalize and generalize the duel with Quin, Barry's espionage for the Prussian police, and the domestic life and style of Lady Lyndon. The *Adagio* from the Schubert *Trio* would appear to reach beyond such formalities to touch upon more intimate feelings: It is associated with Lady Lyndon and her tragic love for Barry and also his conniving courtship and many betrayals. The musical accompaniments—arranged by Leonard Rosenman, who complained about Kubrick's insistence on using the anachronistic *Trio*—explore and reveal very little about the principals as individuals—like the painterly stillness of the film's photography and direction, and the narrator's tendency to translate Barry's life into general human principles.

The Shining returned to a more eclectic score, drawing on Penderecki's *The Dream of Jacob*, Bartok's *Music for Strings, Percussion, and Celesta*, and Ligeti's *Lontano* as a musical correlative to the film's psychic indeterminism. If Ligeti seems an inspired and unforeseeable choice for a "science fiction" film, Penderecki seems a natural choice for a "horror movie." Along with contemporary and modern masters like Ligeti and Bartok, Penderecki brings to *The Shining* a startling air of "seriousness" and mythic introspection, as well as a kind of cultural dissonance: It is not the kind of music one would expect to hear in the lobby during high season—it suggests an underworld of atonal vibrancy and violence. It is clear enough, though, that the music in the film is a constant reminder that Kubrick wanted to make "the best horror film ever" by going beneath the horror genre to fairy tale, myth, and religion. All of this music, then, has a dominant tone of foreboding—an awakening sense of incipient horror. Thus, Penderecki's *The Dream of Jacob* or *Jacob Awakes* (*Als Jakob Erwachte*) is associated with Grady's murders at the Overlook, the locker for the dried goods where Jack will be confined, the maze-like carpeting, and room 237. If Penderecki's title evokes Jacob's dream of angels climbing on a ladder between heaven and earth, in *The Shining*, it musically evokes a descent into the hotel's past or psyche. Kubrick also includes portions of Pendercki's *Utrenja*, *De Natura Sonoris #1* and *#2*, *Kanon*, and *Polymorphia* (which William Friedkin had used in *The Exorcist* in 1973). The Bartok is associated with the hedge maze outside the hotel and Jack's stunned visions, his typing, and room 237. Ligeti's music is employed in the concluding chases in the film. In each case, the music works in contrast with the bright banality of the hotel décor and the tabloid-like scenario. The double register of *The Shining* is similarly heard in the contrast of "serious" music with the songs from *The Road Runner* ("Road Runner/The coyote's after you./ Road Runner,/If he catches you you're through.") and *Midnight, the Stars and You*, played by Ray Noble's Orchestra, with vocal by Al Bowlly. In fact, in the context of the classical compositions, these popular pieces begin sounding uncanny, or simply creepy.

With the exception of the background score composed by Abigail Mead (Vivian Kubrick), music in *Full Metal Jacket* is restricted to pop music from the sixties and the songs sung by the recruits at Parris Island and the City of Hue. The absence of music from the classical repertoire is unique in the later Kubrick and leaves the film with a less allusive resonance—but this in keeping with its minimalist portrait of war. The pop music is not without its own contributions to an implicit interpretation of the action. "Hello Vietnam" plays during the credits as the recruits and draftees have their heads shaved. Johnny Wright sings of Uncle Sam's "bugle call" to war, a farewell to his "darling," and a resigned "hello to Vietnam." Introducing the film's theme of the renunciation of the feminine for war, the song makes no patriotic claims: "I don't suppose that war will ever end." This and subsequent pop songs—"These Boots are Made for Walking," "The Chapel of Love," "Wooly Bully," "Surfin' Bird"—ground scenes in the cultural atmosphere of the 1968 while adding an absurdly alien element to the Vietnamese setting—needless to say, we hear no Vietnamese music.

The training songs deconstruct pieties of family ("Momma and Papa were laying in bed./Momma turned over and this is what she said:/ Uh Give me some") and religion ("Happy Birthday Dear Jesus, Happy Birthday to you"), while clearly establishing one function of the Marine Corps ("I love working for Uncle Sam/Let's me know just who I am"). In contrast, Mead's sonic score for the critical scenes—Pyle's punishment by his fellow Marines; the murder of Hartman and Pyle's suicide; the scenes of dead men; and the killing of the Viet Cong sniper—operate in an utterly different musical space. Here the comic or manic absurdity of "Hello Vietnam" and the others is answered by an uncanny, atonal background that emphasizes the irreversible, tragic elements at work. When the Marines sing the theme song from "The Mickey Mouse Club" in the last, fiery scene, they are both facing and turning away from the execution of the female sniper. Seen in this light, the Corps is nothing more than a Disney confection, a "club" and no kind of immortal cultus. The pop music works to distance or deny the psychic costs of training and war, while Mead's music brings them to tragic awareness. In this sense, one can hear a dialog of repression and the return of the repressed. Only with Rolling Stones' concluding "Paint it Black" do these two musical realms converge.

In his last film, Kubrick returned to the classical repertoire (Shostakovich, Ligeti) and also commissioned work from the contemporary composer Jocelyn Pook. Shostakovich's waltz from his *Jazz Suite # 2* (also titled *Music for Variety Stage Orchestra*) introduces and concludes the film, as well as serving as score for a montage of scenes establishing the daily lives of Bill and Alice Harford. It is a strikingly apt choice for this purpose, suggesting a worldly and ironic attitude toward life's inevitable disguises and deceits while also expressing a powerful vitality. Its waltz-like rhythms serve as a link to the Viennese ambience of Arthur Schnitzler's *Traumnovelle* and as a strong contrast with a few notes from an icy movement from Ligeti's *Musica Ricercata* and Pook's brooding compositions "Naval Officer" and "Masked Ball." The Shostakovich accompanies the opening credits and the scenes of the Harfords dressing for the Christmas party at the Zieglers' mansion, creating an atmosphere of sophisticated pretense and deceit. Appropriately enough, it turns out to be diegetic: Bill turns the music off with the flick of a switch as the Harfords leave for the party. We know, in other words, that their marital pretenses will be disrupted at a later point.

Pook's compositions evoke the secret lives of the couple and the secret life of society at large. "Naval Officer" accompanies Alice's account of her passionate fascination and Bill's brooding imagination of them making love. "Masked Ball" is the apparently diegetic accompaniment for the ritual orgy at Somerton, as the masked Nick Nightingale plays a keyboard that seems connected to a synthesizer. Sounding like an Orientalist fantasy in which the hieratic and the erotic seem to merge, "Masked Ball" is an uncanny and absorbing accompaniment of the cultish rituals of Manhattan's movers and shakers. The Orientalist motifs in the composition complement the Moorish or Turkish elements in the architecture of Somerton—and suggest a fascination with Sultanic excesses across the Bosporus from Schnitzler's Vienna. (The piece is, in fact, a reworking of her *Backward Priests*, which uses Romanian lyrics played backwards.) Pook's music is humorless and primal: There is no sense of self-awareness or detachment—it expresses something erotic and sacred, something enticing and frightening. It also introduces a Tamil song performed by Manickam Yogeswaran, as Bill wanders through room after room of naked, copulating couples. By the time Bill is warned by the Mysterious Woman, all of these musical evocations are supplanted by the Frank Sinatra standard "Strangers in the Night." In this progression, the musical score sketches a range of subjective reactions to the orgy, from the sublime to ridiculous.

In response to this dialectic of a superb detachment from, and an abject investment in, the passions, the second piece from the piano suite *Musica Ricercata* sounds like a summoning to responsibility and the law. It is first heard when Bill has been discovered as an interloper. The ritual orgy now becomes a summary tribunal, and Red Cloak, who swung a censer around the disrobing women, now appears as prosecutor and judge. This plangent composition is heard another four times, each time in a scene of reckoning or unmasking: when, the next day, Bill stands at the gate to Somerton; when he is followed during his night-time walk; when he reads the newspaper account of the death of Mandy Curran; and when he sees the carnival mask on his pillow beside his sleeping wife. These musical summonings will finally bring the Harfords to a dangerous moment of mutual recognition. After they reveal their secrets to one another and see the necessity of "waking up," the Shostakovich is heard a final time with the closing credits. If the waltz originally suggested deceit, desire, and blindness, it now points ahead to an ironic and enlightened participation in the formal nature of social existence.

Effective and moving as the scores of Franz Waxman, Bernard Herrmann, Jerry Goldsmith, and the other masters can be, they sound out an affective world far anterior to the modern cinema. By allowing for citational complexity into the score, Kubrick was able to deepen and ironize the very nature of the emotion aroused by music. And by opening up the cinema to avant-garde composers, Kubrick encouraged trends toward more sophisticated and adventurous musical citations. The consequence is not simply to complicate the nature of musical affect but to introduce a transcultural element into the musical unconscious of the viewer. Music in this way has a greater chance of being heard, and to play its own equal and complex role in the cinematic poiesis of light, time, and speech.

8

Technology

Kubrick's persistent attention to human embodiment and corporeality is the foundation of his vision of human affairs. The gastrointestinal axis of eating and defecating provides his cinema with a constant reminder of human limits, even as it motivates hopes of technological transformation and transcendence. Yet as one surveys the films, one recognizes that technology is never rid of its corporeal designers: It carries within a kind of transmuted human psychology and intrinsic waywardness. Indeed, a cursory review of Kubrick's films would discover, with some consistency and satiric hyperbole, the "failure" of technology. We have only to recall that the nuclear holocaust and destruction of the biosphere in *Dr. Strangelove* are the consequence of American and Soviet Defense technology designed, like the computer HAL, to be "incapable of error." While Kubrick saw promise and beauty in technology and technical artifacts, he also realized that they remained, in a sense, all too human. Although he exhibited time and again the madness that humans channel into technology, he personally *loved* technology; indeed he made the technology of film production into his own fully human esthetic instrument. Technology, in other words, is human and fallible and thus capable of surprise—and even revelation.

Kubrick's films often focus precisely on this conflict between highly rationalized technologies and unknown, unconscious drives. As Michel Ciment writes, "Kubrick's world is forever on the brink of collapse, whether it be that of an individual or a society."[1] The "brink of collapse" is also a point of contact between technological mastery and instinctual demands that remain obscure to rationality.

Consider the minute detail and attention that Kubrick lavishes on computers, telephones, jet bombers, control panels, radar dishes, nuclear bombs, interplanetary spacecraft, space stations, and moon bases. Consider the dark pebbled surface of the control panels of the B-52 in *Dr. Strangelove* when the attack code suddenly erupts. Picture the "eye" through which HAL looks at Frank Poole and Dave Bowman in the Pod as they discuss the predicted breakdown of the AE 35 Unit and the feasibility of disconnecting HAL: Its red "iris" and yellow "pupil," rounded and gleaming, have a numinous quality as well as a distinctly technical coolness. These technical artifacts, and many others in Kubrick's films, have powerfully beautiful appearances: They also seem about to reveal something.

We can find a premise for a reading of the esthetic aspect of technology in Martin Heidegger's "The Question Concerning Technology" (1955). Heidegger dismisses the views that the essence of technology is itself "technological" and that it should be seen as purely "neutral." This is the view, maintained by its champions, that technology is merely a tool that can be used wisely or foolishly. For Heidegger, technology more properly evokes Greek etymology and Greek art:

> In Greece, at the outset of the destining of the West, the arts soared to the supreme height of the revealing granted them. They brought the presence of the gods, brought the dialogue of divine and human destinings to radiance.[2]

To see this buried aspect of *technē* within technological artifacts and culture requires a freshened gaze. We must look at technology without regard to manifest use and familiarity. Seen in this light, another face of technology is disclosed. "Technology," Heidegger writes:

> is therefore no mere means. Technology is a means of revealing. If we give heed to this, then another whole realm for the essence of technology will open itself up to us . . . Technology comes to presence in the realm where revealing and un-concealment take place, where *aletheia*, truth, happens.[3]

Seen in this light, technology as *technē* sheds its merely "mechanical" appearance and recalls its esthetic roots in crafting, expression, and revealing. In this light, again, we see technology's hidden face, its human aspect.

According to Albert Borgmann, contemporary technology is characterized by what he calls the "device paradigm," the interface that separates the consumer from the actual functioning of the machinery of information, computation, transportation, and other modern "wonders." For Borgmann, this consumerist device paradigm acts to alienate users from the actuality of their dependence and ignorance of how technology actually happens.[4] A kind of "magical" aura, aided by design, branding, and imagery, surrounds computers, televisions, jet airplanes, and the like. By encouraging delusions of consumer mastery, the device paradigm transforms human beings into aspects of technology. The "send button" on an email program floats atop an abyss of circuitry and "magically" abridges time and space. At the same time, of course, all messages—ostensibly a medium of human intimacy—are subject to third-party inspection. Dependency on such forms of "intimacy" has grown exponentially in recent years. Sold according to an appeal to notions of "freedom" and "independence," they instead continue to involve human subjectivity into a network of dependency and alienation. And the same kind of effect has been accomplished by air transportation for decades. Passengers enter a Boeing 747 through a "jet way" that translates them from the lobby of the terminal to an aluminum tube. The facts of jet propulsion are concealed behind a physical and semiotic facade of consumer "comfort" and "freedom." And yet, as everyone knows, to fly is to surrender one's independence and one's dignity to a vast network of coordinated flights to destinations that become increasingly similar.

In Kubrick's films, technology assumes an esthetic and an apocalyptic function that is initiated by the destruction of the illusions of the "device paradigm." The Strategic Air Command (SAC) and the National Areonautics and Space Administration (NASA) present themselves as user-friendly devices that confront danger and distance with assured mastery. But pilots and astronauts sit before a panel of devices that facilitate and alienate at the same time. The "purposes" of technology as they are represented by the device paradigm—and the corny iconography of SAC and NASA—are overmastered by the abyssal forces of energies and machinery that reach below them. The actual machinery, then, the technology, as opposed to the consumerist interface, has its own intentionality. Beneath the devices arrayed before Major Kong's gaze is a circuitry reaching back to an elemental death drive that men have wired into their technology. Beneath HAL's placid eye are the dark and mysterious motives of the beings that placed the monolith on the earth, the moon, and Jupiter space. These devices only nominally control technology; in actuality, they facilitate its apocalyptic potentials.

The films most directly dedicated to technology's disclosure, *Dr. Strangelove* and *2001*, operate in terms of dialectic. With *Dr. Strangelove*, Kubrick attempted to discover the actual conditions and capacities of the Defense Department in the early sixties and to represent them in terms of a kind of revelatory satire. In *2001*, Kubrick and his design team were free to invent technologies for the dawn of the next millennium. With the escape from earth gravity, Kubrick's technological esthetic achieves a kind of mythic freedom and promise. In these two films, we see technology as antithetical, as nightmare and as idyll—the strange love of the death-drive and a nearly realized deliverance from the earth.

In this synoptic analysis of Kubrick's esthetic disclosure of the essence of technology, we will focus on the following modes: automata, computers, information, communication, and transportation. The practical purposes of these technologies, ostensibly dedicated to aiding and advancing human beings, in fact barely conceal a contempt for corporeality and advance in its place an ideal of technical spirituality.

Automata and computers—the culture of Artificial Intelligence—offer what could be called "successor-concepts," materially realized, to such discredited metaphysical principles as the soul, omniscience, and immortality. Kubrick's interest in automata, both human and artificial, indicates the realization of a dilemma that has no solution. If HAL is the expression of a desire to escape from the body and the limitations of human cognition, "he/it" is also the expression of a human desire to remain human. Bodiless and Argus-eyed, HAL's intellectual superiority is evidently no compensation for his desire for society and fraternity. His attempts at friendship come off as awkward or arrogant. When he learns that Poole and Bowman plan to disconnect him, he determines to terminate all organic life on *Discovery*, as if to insist on his own form of subjectivity as the new norm. And yet his own programmed "humanity" is in contrast with the deadened and disciplined natures of Bowman and Poole: Their training has made them only marginally more alive than the crew traveling in hibernation. In this way, the human and the technological seem to be developing in opposite directions: If scientists and engineers are no longer capable of subjective stances, they are at least able to program a machine to simulate them. HAL's madness appears, in this light, as a compensatory overreaction to the gap that separates human technologists and their technologies.

If HAL is Kubrick's ultimate expression of technology's failed attempt to transcend human contingency and corporeality, the CRM 114 is his ultimate expression of technology's attempt to establish communication at a distance free from interference and distortion. The paranoid-schizophrenic General Ripper has ordered Wing Attack Plan R in response to a supposed disruption of the chain of command from the president. The deterrent effect of Plan R was, of course, meant to prevent the Russians from attempting a sneak attack that would prevent a US nuclear response. It was not foreseen that Plan R would instead encourage an American sneak attack. Thus, a plan to prevent nuclear war actually brings it about. Once the B-52s of the Wing switch on the CRM

114s no one without the three-letter code prefix can contact them: the planes are "safe" from "unauthorized" communications and are thus completely "secure" and "dedicated"—to a mad man's insubordination. Technical subjects—whether they are automata, constituted human beings, or simulacra—and technical communication alienate traditional manifestations of organicism and presence via artifice and the abrogation of distance. Both seek to overcome organic presence with simulation.

Aviation and space travel were the realization of perennial myths and dreams of transcendence—just as the making of automata and communication at a distance were. Yet once these myths and dreams yielded to business, the government and the military, flight became resolutely terrestrial and anti-transcendental. Flight would change no one: It was designed as an elimination of distance and difference and the preservation of the subjectivity of the traveler. Mankind would escape the earth and gravitation, but it would then recreate them on its own terms.

Automata and computers

Kubrick's interest in automata (simulacra, cybernetic systems, computers) and para-automata (by which I mean constituted or conditioned human beings) is evident from *Killer's Kiss* to *A.I.: Artificial Intelligence*, his long-planned film that was ultimately made by Steven Spielberg in 2001. The question he asks throughout is elemental: Is there a significant difference between a dedicated machine and a human being who has surrendered agency to an obsession, an ideology, a bureaucracy—any protocol that overrides his own potentials for freedom. Kubrick's films represent the ways in which machines develop human freedom and human beings submit to mechanical regularity. Burdened with a computational hyperrationality, HAL aspires to a fully, and finally mad, human ontology while General Turgidson, swollen with fears and desires, aspires to the aerodynamic efficiency of a B-52 delivering a nuclear payload.

Killer's Kiss presents Kubrick's first images of automata and simulacra in a Times Square shop window: a furry wind-up bear endlessly bringing candied apples to its mouth and a wind-up infant swimming around a bowl of water that resembles a toilet. In Kubrick's noir vision of New York City, automation is a general condition, but these automata have a bright emptiness about them. They seem to solicit empathy, to ask us to grant them our own subjectivity. To this extent, they parallel the main characters, Davy and Gloria, themselves little more than generic captives of the city. Davy is a "boxer" and Gloria is a "hostess" in a dance club: Both perform a mechanical routine for the agent and boss who wind them up. It is appropriate, then, that the final confrontation between Davy and Gloria's boss Vince takes place in a manikin warehouse. As they battle each other for Gloria, the manikins appear as doubles, and finally as weapons, as the men heave them at one another. The subjectivity or interiority of the principal characters appears, in this context, dubious, since even their "love" for one another seems fluxional, depending on whatever "fix" they are in.

Kubrick's investigation of simulacra and automata is more broadly conducted directly with human bodies—thieves, soldiers, and astronauts. With the alienating and constitutive uses of masks, uniforms, space suits, helmets, and weapons, these bodies seem to be striving for—or driven to—a post-subjective, para-automated form of existence. The thieves who rob the racetrack in *The Killing* have organized their movements with timed precision, each performing a single function as a part of the larger mechanism. The mastermind, Johnny Clay, assumes a mask when he stuffs the money into a sack: It is as if the whole gang were a single, self-less machine. Likewise, in *Paths of Glory*, *Spartacus*, *Dr. Strangelove*, *2001*, *Barry Lyndon*, and *Full Metal Jacket*, military culture is understood as the constitution of a mechanized or technical subject. When the trainees in *Full Metal Jacket* sing, one hand on their genitals and their weapons at their shoulders, "This is my rifle, this is my gun," they are asserting a distinction without much of a difference. The song implies that a clarification is needed but also that fighting and fun, violence and sex, are aspects of one another. The officers and men in these films often assume the dedicated emptiness of automata. Sheathed in uniforms, packs, martial regalia, helmets, they are human beings fully "weaponized." Like a round of ammunition, each soldier, general, astronaut assumes a "full metal jacket."

A striking instance of these developments can be observed in the character of Dr Strangelove. A former Nazi scientist who has become an American "defense" expert, Strangelove has lost the ability to control his limbs: He can neither walk nor prevent his gloved hand from seizing his own throat. His body in rebellion against his will, Strangelove is the intersection of the human desire for technological transcendence and the technological usurpation of human agency. Seated in his wheelchair with his dark glasses, dapper suit, silver hair, and cigarette, Strangelove appears as a human-technological hieroglyph. Once the "doomsday shroud" spreads around the earth, then Strangelove rises from his chair and cries out, "Mein Führer, I can walk." Only in a dead world can Dr Strangelove realize his autonomy.

Dr Strangelove remains, however, more hieroglyph than agent: He may represent the usurpation of human agency by technology, but he is himself only an "expert" and a "planner." Actual agency in the film is a meeting of human madness and a technology which has been devised to operate beyond human control. In a sense, the paranoid–schizophrenic Gen. Ripper is the perfect expression of this post-human agency, since he is himself beyond his own control. Ripper directs the 34 B-52s of his 843rd bomb wing to attack their targets inside Russia, but it is "Plan R" that is finally in charge. And "Plan R," for Romeo—there is a love of death scarcely concealed in this Plan—is a linkage of discriminating computers, communication technology, jet transportation, trained pilots, and nuclear bombs. No "one" is really in charge, except the plural, distributed, and selfless agency of the technology which was erected by American corporations, like IBM and Boeing, under contract to the Defense Department and the Strategic Air Command. This massively distributed technical subject represents an empty form of agency, without consciousness or volition. It is, in principle, nothing more than a clockwork bear eating candied apples or a clockwork doll swimming in a toilet.

The development of computing in Kubrick's films follows the same movement from tool to agency. The computers in *Dr. Strangelove* have purely instrumental purposes: They can, for instance, derive and send all the 17,000 permutations of the three-letter code group prefix to the bomb wing heading to Russia. They can operate the Doomsday Machine; they can select which elites will be allowed to survive its radiation. These computers have a discrete physical presence and, as such, they have a kind of technological body and "space": They are, in other words, appliances.

The status of computers changed radically in *2001*. According to Michael Mateas, HAL is more than a fictional computer: HAL "was a representation of the goals, methodologies, and dreams of the field of Artificial Intelligence."[5] Its "nature" is thus, especially in retrospect, both technical and mythological. In *2001*, the HAL 9000 computer is, despite its technical construction, a mysterious presence: not only is it conscious (and self-conscious), its hardware and applications are indistinguishable from the space ship itself—and its surveillance and communication range. It is both nowhere and everywhere, a kind of divine ubiquity. Its only discernible presence are the "eyes" positioned throughout *Discovery*: These are encased in a silver ring and composed of blending bands of dark red and vermilion in the "iris" and a yellowish "pupil." Although these eyes are ostensibly video camera lenses, they appear as a symbolic expression of HAL's "nature" and technical subjectivity. The eyes look something like a glassy mandala—an instrument dedicated to transcendence. But this expressive aspect is brought into doubt by its multiple locations. Moreover, its voice is soft and mild, its intonations subtle, and its language mannered. Its memory base is a space bathed in vermilion light and large enough for a man to enter and walk about. Its memory is stored in cassette-sized crystals. All told, the physical manifestations of HAL indicate spirituality and mechanism in equal measure. HAL's strangeness derives from these simultaneous manifestations of interiority and decenteredness, of subjectivity and mere computational complexity. As such, HAL stands as an expression of our desires for technical transcendence and fears of our essential materiality.

While Drs Bowman and Poole and Mr Aimer of BBC can only wonder whether HAL has "real emotions" or only simulates them, HAL itself is in no doubt—any more than any human being is. His/its exchanges with Aimer evince pride, superiority, and condescension. Although HAL appears to be simply "another person" (according to Poole) and the "sixth member of the crew," he has ultimate control over the spacecraft, for, as Mr Aimer says, HAL is the "brain and nervous system of the ship." While these may not be literal statements, they are metaphorically true. HAL speaks of only wanting to be of the "fullest possible use," just like any other "conscious entity." But this seems to be a hypocritical courtesy veiling his absolute control of the ship and crew. HAL's subjectivity and agency become fully manifest only when he kills Poole and the three hibernating astronauts—and then tries to kill Bowman. This manifestation of the self through murder repeats the human trajectory dramatized in the "Dawn of Man" section of the film: Moon-watcher becomes individuated from the hominid clan only once he has conceived of the technical potential of an animal femur and used it as a weapon.

A.I. Artificial Intelligence (2001), Steven Spielberg's film based on a secretive collaboration with Kubrick and his extensive preproduction archive, moves well beyond the year 2001 to approximately AD 4001. The narrative is in fact that of an artificial being, named the "Specialist," and concerns the last surviving "mecha" (mechanical) with any experience of human beings. David, produced by a god-man named Hobbie (Ezra Pound once referred to Yahweh as an "old man with a hobby"), had spent 2,000 years in the underwater—and then frozen—world of Manhattan before being excavated by a self-replicating society of artificial beings. Although the Specialist and the others appear to be the apotheosis of rationality and compassion, they also seem beset by melancholy. Having transcended organic existence and human control, they are drawn to a kind of romantic archaeology of human civilization and grant David his greatest wish, a final day with his "mother"—the woman whose son he had replaced for a time.

While HAL's existence is distributed throughout the *Discovery* and has no anthropomorphic existence, David appears to be a "real boy." If the smug and aloof HAL still seems to want human acceptance, David wants above all else the love of his mother. While HAL's artificiality is manifest essentially in terms of his "enormous intellect," David's artificiality is manifest essentially in terms of simulation. He is indeed an eternal simulation of a ten-year-old; there is nothing otherwise remarkable about him. If HAL represents a deliverance from corporeality, David longs for "reality"—in this context, a condition requisite for eliciting maternal love.

It is only at the end of the film that one realizes that the refined English voice of the narrator is that of the Specialist. Suffused with melancholy, he surveys a drowned world: Venice, New York, Amsterdam. We can hardly imagine that the speaker is in effect a robot mourning the ecological cataclysms that brought the human race to an end. Just as the soulful voice of the narrator is revealed to be a robot at the end of the film, so, moving in the opposite direction, does David appear initially as an artificial boy but dies as an apparently "human" being. In the early scenes, David's skin is evidently plastic, his movements mechanical, but by the end, his skin is natural, his movements lifelike, and his emotional life deepened by love and loss.

The crucial question in the film, what is it that distinguishes a perfect simulacrum from reality, a programmed emotion from a genuine one, is of course central to all of Kubrick's films. Having gone in search of the Blue Fairy from *Pinocchio*, David has found a theme village in a submarine Coney Island and spends 2,000 years gazing at the Blue Fairy. What a fairy simulacrum cannot grant, the robot race can—in a manner of speaking. They make him a "real boy" by making his "mother" a clone or a simulacrum. Roused from 2,000 years of death, she appears now as a perfect simulation of the original woman. In this way, she and David spend an idyllic day together, an Oedipal fantasy nearly realized. Waking her from a sleep of two millennia, he falls "asleep" with her in bed as the sun sets. Thus, through the kind of simulations imagined by robotic enthusiasts such as Hans Moravec, Frank Tipler, and Ray Kurzweil, the Specialist and his technology realize David's fantasy. But David becomes real only when he "dies" next to his "mother" in bed.

But a curious theme remains unaddressed in Spielberg's film: Why does David equate reality with love? His quest for maternal love is a quest for reality—a reality that can only be granted by a fairy from an Italian fable. If the Specialist and the other artificial beings take such an interest in David, it must be because they understand David's dilemma. The perfection of artificial, simulated existence inspires an atavistic desire for "reality," which can only be understood according to a fundamental loss: of the mother, for David, and the human race, for the Specialist. In a civilization dominated by simulation, "reality" would appear to be the ultimate desire, just as "spirit" would be the ultimate desire for a civilization dominated by transient corporeality. Fulfillment, in other words, points ahead to the Utopia of technological transcendence or behind to the Arcadia of natural presence. Kubrick seems to be showing us that it is allied either with technology or nature—yet each, by itself, inspires abjection and melancholy. *A. I. Artificial Intelligence*, as realized by Steven Spielberg, brings Kubrick's meditation on the allure and the dilemma of automata to a mordant and ironic conclusion.

Information and communication

The ambition concealed by modern information and communication technology is, in essence, mythical: It is spiritualized or disembodied knowledge projected across limitless distances. Information, in this mythic context, is knowledge purified of human subjectivity; communication is information joining subjects without regard to space. In Kubrick's films, however, information and communication technology do not submit to such mythic ideals: They assert their own presence and demands. Information and communication, in other words, want to have their own say.

The information and communication interfaces dramatized in *Dr. Strangelove* can be seen as the concrete manifestation of the worldview attributed by Nietzsche to Socratic or "theoretical man," the "mystagogue of science," who aspires to throw across the "entire globe" a "common net of thought."[6] The theoretical mastery, implicit in the net of longitude and latitude thrown across the earth, becomes hardwired in the twentieth century with the advent of universal communication, surveillance, and air travel. In this way, with the coming of radio, radar, computers, jet travel, and nuclear warheads, the "earth"—quaint term—is supplanted by a simulated "globe" which is formed and mounted by a constant streaming of information. This technological replacement of a living and indeterminate state of affairs by an electronic representation is dramatized in the opening scenes of the film. The confusion of the precedent and the simulated world is the essential revealing of technology. Reality can no longer be entrusted to the human senses; it must be assembled electronically, synthesized, and projected on the "threat board" in the war room. The "world" yields, as Heidegger demonstrates, to the "world picture":

> The fundamental event of the modern age is the conquest of the world as picture. The word "picture" [*Bild*] now means the structured image [*Gebild*] that is the creature of man's producing which represents and sets before. In such producing, man contends for the position in which he can be that particular being who gives the measure and draws up the guidelines for everything that is.[7]

The technological media of inspection discover what is "real" by positing an alien yet alluring kind of representation. In this study of technology, Kubrick chooses to use black and white stock—suggesting Defense Department documentaries and film noir—in order to establish both a sense of realism and gothic menace: The world is in thrall to a shadow. Kubrick's masterful simulation of technical elements serves as a sobering and a paradoxical context for the satiric vision of hyperrationality blending with delusion and madness.

Radar, the primary instrument of this world surveillance, plays an iconic role in the expository scenes early in *Dr. Strangelove*. We see a radar dish turning against a darkened sky. Although we may not be certain, it seems to be moving, if not too fast, then a little frenetically, a little imploringly. Like the other technological manifestations in the film, it suggests an older precedent in mythology, metaphysics, and religion, confusing our comfortable sense of its reliable and "technical" nature with a barely realized sense of its bereavement, exposure, and anxiety. Radar is constantly listening for echoes of its own constant stream of signals.

But if the radar dish appears like an anxious listener to darkened skies, the radar screen appears quite differently: It translates distance and darkness into infallible, luminous imagery. When Major Kong's B-52 is headed for its primary target, Kubrick provides an extended and dramatic episode in which the bomber's radar screen picks up what the DSO—the Defense Systems Operator—calls "an unidentified radar blip" that soon "looks like a missile tracking [them]."

Throughout this dramatic episode, the radar screen acquires a nearly numinous quality, a luminous precision and evocativeness, as the DSO acts as its interpreter and spokesman. The scene is a familiar one from war films: The graded precision of the screen's representation of space—the flashing blip and the concentric rings centered on the moving bomber—acts as an uncanny medium to appreciate the facts of death and destruction. The DSO interprets the screen's information for Kong in the dispassionate, pitch-perfect tone of someone far removed from danger.

If Kubrick's account of surveillance and information has a divine aspect, his representation of communication is consistently satirical and ironic: Attempts made by human beings to make contact nearly always generate buffers, relays, delays, and barriers. Attempts to establish or guarantee secure communication tend instead toward isolation and alienation. Here is an incomplete list of such instances from *Dr. Strangelove* and *2001*:

> When Gen. Ripper calls Mandrake to tell him that "we're in a shooting war," he first seeks confirmation that Mandrake recognizes his voice. Claiming that word came in "on the Red Phone," Ripper orders Mandrake to transmit plan R to the wing and have the base sealed from outside communication. Since all forms of communication can be compromised, it's best to remain incommunicado.
>
> When Major Kong receives the order and has it "confirmed," the CRM 114 is activated, preventing the bomber from receiving any message without the code prefix, which is in the keeping of a madman.
>
> When Col. Butridge calls Gen. Turgidson about the Wing attack, he's in the toilet. His message is relayed by his secretary Miss Scott. He soon learns that "all communications are dead" at Ripper's base.
>
> When President Muffley asks the source of Turgidson's information about Ripper's actions, Turgidson reads a "partial transcript" of Ripper's phone call to SAC. When Muffley asks to speak with Ripper, Turgidson tells him "that's impossible, sir." Muffley then orders an army unit to "enter the base, locate Gen. Ripper, and put him in immediate telephone contact with me."
>
> When Soviet Premier Kissov cannot be reached by phone, the Russian Ambassador DeSadesky supplies a private number, B86543 Moscow. Kissov is drunk.
>
> Strangelove asks DeSadesky how the Doomsday Machine could work as a deterrent if the world doesn't know about it. "It was supposed to be announced at the Party Congress on Monday . . . the Premier loves surprises."

When Mandrake has nearly figured out the code, he discovers that the red telephone to SAC has no cord. When he tries to call the President on a pay phone, he finds he's short of change. The Pentagon won't accept his collect call.

After a missile attack on Kong's bomber, the CRM 114 and radio are destroyed. Even with the correct code prefix employed, the plane remains incommunicado.

When the Teleflex drive cable to the bomb bay doors is sheared off, it seems that nuclear holocaust is averted. But Kong connects the cable and rides the bomb to detonation.

Once the monolith is discovered near Clavius, the moon base is made incommunicado for security purposes.

When Dr. Heywood tries to call his wife on the video-phone from *Space Station V*, she is in the bathroom. He has his daughter relay a message to her.

When Bowman, Poole, and HAL are interviewed by BBC, the seven-minute delay in the radio transmission is edited out for broadcast. The men and the computer watch themselves being interviewed.

Poole passively watches a birthday video message from his parents while sunbathing. The communication is one-way and Poole appears bored by it.

HAL predicts a failure of AE 35 communication unit as a stratagem to kill the astronauts and take over the ship during the lapse in communication with earth.

After Bowman has gone after Poole's body in the Pod and returned to the bay doors, HAL refuses to answer his request to open them. Like Kong, he manages to get them open with human initiative.

Once HAL is dismantled and everyone on board but Bowman has been killed, a taped message plays: "This is a pre-recorded briefing made prior to your departure and which for security reasons of the highest importance has been known on board during the mission only by your HAL 9000 computer. Now that you are in Jupiter space and the entire crew is revived it can be told to you."

Technology, then, does not act to overcome barriers to communication; instead it creates new potentials for solipsism and misapprehension. For instance, Ripper's order to transmit the formula FGD 135 not only initiates Wing Attack Plan R, it strongly infers a "reality," implicit in the technological protocols, that is utterly unfounded. With the three-letter code prefix OPE, which only Ripper knows, and who is soon to be a dead man, in place, the plane is completely isolated and "secure," both dedicated and rogue.

The sophistication and apparent mastery of technological surveillance and communication encourages a renunciation of skepticism and sensory experience. Thus the world-picture eclipses the world, according to unconscious or covert desires to "secure" or "spiritualize" reality. Devised by human beings to serve conscious human purposes, information and communication appear driven toward autonomy, autonomy that can only be achieved by the subversion of those very purposes. If the information and communication do not *work* in these films, it is only with respect to human intentionality; they do work according to the selfless insistence of the technical media themselves.

Transportation and teleology

In turning to the technology of transportation, we may ask one fundamental question: Where is it that human beings want to be taken by their trains, airplanes and spacecraft? What is the *telos* of transportation? Is it movement in space or metaphoric transport? In Kubrick's earliest films, planes and trains are modes of escape. *Killer's Kiss* begins and ends in Penn Station, as Davy tells his story and waits to see if his girlfriend Gloria will join in his escape from the labyrinthine prison of New York. In *The Killing*, Johnny Clay and his girlfriend Fay try to escape from Los Angeles on a plane bound for Boston. Transportation in these instances represents an enactment of a deep human desire for rebirth: Technology is the reliable instrument for fulfilling desires. In *Dr. Strangelove*, transportation's purpose is the delivery of nuclear payloads. Major Kong's final ecstatic ride on his bomb suggests that more is in play. In *2001*, the purpose of transportation is the "conquest of space." Captain Bowman's ecstatic final ride through the star-gate likewise suggests that more is in play.

In dramatic counterpoint to the war room is the B-52 Stratofortress, the massive, gleaming bomber being refueled in the first scenes by the KC-135 Stratotanker, to the romantic melody "Try a Little Tenderness." Once it is retracted, the refueling boom droops a little sadly: In this way, Kubrick begins with a visual anecdote of technology and its emergent and strange loves. This refueling makes it possible for a B-52 fleet to be constantly airborne and within 2 hours of checkpoints outside the Soviet Union—each with a nuclear payload of 50 megatons—more, as the strident narrator informs us, than all the explosive power deployed by all the forces of World War II. In the opening scenes, we see the pilot, copilot, and crew eating, doing card tricks, reading, and looking at a Playboy Magazine. The B-52 has its appetites and its crew theirs.

The B-52 is the agent and executor of the spiritualized information devised and disseminated by radar and computer, an aircraft as beautiful in design and symmetry as it is sublime in its speed, dynamism, and terror. Designed by Boeing with eight turbojets hung in pairs, the B-52 had the longest range of any jet bomber. But it is more than a mere airplane: As we have seen, the "Stratofortress" exerts a powerful influence on Turgidson, who is so swept away while describing it that he stretches his arms, sways, and mimics its descent. Technology, in other words, can function as an idealized expression of human power and invulnerability. Kubrick further suggests that the B-52 is an abstracted version of the human body by paralleling a shot of the bomber, lit by a battery of lights on the flight line, with the first shot of Turgidson's mistress, Miss Scott, lying prone in a bikini beneath the glare of tanning lights. Her function as an instrument of transport and release is underscored when Turgidson assures her that he will be back from the Pentagon soon enough: "You just start your countdown, and old Bucky'll be back before you can say . . . Blast Off!"

From the moment the attack code is received, Kong maps his B-52 onto a cowboy conceit, both modernizing the Western myth and naturalizing his technological mastery. For Major Kong, this massive and complex defense posture and engagement is nothing more than "nuk-ya-lure combat, toe to toe with the Russkies." Once he has managed to hot-wire the bomb-bay doors, he rides his nuclear bomb like a rodeo-rider. Like Strangelove, Kong's body is fused with the machine, his sexual fantasies supplemented by a nuclear phallus which he guides to its target, the ICBM complex at Kodlosk.

In designing and making a global, interlocking technology of surveillance, communication, and destruction, SAC mobilized an unprecedented work of technical art—as sublime in its way as the Pyramids, Cathedrals, Palaces, and Fortresses of the premodern world, structures whose sublimity likewise shines with spiritual and political utility. In a world where symmetry and immensity have often been abandoned by contemporary artists, technology has—for purely practical reasons—become the bearer of these traditional esthetic potentials. We witness in Defense Department culture a patient, immensely detailed exhibition of technology as esthetic artifact and mythical agent.

With this battle—or mating—of nuclear devices, the greatest of all weapons is engaged and engendered. The Doomsday Machine, its deterrent value wasted because of a lag between its deployment and its announcement, is described by Ambassador DeSadesky in the sublime terms of awe and dread:

> A device which will destroy all human and animal life on earth . . . When it is detonated, it will produce enough lethal radioactive fallout so that within ten months, the surface of the earth will be as dead as the moon . . . Cobalt thorium G has a radioactive half-life of ninety-three years. If you take, say, fifty H-bombs in the hundred megaton range and jacket them with cobalt thorium G, when they are exploded they will produce a doomsday shroud. A lethal cloud of radioactivity which will encircle the earth for ninety-three years!

Invested with this apocalyptic capacity, the Doomsday Machine conserves a perfect autonomy: It is "designed to trigger itself automatically . . . It is designed to explode if any attempt is ever made to un-trigger it."

When Kong's "device" triggers the sensors of the Doomsday Machine, we witness the ultimate epiphany of technology: A human invention freed from human control assumes the capacities of a world-destroying divinity. When Yahweh destroyed the earth by water, he fixed a rainbow in the firmament as a sign. When technology, man's successor, destroys the earth, it fixes a shroud in the firmament to reign over a planet as barren as the moon. Although the Strategic Air Command was designed ostensibly to "defend" the United States through an implementation of the doctrine of deterrence, in Kubrick's film, it engages the Soviet Union's own implementation of a mirroring doctrine of MAD. The question we are left with, then, is this: Has technology in *Dr. Strangelove* truly failed? Or has it realized a desire for a post-human, post-organic world that it has barely attempted to conceal?

If *Dr. Strangelove* moves toward apocalypse, *2001* moves toward apotheosis. From the femur of a tapir thrown into the air by Moon-watcher, to the *Orion*, *Space Station V*, the *Aries*, *the Discovery*, and its Pod journeying through the star-gate, the journey is toward self-realization and the discovery of technology's origins. Yet the human beings who designed this technology were consciously motivated only by a desire for *transportation*—not *transport*. By the year 2001, none of the passengers on these crafts evince the slightest sense of spiritual transport. Floyd's journey to the moon echoes the glory days of pre–World War II travel, not the mythic traditions of soul travel or transcendence. Likewise, Bowman's and Poole's journey to Jupiter is a moribund transportation of deadened men, a computer, and three hibernating members of the exploration team. It is left to Bowman, once everyone else is dead or dismantled, to discover the difference between transportation and transport: In this sense, his psychic journey is a compensation for the doldrums of mere "space" travel and a recovery of its original or unconscious motives.

Kubrick and his crew of designers lavished attention on these spacecraft, evoking a sense of the ideal and the potentially real. It is the meeting of these two standards that makes for the film's success as a technological tone and picture poem. They also have marked organic and anthropomorphic aspects: Their docking bays often have a crimson-tinged, blood-like hue that suggests organic interiors. When the *Orion* enters the hub of *Space Station V*, it suggests a kind of intercourse, reminiscent of the refueling of the B-52. The *Aries* has two apertures at the command level that suggest eyes in a gigantic hieratic face. It too, when it enters Clavius base in a crimson light, seems to be returning to its womb. *Discovery* has a skeletal aspect—from its whitened "skull" to its long "spinal" column—that evokes its solitary and monastic penetration of space. From another perspective, *Discovery* resembles a technological spermatozoon destined to impregnate Jupiter's massive ovum. Its pod, likewise, emerges and returns to the mother ship, first as a two-armed engine of destruction, then as a grieving mother with Poole's lifeless form in those same arms. Kubrick's cinema thus continuously undermines the supposed gap between inorganic and organic forms, technological and human agency—preparing the way for our ultimate realization that mankind's genius has, in some way, been inspired and promulgated by the monolith—which itself remains elusive of such categories, being both a technological device and a metaphysical symbol.

9

Speech

Kubrick aspired to be the Wagner of cinema. Having dismissed the musical score and raided the classical repertoire, he could "compose" his own scores. A master photographer and an expert cinematographer, he could achieve a visual distinctiveness and éclat found only in the greatest directors. But he was never the master of screenwriting, and so could not claim to be the sole begetter of his films. His two solo screenplays were dependent on novels, like *A Clockwork Orange* or *Barry Lyndon*, that were filled with memorable dialog and narrative voice. In all the others (with the exception of *Killer's Kiss*, the weakest of his scenarios), he employed collaborators or worked freely with a commissioned screenplay.

Despite his inability to be in complete control of his screenplays, Kubrick was certain about what he did not want, even if he could not always explain it. Certainly, he did not want the dead weight of formulaic or expository dialog. He listened for something else, something that could match his distinctive visual and musical idioms. He recognized, in effect, that there is no such thing as "language" or "English" per se. All speech is, to some degree, an idiolect, a jargon, a style, and so serves as a mask of justification or a symptom of a particular mode of life. The language of the screenplays has a quirky energy of its own.

All language in the mature Kubrick is, so to speak, spoken in italics; that is to say, speech is exhibited with a tacit irony, suspended by aural quotation marks. The main point is to get past the clichés of screenplays and discover the living and the strange: Kubrick's aim is to suffuse all the elements of cinema with revelatory vibrancy. Dialog and narration in even the best films are drawn toward either theatrical cleverness (the films of Joseph Mankiewicz) or "naturalism" (countless examples). Such speech is too often formulaic, too often suggestive of movie talk. Narrative and dialog in Kubrick's great films are instead highly stylized, idiosyncratic, exhausted, patently stereotypical, and strange. These qualities of speech disappoint any expectation that reality, as reflected in speech, has uninflected or clearly established aspects.

Fear and Desire, written by Howard Sackler, is prefaced by a narrator who orients what is to follow in terms of a philosophical thesis. Human beings are thrown into a world they cannot grasp and whose elements are universal and psychological. The narrator's point of view is shared obliquely by Lt. Corby's sardonic reflections in a diction that is artificial, ironic, steeped in existentialist cliché and literary allusion (John Donne, for instance). Sidney's excited, neurotic, and finally maddened voice is filled with references to *The Tempest* delivered in an offbeat New York accent. Fletcher's slow Southern drawl manages to liken the plan to escape down the river on a raft to *Huck Finn*. *Fear and Desire*'s humorless, high seriousness is established by a kind of speech that remains cold, flat, and uninflected by idiosyncrasy.

Killer's Kiss and *The Killing* abandon this high, generic diction for the "naturalist" code of film noir, the first tending toward pathos and the second toward an ironic distance. Since the film noir is, in effect, a genre based on an existential outlook, this was a natural shift for Kubrick to make. Davy's narrative and the dialog in *Killer's Kiss* are equally hard-boiled. Davy begins by pondering a paradox of consciousness: "It's crazy how you can get yourself in a mess sometimes and not even be able to think about it with any sense and yet not to think about anything else." This kind of rough philosophizing can yield easily to the classic tough-guy talk managed by Vince when talking to Gloria: "What do you take me for, a 14-carat sucker? You and lover boy aren't gonna put me in the hot seat." There is little intonational complexity in *Killer's Kiss* that goes against generic expectation. *The Killing*—drawing on Lionel White's novel *Clean Break*, with additional dialog by Jim Thompson—is likewise grounded in hard-boiled locutions, as for instance, in Johnny's assessment of Sherry: "I know you like a book. You're a no good, nosey little tramp. You'd sell out your mother for a piece of fudge, but you're smart." But it also has a curiously rich range of verbal styles—from Sherry's mordant ironies and Maurice's Greek-inflected, nearly Socratic, utterances to Nikki's clenched-teethed laconism, Johnny Clay's bluster, the narrator's obtuse and pompous delivery, and the practiced sales-speak of the American Airlines agent Mr Grimes ("Sir, those are the regulations, designed for your comfort and safety"). The perspectival and temporal complexity of the film is nearly matched by a variety of voices, none of which—certainly not the narrator's—carries the slightest cognitive or moral authority. With the fading of generic speech and narrative, moral and romantic conventionality also fades.

The two films that Kubrick made with Kirk Douglas do not advance this trend toward distinctive speech. Both *Paths of Glory* (written with Calder Willingham and Jim Thompson) and *Spartacus* (written by Dalton Trumbo, in his first credited effort since the blacklist), as different as they are, have the defects typical of period dramas set in non-English cultures. The French general officers in *Paths of Glory* speak a mid-Atlantic, theatrical English. The narrator, who also plays the Colonel Judge of the Court Martial, provides historical orientation for trench warfare in a crisp British English that insinuates the hypocrisy to come. The field officers and men speak an American English. Such a hierarchical organization of styles of English is also heard in *Spartacus*. The Roman speakers are largely British; the mutinous slaves are Americans speaking without reservation or modification. The accented speech of Antoninus and David could easily have served for the New York toughs in *Killer's Kiss*. Kirk Douglas, in both films the pivotal figure between corrupt power and the people, speaks his own English, neither pretentious nor demotic. His is the voice of the human subject, universal and noble. This kind of vocal conventionalism, especially in *Spartacus*, is not to be heard again in Kubrick's films. Indeed, it would appear that the vocal conventions of *Spartacus* drove Kubrick's subsequent deconstruction of film speech.

In *Lolita*, the rivalry for the affections of an underage girl between a European literary scholar and an American writer for stage, screen, and television has everything to do with language. As the narrator and protagonist of the film, James Mason's Humbert speaks a richly insinuating English that butts up, first, against Charlotte Haze's Club-Woman's American English, then Lolita's mass-cultural battery of cliché, and, finally, Clare's range of impersonations—the regular guy, the German psychiatrist, the droll hipster, and the slack libertine. Given the fact that Kubrick could bring over precious little of Nabokov's novel and screenplay into the film, these "intonational quotation marks"—to cite Bakhtin's phrase—must stand for much that Kubrick could not adapt. Amid this mixture of voices, Kubrick's cut of Nabokov's script relies on a rash of sophomoric double-entendres that suggest all too well the limitations on expression demanded by the dutiful censors of the early sixties. Showing her house to Humbert, Mrs Haze says flirtatiously, "Oh Monsieur, if what you're needing is peace and quiet, I can assure you couldn't get more peace anywhere." What Kubrick did accomplish was a linguistic equivalent to the battle for American youth by traditional European culture and mass American culture:

Humbert: I always write my po-ems in a diary. It's one of my little idiosyncrasies.

Lolita: Umm. Afraid someone's going to steal your ideas and sell them to Hollywood?

It is a battle that the hack Quilty wins, but in the end, he has no interest in possessing the girl—like the culture he represents, he has a short attention span.

The same kind of linguistic conflicts can be heard in *Dr. Strangelove*, written with Terry Southern, with substantial improvisation by Peter Sellers. The script features, as James Naremore has demonstrated, nearly direct citations from Herman Kahn's *On Thermonuclear War*.[1] Kahn's (serious) phrasing and logic is inverted and ironized when spoken by satirical types such as Dr Strangelove and General Turgidson. The serious and the absurd, the learned and the mad or ignorant collide and exchange position through "objective," military and aeronautical jargon, Major King Kong's cowboy dialect, and Ripper's nuanced explication of the communist conspiracy.

Consider Major Kong's address to his men as they head into nuclear combat.

> Kong: Now look boys, I ain't much of a hand at makin' speeches. But I got a pretty fair idea that something doggoned important's going on back there. And I got a fair idea of the kind of personal emotions that some of you fellas may be thinking. Heck, I reckon you wouldn't even be human beings if you didn't have some pretty strong personal feelings about nuclear [nuk-ya-lur] combat . . .

Although Kong's remarks sound like a perfectly authentic Texan dialect, they are also oddly insistent—as if registering an unspoken fear—that feelings and emotions are "personal," neither generic nor government issue. Kong poses the question of how a "human being" can be willing to drop nuclear bombs on other "human beings."

These quandaries are quietly vanquished when Kong and Goldie engage the CRM 114 that will protect them from any unauthorized communication:

> Goldie: Roger. Ready to set code prefix.
> Kong: Set code prefix . . . Lock code prefix.
> Goldie: Code prefix locked.
> Kong: Switch all receiver circuits to CRM discriminators.
> Goldie: All circuits switched to CRM discriminators.
> Kong: Check auto destruct circuits.
> Goldie: Auto destruct circuits checked.

The speech to the crew and the checklist demonstrate the schizoid or alienated nature of speech and subjectivity in *Dr. Strangelove*.

In *2001* (written with Arthur C. Clarke, from the novel commissioned by Kubrick for the film), the same opposition holds between the hominids' lusty, but lexically thin, grunts and the worn-out, technical platitudes of the State bureaucrats and astronauts schooled in the discourse of national security. Heywood Floyd's chilling instructions to the worried and restless men at Clavius who have uncovered the monolith are delivered in an affable yet hollow voice:

> And of course you know that the Council has requested that formal security oaths are to be obtained in writing from everyone who had any knowledge of this event.

Nevertheless, Halvorson later assures Floyd that his remarks "beefed up morale a heckuva lot." All of the speech on the space station and the lunar base is impersonal, bureaucratic, and yet suffused with a certain measure of affected camaraderie and deceit. Floyd's conversation with the Russian scientists, in which deceit and politeness are indistinguishable, ends with a *sotto voce* comment in Russian by Dr Smyslov.

On the *Discovery*, Bowman and Poole speak in a low-keyed, dispirited way that conveys both their solitude and duty: Poole is blunter than Bowman, but both seem remote from the language they speak. Two other linguistic styles are introduced by HAL and Mission Control. HAL's suave, human voice is suited to a language of quiet precision and formality. When asked by the television interviewer if he ever feels lack of confidence, he answers:

> Let me put it this way, Mr. Aimer. The 9000 Series is the most reliable computer ever made. No 9000 computer has ever made a mistake or distorted information. We are all, by any practical definition of the words, fool proof and incapable of error.

When further questioned whether he feels any frustration because of his dependence upon human beings to carry out actions, HAL responds:

> Not in the slightest bit. I enjoy working with people. I have a stimulating relationship with Dr. Poole and Dr. Bowman . . . I am putting myself to the fullest possible use, which is all, I think, that any consciousness entity can hope to do.

By contrast, Mission Control addresses Bowman and Poole this way:

> X-Ray Delta-One, this is Mission Control. Roger your 2013. Sorry you fellas are having a bit of trouble. We are reviewing telemetric information in our mission simulator and will advise. Roger your plan to go EVA and replace Alpha Echo 35 unit prior to failure.

NASA-speak is a highly artificial, oddly stressed speech performed by a human being; HAL's speech is an insinuating, personable, and elegant, actor-like speech simulated by a computer. It is HAL's simulated voice that introduces a curious sexual and post-human ambiguity into the verbal texture of the film which includes pre-human, human, and post-human idiolects. HAL's is, ironically, the only fully human speech in the film, expressing a range of emotions: pride, suspicion, condescension, fear, and panic. There is, in other words, no authoritative or "normal" perspective or voice in this space odyssey.

These trends toward opaque or italicized speech reach their peak in the Nadsat dialect spoken by Alex and his droogs in *A Clockwork Orange* and Sergeant Hartman's training language and the "Nam-speak" of the grunts in *Full Metal Jacket*. In both films, gangs of young men, dedicated to a cult of violence and misogyny, make war on civilian society—which speaks another language. Their dialects are a kind of armor and fraternal code.

The mélange of Russian and modern English Anthony Burgess invented for his novel was formulated for a future in which Soviet Socialism would exercise cultural hegemony over young Britons. It also reflects the alienation of the young from the traditional hierarchies of British speech. Not only a blending of English and Russian, Alex's Nadsat is characterized by Renaissance conjugations, syntactic inversion, and poetic figurations. Before the brawl in the abandoned theater, Alex addresses his rival:

> Ho, Ho, Ho . . . Well, if isn't stinking Billygoat Billyboy in poison. How are thou, thou globby bottle of stinking chip oil? Come and get one in the yarbles, if you have any yarbles, you eunuch jelly thou.

In response to Deltoid's question "Do I make myself clear," Alex responds: "As an unmuddied lake, Fred. As clear as an azure sky of deepest summer."

Speech in *A Clockwork Orange* is heard in contrast between the natural conventions of British English as spoken by figures of authority and the powerfully poetic idiolect of Alex and his droogs. In a sense, it is a synthesized version of English, bringing to the movie the density and figural richness of a Jacobean play. Burgess claimed that Nadsat would "act as a kind of mist half-hiding the mayhem and protecting the reader from his own baser instincts."[2] In the film, Nadsat operates in a similar way. It is not "natural" speech, anymore than Walter Carlos's synthetic music is: and yet both bring an energy and odd beauty into a film dedicated to the proposition that violence and free will are indissociable.

Full Metal Jacket (based on Gus Hasford's *The Short-Timers* and cowritten with Michael Herr, with substantial contributions by Lee Ermey) is dominated by two idiolects: Sergeant Hartman's abusive, obscene, but hilarious training language and the dialect invented and spoken by enlisted Marines in Vietnam. Hartman's richly metaphorical and metonymical idiolect is meant to destroy his recruits' identity and pieties (Mom, God, the Virgin Mary, high school sweetheart) and reconstitute them as post-moral agents of death and inductees into the Marine cult: "the first and last words out of your filthy sewers will be 'Sir!' Do you maggots understand that? You are nothing but unorganized grabbastic pieces of amphibian shit!" Hartman's poetics are dominated by figurations that bestialize, feminize, and excrementalize. The impressive fluency and inventiveness of this jargon at first appears to Joker and Pyle to be humorous; by the end of their training, it is simply the reality they have come to inhabit. Nam-speak by contrast is a cultish expression of solidarity articulated with antisentimental, hostile, and self-conscious irony: "If you get killed," Joker tells the new guy, Rafter Man, "your mom will find me after I rotate back to the world and she'll beat the shit out of me. That's a negative, Rafter Man." And Payback answers Chili's claim that he wasn't "in country" during operation Hastings: "Eat shit and die, you fucking Spanish-American. You fucking poge! I was there, man. I was in the shit with the grunts." Nadsat and Nam-speak enforce a sense of proud exclusion from a dominant speech, while transmuting violence and death into an alien yet intimate lexicon. Narration and dialog in both films are thus largely conducted in a private speech, alien to the norms of English-language films, acting as a means of derealizing the violence, both for the young men and the audience. These argots accomplish this not by denying the facts of violence, as it were, but by denying its human or affective meaning.

Speech in *Barry Lyndon* and *The Shining* represents the poles of formal gentility and informal vulgarity to be found in the source novels by Thackeray and Stephen King. Drawing heavily on both for dialog, Kubrick—along with Diane Johnson, who cowrote the screenplay of *The Shining*—creates two radically different linguistic worlds. The first film contrasts the voices of a mellow English narrator and the English aristocracy against the Irish–English of Barry and his kin. Barry's subject-position is as clear as his brogue. *The Shining* contrasts the flat American accents of the Torrances against the theatrical voices and diction of the English butler Grady and cook Halloran.

Both films are about men who aspire to live in great houses where a different language is spoken—the language of privilege, prestige, and ultimately the past. For the Irishman Redmond Barry, the English Castle Hackton is the penultimate goal—the ultimate being granted a peerage. And yet, he never learns the language of his Lady's and son's house and world. Redmond Barry's Irish-inflected English constantly betrays him—both with the British and the Prussians—as Ryan O'Neill's brogue has betrayed him to Irish audiences. Jack Torrance comes to the Overlook Hotel as a caretaker and ends by making it his permanent, ghostly residence. Planning to use the winter to write a novel, he is distracted from his own imaginative ambitions and becomes a student of the hotel's past. If Barry aspires to transform himself into a nobleman, Jack aspires to transform himself into a Jazz Age tycoon.

The narrator of *Barry Lyndon*, wonderfully performed by Michael Hordern, is sympathetic, worldly- wise, and ironic. Although his identity and perspective are not established, the narrator emerges as a central character in the movie, a voice beyond fear and desire, a rich and mellow complement to the painted world he describes and analyzes. He thus tends to slacken whatever suspense accumulates by anticipating events and placing them within the context of human affairs at large. The narrator is sympathetic to Barry, but his real concern is with what he represents as a type of human nature. In this way, he speaks in the spirit of Dr Johnson—cited by Colonel Dax in *Paths of Glory*—who claimed that great art must aspire to "just representations of general nature." This anticipatory and interpretive narration fits neatly with the film's impersonality and formalism. The narration in *Barry Lyndon* tends to spatialize time; it moves from specific concerns rooted in time to knowledge beyond time. Thus, the narrator informs us of Barry's fate as he flees to Dublin after the duel with Capt. Quin and just as he is about to be robbed and forced to enlist in the Army: "But Barry was destined to be a wanderer." Later, just as he plans to desert, he informs us that "Fate did not intend him—." And, finally, once Barry has gained a Lady Wife, an estate, and a son, the narrator tells us that Barry was fated to be sonless. By keeping the end constantly in view, the narrator balances his function as guide and informer against his function as philosopher and fatalist. Formal speech is more, in other words, than a necessary feature of a film about the aristocracy of a formal age. It implies a completeness and explicitness that leaves nothing unsaid.

Dialog in *The Shining* has many styles: Ullman's managerial, empty cheerfulness, Danny's kid talk, his imaginary friend Tony's throaty warnings, Wendy's chipper or hysterical extremes, Halloran's highly mannered emotiveness, the (actual) television news anchors' practiced informalities, Grady's butler-isms and, most importantly, Jack Torrance's many voices and tonalities. The thematic contrast implicit in these verbal styles is between a recognition of language as a form of stylized repression (Ullman, Wendy, Tony, Halloran, the television news anchors) and as a channel for the eruption of the repressed.

Oftentimes speech sounds like a form of appeal or performance—not as a simple medium of expression. The speech of the television anchors—Kubrick used a real video clip—establishes the gold standard of such simulation, reading from their Teleprompters ("Good evening. I'm Glen Rinker, Newswatch Ten"). Speech becomes here, in other words, less a medium than an object, a thing. It is perhaps in this context that we can understand why telepathy or "shining" seems so attractive to Halloran, who is saddled with an elaborate and labored style of speech. Danny speaks as the child he is, but Tony, who lives in his mouth, speaks like a sinister adult, filled with knowledge and portentousness.

Jack does a number of voices in *The Shining* that suggest the abyssal nature of his own identity. He can appear bright and cheerful with Ullman, but with his family, his words are always on the point, or beyond the point, of irony and sarcasm. When he talks with the bartender Lloyd in the phantasmal Gold Room, he suddenly assumes the bygone argot of male intimacy ("You were always the best of them. Best goddamn bartender . . . from Timbuktu to Portland, Maine. Or Portland, Oregon for that matter"). When Wendy tells him that Danny needs to be taken to a hospital, he repeats her words sarcastically ("You think 'maybe' he should be taken to a doctor?") but when he tries to persuade Wendy to let him out of the dried goods locker, he reverts to a little boy's wheedling voice ("I think you hurt my head real bad. I'm dizzy. I need a doctor"). When he breaks into their apartment with an axe, he channels television sitcoms ("Honey, I'm home"), late night television ("Here's Johnny!"), and then a fairy tale ("I'll huff and I'll puff . . ."). Wounded and lost in the freezing maze that his son has led him into, he howls like a dying wolf. In this Babel of voices, one hears the elements of a novel that he might have written, had he not instead become subject to the Overlook's own dictations.

By severe contrast, speech in *Eyes Wide Shut* is entirely unmemorable. Frederic Raphael's *Eyes Wide Open* observes how little of his efforts were audible in the film.[3] But this is by intention, for in this film, speech is suspended in a dream-like stasis where characters repeat or nearly repeat each others' words, as if caught in an oneiric logic of indecision and impasse.

Michel Chion has cataloged instances of this dialogic stutter, which he calls "parroting":

Bill:	Once a doctor, always a doctor.
Nick:	Once a doctor, never a doctor.
. . .	
Gayle:	Where the rainbow ends.
Bill:	Where the rainbow ends?
. . .	
Domino:	Come inside with me?
Bill:	Come inside with you?

This is but a sample of the 46 instances that Chion finds in the screenplay. He interprets this parroting in a number of ways, the most significant one for a reading of the film as dream is that it alters the sense of time: "we no longer know when this game of echoes began, and who said what first."[4] These suspended phrases hold up the action, put the drama to sleep, allow for a kind of hypnogogic waywardness to direct the scene into a dreamy timelessness and ambiguity. At the same time, as we have observed before, these repetitions reveal speech in all its opacity and materiality.

Another means by which this is accomplished is through pastiche. We hear it in Bill's bedside manner, Nick's "good guy" greeting ("How the hell are you buuuuudyyy?"), Milich's immigrant English ("It's starting to fall down, too fast. I lost in two weeks a lot of hair"), and Red Cloak's inquisitorial diction ("That IS unfortunate"). The most elaborate pastiche can be heard in Sandor's attempted seduction of Alice:

Szavost: My name is Sandor Szavost. I'm Hungarian.
Alice: My name is Alice Harford. I'm American.

. . .

Szavost: Delighted to meet you, Alice. Did you ever read the Latin poet Ovid on *The Art of Love*?

. . .

Szavost: Don't you think one of the charms of marriage is that it makes deception a necessity for both parties?

This is the "Hungarian lover" who lives only in the movies, with his pronounced accent and "sophistication." The conversation, in any case, lasts too long: It is one of those elaborately suspended moments of temptation and indecision found in dreams. Speech in all these instances is "cited" as much as it is spoken. This is not to say that it is "unreal" so much as it is impersonal and archetypal.

Kubrick *disables* cinematic speech and strips it of its pretensions of intimacy, transparency, and authenticity. This is not a matter of representing hypocrisy or deceit, or of an intentional act of disguise. It is rather a revelation of language's artificiality, conventionality and its inevitable inauthenticity. This disabling of speech awakens a sense of uneasiness or suspicion, allowing for deeper, but less articulate, forms of illumination. When speech loses its authority as a conveyance of motive and meaning, it can be folded into the total poiesis of cinema.

10

Poiesis

In the early decades of the twentieth century, Ezra Pound was refashioning poetry to make it capable of dealing with the modern world. In breaking with the decorum and metrical regularity of late romantic verse, Pound asserted that vibrant poetry was a simultaneous expression of three media: logopoeia (the play of words), melopoeia (the play of music or rhythm), and phanopoeia (the play of the image).[1] While Pound could only *write* his *Cantos*, film directors were inventing a fully realized *poiesis* thanks to the new media of the photographic image, recorded music, and dialog. By mid-century, few directors were really interested in this kind of realization of cinema as poiesis. Most were interested in theatrical or narrative application of the new medium. Others saw the possibility of something quite different—a poiesis of image, music, and word: among these are Welles, Kurosawa, Antonioni, and Kubrick.

In coming to an understanding of what Kubrick means by the "illumination" (and what I have called a cinema cogitans) to which his cinema aspires, we have traced a number of themes and the characteristic ways in which he uses light, time, music, and speech. Now we can turn to an appreciation of their combined effects which serve to occupy the audience's sensorium with a fictive world. Ideally, it is a kind of "out of body experience." Kubrick more than any other director I know has found ways to detach the sensorium from local data streams and replace them with his own characteristic poiesis. The primary task is one of fascination: The film has to keep the customer in his seat by subjecting him to an alternate reality that he finds more compelling than the realities in the lobby and the worlds beyond. This fascination is poetic in nature: that is to say, it is the result of a manipulation of media that puts him in a state of anticipation and leaves him in a state of slightly bewildered satisfaction.

In attempting to make the best "horror" film ever made, Kubrick took the genre and reinvented it: As we have seen, he remade the banalities of suburban culture in the seventies and revealed their most ghastly and frightening potentials. If

German expressionism drew cinematic *horror* out of the chiaroscuro metaphysics of gothic literature and art, Kubrick's *The Shining* drew it out of the spectral golds, oranges, and reds discovered and transmitted by "color" television. Yet Kubrick's task was to make of this banal palette something beautiful—just as beautiful as *Barry Lyndon*, but without once showing us anything particularly beautiful.

Kubrick was able, with Diane Johnson, to extricate from Stephen King's novel *The Shining* the scenario for one of his strangest and least interpretable works. He saw past the clutter and tedium of King's prose to its fundamental mythos: The hero Jack Torrance is a man who has been dislodged from eternity into time. His mythic quest for return is motivated by this sense of temporal malaise and spiritual alienation. His interest in literature and writing fiction manifest his search for a way beyond the temporality that has imprisoned him in a loveless marriage and burdened him with a son who possesses the faculty he is lacking: what King calls "shining," the psychic power of illumination or vision that transcends time and space.

His son Danny's powers expand and spread to his father and his mother once they have removed themselves to the vast and remote Overlook Hotel. As Jack is drawn more and more into the hotel's past, the nature of his quest becomes apparent to him: He must murder his son and his wife so that he can escape from his temporal confinement into the eternal or timeless psychic space of the hotel. While his wife Wendy and his son Danny are the twin monsters who confine him to a cursed existence, Jack is, from their point of view, the monster who has confined them in a haunted house and threatens to murder and consume them. Beneath the cheery and banal colors of seventies' America, a hideous mythic struggle is joined for the boon of shining or illumination—the power to see beyond the tedium of time and then to take up residence there. Despite all their differences, the theme of *The Shining*, like *2001*, is a gradually realized quest for timelessness.

Opening and credits

The opening scene of *The Shining* is a case in point. We can say simply enough that we see a Volkswagen Bug moving on an empty highway along mountain passes on a sunny day. Later we realize that we have witnessed Jack Torrance driving to a job interview at the Overlook Hotel for the post of winter caretaker. It could easily have been dispensed with, but it is an appropriate scene to run the credits, since it gives us the setting and the dominant theme of isolation without the distractions of dialog. As we quickly assimilate the plot factum along with the title, the director, and so forth, we realize that the camera is tracking the Volkswagen from the sky. On a second viewing, we may feel that the camera and helicopter tracking the car have introduced another theme: the double. And yet at first, the point of view seems in search of an object: It skims above a mountain lake and a forested island. Only then does it spot the yellow Volkswagen, as if this transcendent and menacing visual consciousness has settled on its proper subject. Our dawning recognition of the theme of the double is deepened when we see, once again, how the tracking shot is suddenly interrupted when it fails to take the turn with the car and continues its flight over a pristine mountain lake: It seems to have gone off the tracks or, perhaps, returned momentarily to its original focus. So along with the theme of doubling, we witness a surprising digression. The film is in effect assisting us in a fascinated tracking of Jack's journey into madness: Do we follow him all the way or veer off?

But the airborne vision registers more than the road and the Volkswagen and the themes of doubling and digression: The mountains, the lakes, and the trees are captured with a peculiar kind of light. It might be early morning, but the light has already gained a powerful capacity for illumination: The shadows of the fir trees seem to fall in all directions, as if the point of view is fixed but not real. This half-realized sense is encouraged by the credits—in a weird aqua lettering—that are scrolling upward, reminding us that we are watching the beginning of a movie. More importantly, it is suggested by the plangent tones of the score—the *Dies Irae* derived from medieval church music and adapted by many classical and modern composers. If we do not recognize the music, we feel a profound foreboding; if we do, we know that it portends the immanent vengeance of God on sinners—as the supervisory camera position has already implied. It may also sound another, typically Kubrickian, grace note: the ironic undercutting of a theme too clearly in evidence. The "days of wrath" will not be those of a righteous God but of an insane Dad in an empty resort hotel. Mixed into this gothic tonality is the evocation of Native American chants and percussive rhythms, pointing ahead to the revelation of the Hotel's displacement and pollution of an Indian burial ground. So, two quite different kinds of vengeance are announced.

The interview

Now, suddenly without music, the first scene unfolds under a cloud, as it were. The aftereffect of the *Dies Irae* and the surrealistic Native American chants is hard to define: It is as if they have cast a sonic shadow on the scene. We feel, if we do not know, that this absence of music amounts to dissimulation or disguise—and the advent of empty speech. As if to stress this feeling, the first scene is announced by a screen card: "The Interview." While it prepares us for the cards to follow, this initial gloss seems odd, on first consideration, because it appears to be so unnecessary. In a film that will leave much unexplained, this kind of gratuitous assistance has an ironic overtone, especially since the interview that follows is so painfully recognizable: the awkwardness, the forced intimacy, the evident dissimulation, the eagerness for contact. The irony derives from how much is overstated and how much is concealed: It is cramped yet busy, cluttered but rigorously symmetrical. The office is lit by the soft glare of a window and two large rectangular fluorescent ceiling lights. While the lighting is clearly visible in the frame, its illumination is less apparent than real. Concealment in *The Shining*, as I have already suggested, has less to do with darkness than the unilluminating nature of light itself.

The exclusively Middle American décor mirrors the attempts at jocularity and instant intimacy: This is a code everyone knows and, besides, who would not want to participate in it? When Jack enters the office and introduces himself, Ullman replies: "Hey, Jaaaaaack," with the same intonation Nick Nightingale uses when he greets his old friend Bill Harford: "How the hell are you buuuuudyyy." The tonalities of interlocutors, whether old friends or strangers, echo one another: The effaced coin of common parlance is exchanged in a kind of silence.

> Jack: Do you mind if I ask why you do that [close the hotel for the winter]?
> It seems to me that the skiing up here would be fantastic.

Here Jack's attempt to introduce a sense of his own leisure activities, despite the low-level job he is applying for, is answered by Ullman's turning the word "fantastic" around.

> Ullman: . . . the winters can be fantastically cruel, and the basic idea is to . . . to cope with the very costly damage and depreciation which can occur. And this consists mainly of running the boiler, heating different parts of the hotel on a daily rotating basis, repairing damage as it occurs and doing repairs, so that the elements can't get a foothold.

While Jack pretends to rise to the level of a guest at the hotel rather than accepting the fact that he is applying to be its caretaker, Ullman wants to steer the conversation to the threats and dangers—and the duties Jack would have to assume. This is the first pulse of the motive that will direct Jack's desire to take possession of the Overlook.

Despite the "affable" nature of their conversation, the scene works to suggest and conceal a few things. First, Mr Ullman's sexuality here and on Closing Day seems slightly at odds with the Middle Manager ethos he otherwise conveys: His hair style, clothing, and remarks about "Navaho and Apache motifs" in the Overlook sound a mid-seventies' note of gayness which, in turn, suggests more concealed potentials. Second, Bill Watson is a nearly silent and an uncanny element in the scene, as if he were a double, a figure of Jack's own concealed nature. The setting and dialog, then, are carefully established to form a contrasting context for Ullman's revelation. Ullman invokes Bill in a curious way before telling Jack about the murders committed by Grady, a previous caretaker: "Before I turn you over to Bill, there's one other thing I think we should talk about." Once Jack has taken in the news and allayed Ullman's concerns, he is taken away by Bill Watson for his tour of the hotel—and his first experience of its labyrinthine design and his double (Bill).

Cut into Jack's interview are several other interviews back in Boulder at the Torrance apartment: between Danny and Tony, "the little boy who lives in his mouth," between the doctor and Danny, following his vision of the murdered twins at the Overlook and the blood pouring from its elevator doors, and between the doctor and Wendy. These "interviews" put the initial job interview between Jack and Mr Ullman into a context of inquisition and concealment, of a doubling of doubles. The doctor wants to find out how Danny had once dislocated his shoulder, while Wendy does her best to conceal or explain the abuse away. Considered as a whole, then, "The Interview" can be seen as an exploration of the interiority of the Torrance family conducted at the same time in different places.

Kubrick delves into this visionary world through the bathroom mirror into which Danny looks as he questions Tony: Boy and image are both visible at first, but Kubrick moves the camera slowly into the image until the boy disappears and only his double remains. We then see what the reversed "image" is seeing: the closed doors of two elevators in the lobby at the Overlook Hotel. Outer elevator doors, of course, protect people from falling into the elevator shaft, the abyss, as it were, inside the hotel. As such, the doors are images of repression, but they do not serve their purpose: Torrents of blood pour through and, at the end of the vision, engulf the lobby and Tony's vantage point.

The vision is, in this sense, about itself: It dramatizes its own penetration of the abyss. This penetrating vision is amplified by a rising chord from Penderecki's

Awakening of Jacob: The swelling and rising blood is mirrored by the emergence of the *Dream*. Cut into the shot of the twin doors are Grady's twin daughters, holding hands and looking placidly at Tony and the audience from a hotel corridor. An allusion or an homage to "Identical Twins" by Diane Arbus (whom Kubrick knew from his days as a *Look* photographer), the image establishes an objective correlative for the doublings of identity and reality throughout the film. After cutting back to the bloody lobby, Kubrick presents "Danny"—no longer as a mirror image—mouth agape in horror at the vision: Here Kubrick alludes to the stills of David Bowman as he travels through the star-gate in *2001*. Subject and object, viewer and vision are doubled by allusions. Kubrick ends the vision by allowing the blood to swallow up the frame with darkness. After a few seconds, we hear a woman's voice ("Now hold your eye still so I can see") and then see a doctor peering into Danny's eye with a scope—hoping to find a clue to the vision. This opening into the texture of filmic reality takes less than a minute and manages to compress the critical themes and images of the whole film. It is a discrete instance of "shining"—linking image and music—that becomes contagious as the film proceeds and the time frame narrows and deepens. In the end, the film itself seems to have absorbed its inexplicable vision.

The maze

These epistemological complexities assume spatial representation in the hedge maze outside the hotel and the figurative maze of the hotel itself. The film is devoted to vistas of long corridors and turns from one corridor to the next. The mazes represent the complexity of past and present and of the real and the visionary and, in the end, suggest the brain itself with its endless circuitry. The maze or labyrinth, from another point of view, transforms space into time. Ullman warns Wendy: "I wouldn't go in there unless I had an hour to spare to find my way out." When, in the end, Danny leads Jack into the snowy hedge maze and then retraces his steps in the snow by walking backwards, Jack is trapped: The maze acts as a conduit to death and beyond into timelessness—or perhaps less portentously an infinite riddle, an aporia.

If the hotel is a figurative maze, the hedge maze outside is its literal double: the two mirror one another. But there is also the map outside the hedge and the model inside the hotel. Together, then, we have four mazes: the maze itself, a metaphorical maze, the map of a maze, and the model of a maze. Taken all together, this would seem to be a kind of postmodern allegory, in the spirit of Borges and Jean Baudrillard.

Indeed, Thomas Allen Nelson has made of the maze or labyrinth the symbol of Kubrick's "aesthetics of contingency."[2] But Kubrick did not have a fixed epistemological stance: He may have recognized much of what theorists call simulation and contingency but he remained exploratory, a weird combination of theorist and visionary, of existentialist and spiritual seeker. *The Shining* is not an attempt to demonstrate the purely psychological origins of supernatural notions: It is a recognition that we can never finally know, one way or another. The maze is not an allegory, then, but a symbol: a way of approaching matters that cannot finally be known.

The maze scene begins with Jack, his typewriter abandoned, his page blank, playing handball in the Overlook lounge. The typewriter's keys conceal the novel he wants to write, but he is unwilling to throw himself into the maze of letters and words. His game of handball is a perfectly specular activity: He throws and he catches. Meanwhile, Wendy and Danny are running outside toward the maze. They ignore the map and walk inside. As they enter, we hear the Adagio—sometimes called a "night-piece"—from Bartok's *Music for Strings, Percussion, and Celesta*: It is eerie, tentative, and exploratory, but it will be punctuated by an unexpected spike from the xylophone and later by a powerful crescendo, both seeming to declare decision, recognition, and certainty. The Steadicam tracks them from behind and in front as they casually wander into the labyrinth, chatting happily. They come to a dead end, but instead of being frustrated, they turn back good-naturedly. While Jack is overwrought and nearly at wit's end at the task of writing he has assumed, they have thrown themselves into the abyss without hesitation. Cutting back to the lobby, Kubrick presents a brutal contrast: Jack throws the ball down forcefully, timed to Bartok's crescendo. He then wanders toward the model of the Overlook maze: With a sudden indifference and composure, he looks down into the model and, mysteriously enough, seems to see, from a great height, his wife and son as they reach the center. It is as if he is viewing his family from a divine perspective.

The cut from Jack's point of view as he ponders the model to the subsequent, nearly celestial, perspective of the maze itself cannot be located: Kubrick has abridged the gap between model and reality, Jack's limited point of view and a divine one, which alludes to the opening tracking shot of the Volkswagen as it wends its way through the Rockies. This shift in perspective suggests Jack's megalomania and the origin of his mission of vengeance: He sees his family from the point of view of the avenging God we are warned of in the opening credits. Leaving Jack behind, the elevated perspective closes in on mother and son as they walk contentedly at the center of the labyrinth. And now Bartok's night-piece rises to its second, percussive crescendo, as the scene and section end with the card for the next time frame: Tuesday.

From a thematic point of view, much is accomplished in this scene: We witness a powerful contrast between the ways that Jack and his family address the maze, the challenges of life, and the labyrinth of the mind. From the point of view of pure cinema, something subtler is accomplished: The juxtaposition of conceptual, simulated, and actual mazes is amplified by the Bartok Adagio, which moves from an errant eeriness to sudden explosions of apparent decisiveness. The music critic Alex Ross describes the effect this way:

> The glistening nocturnal mood of the movement, with its glissandos and trills, is broken by a large, frightening crescendo in which celesta, harp, and piano flit wildly up and down their range while the strings pile on dissonances in four-note groups.[3]

If Wendy and Danny are content to wander happily to the center, Jack's choleric and frustrated moods presage a violent percussion and penetration.

In order to activate and explore the figure of the maze, Kubrick employed Garret Brown and his recently invented Steadicam—a device that allows the cameraman to track his subject with enormous freedom and flexibility—especially the low tracking shots of Danny in the corridors. Brown uses an arresting phrase to describe the Steadicam's function: It can "penetrate space."[4] To "penetrate space" is a way of saying that the camera's eye can see "beyond" the surface of space represented by dolly or fixed shots and discover what lies within and beyond it. It is a way of making the camera shine.

When Danny sees the twins the third time, he has been driving his Big Wheel tricycle through the hotel corridors. In a service wing corridor, the tracking is distant and at the level of the child. We are listening to Penderecki's *De Natura Sonoris I* which, inspired by Lucretius's *De rerum natura*, seems to present a parallel account of the nature of sound to Lucretius's account of nature. As we have seen already, Kubrick's use of contemporary classical music is always in relationship to uncanny or sublime experience. There is, here too, a linkage between atonal music and anomalous experience: As an aspect of Kubrick's cinema, it aurally explores the abyssal, vanishing point that the tracking shot discovers in the dimly lit corridor. When Danny turns right, the camera loses him for a few seconds: If there is a subject element to this tracking, one would say that it is reluctant or discrete, perhaps ambivalent. But it catches up in the next corridor, passing doors and housekeeping carts, now tracking closely and from a higher angle. This must be the staff wing: It prepares us for the vision of the caretaker's twins in their old-fashioned party dresses. When Danny turns left and suddenly stops, the tracking shot, just behind and above his head, discovers the girls standing at the end of the hall, holding hands. Cutting back and forth between the girls and Danny's frightened face, Kubrick gives us a sense of Danny's fearful moment in time and the girls' cold and fixed timelessness.

As they greet him ("Hello, Danny. Come and play with us"), Kubrick splices several still shots of the girls' axed bodies sprawled on floor, the walls smeared with blood. Within his vision, then, Danny sees the girls in timeless and temporal frames. As the visions of the girls alternate, they qualify the nature of their invitation to come and play: "Forever and ever and ever." The chilling image is complemented by their studied and cold upper-class English accents. (We may wonder why they should be English girls. Ullman had told Jack that the caretaker who murdered his daughters was Charles Grady, a "completely normal individual," presumably an American. But Danny knows nothing of this and sees and hears for himself. Ironically enough, however, during Jack's moment of shining in the Gold Room, he is advised by an English waiter, who calls himself Delbert Grady and explains that his daughters are "somewhere about" the hotel. This would suggest that the Overlook's spectral aspect is not fixed, but is seen differently in different instances of shining. It would appear that Danny's vision has somehow influenced Jack's.)

Covering his eyes and then slowly uncovering them, he sees the empty, bloodless hallway. The movement from history into eternity is accomplished through the movement into the maze and the penetration of space. Danny's constant cycling through the Hotel acts, in other words, as a conjuring against the illusion of time as a fixed and linear dimension: Against his own wishes, he is drawn into its horrifying past and its potential repetition in the future. In his fear, Danny may recall Mr Halloran's commentary on shining ("It's just like pictures in a book. It isn't real"), but *The Shining* leaves us with a less conclusive view.

The Gold Room

We see with Jack the Gold Room in three scenes in three different manifestations: (1) disenchanted, when it is being cleaned on Closing Day; (2) enchanted, when Jack conjures the bartender Lloyd after a fight with Wendy; and (3) in its full glory, during a ball from the twenties, after another fight with Wendy. The ballroom is the *locus amoenus* of the Overlook: It is here that Jack fully realizes his awakened sense of what was once the world of the fathers, the age of patriarchy in its fullest and most confident expression. Here a man can malign his wife to a sympathetic bartender; here his "credit is fine" and his "money's no good." These are the "orders from the house." But this sweet spot can only be entered because Jack's rage has awakened his abilities to shine. Like Danny's vision of the twins, Jack's vision is mediated and promoted by his penetrations of space, his marching through the corridors of the hotel and, correspondingly of his own mind or brain: at the center of the maze is the timeless, the Golden, place.

While Danny rides his Big Wheel into intersections of space and time and of shining, Jack's furious prowling of the hotel's labyrinth provides him with a point of entry. As he turns the corner of the corridor leading to the Gold Room, we enter with him into an atmospheric, yellow or golden light provided by the chandeliers and we hear the violent and disarticulated sounds of Penderecki's *De natura sonoris #2*. As so often in the film, the corridor suggests a vanishing point that prepares us for another collapse of space and time. Yet this imagery and music would hardly suggest that Jack is about to discover solace. Tracking Jack from the front, Kubrick draws him to the entrance, where photographs on a placard announce a seventies-style guitarist: Inside it is a quite different temporality. Once he has entered and flicked the switches, the sconces, table lamps, and bar lights illumine the golden ceiling and transform the room. The bar, with its lit counter and shelves, has a nearly hieratic look, awaiting only the magical invocation of a bartender and an array of liquors. As Jack sits down at the bar, the Penderecki tapers off, and we hear only the sound of wind. Once Jack has made his Faustian bargain for a drink ("My god damn soul, just a glass of beer"), Lloyd the bartender appears—a classical and appropriately hieratic minister and confessor—in formal attire from the twenties.

The time shift is reflected in a shift in Jack's speech: a new-found jocularity expressed as a pastiche of male buddy talk from the old days:

> Jack: That's swell. I like you, Lloyd. I always liked you. You were always the best of them. Best goddamned bartender from Timbuctoo to Portland Maine—Portland Oregon for that matter.

Along with this shift into ironized speech, Jack's expressions and bodily movements become suddenly mannered and motivated by some notion of another self and time, when men speaking to other men behaved with a stylized intimacy and concern, far from the interference of women:

Lloyd:	How are things going, Mr. Torrance?
Jack:	Things could be better, Lloyd. Things could be a whole lot better.
Lloyd:	I hope it's nothing serious.
Jack:	No, nothing serious.
Jack:	Just a little problem with the . . . old sperm bank upstairs.
. . .	
Jack:	Nothing that I can't handle though, Lloyd. Thanks.
Lloyd:	Women! Can't live with 'em. Can't live without 'em!

The scene, in fact, becomes a parody of man talk from the cinema of the forties, as Jack's unconscious mind struggles to find an adequate voice for the alien temporality he has broached. This scene ends, appropriately, when Wendy bursts in—the bartender, the liquor, and the time itself suddenly disappear.

In the third scene, the Gold Room is fully realized, like a film within a film, a parallel cinematic world. After Wendy has argued that they must leave the hotel in order to save Danny, Jack flies into another rage. In the elevator lobby, he sees scattered balloons and hears the faint strains of big band music—Jack Hylton and his Orchestra playing "Masquerade." When he enters the smoky hallway leading to the ballroom, we hear a band playing "Midnight, the Stars and You." He enters and sees that the Gold Room is filled with revelers in twenties' attire. The Maître d' greets him by name. Completely at home as he is in this scene, Jack is attired in a ragged red jacket and jeans. No matter. Jack's return to this moment in time is mediated, not by the violent exertions of Penderecki's *De natura sonoris*, but by Art Bowlly's haunting, romantic phrasing:

Midnight, with the stars and you;
Midnight, and a rendezvous.
Your eyes held a message tender,
Saying, "I surrender all my love to you."

Midnight brought us sweet romance,
I know all my whole life through
I'll be remembering you,
Whatever else I do,
Midnight with the stars and you.

The contrast in musical scoring emphasizes the shift from a traumatic breakthrough into time and a sense of nostalgic familiarity and return—not only to his true home, but also to his true duties. Welcomed back by Lloyd with the formulaic "What'll it be," Jack is soon handed off to his next counselor, the waiter Delbert Grady. As Grady ministers to his soiled jacket in the men's room, Jack is reminded of his deepest memory.

Jack:	Mr. Grady, you were the caretaker here. I recognize you. I saw your picture in the newspapers. You, eh . . . chopped your wife and daughters up into little bits, and eh . . . and you blew your brains out.
Grady:	That's strange, sir. I don't have any recollection of that at all.
Jack:	Mr. Grady, you were the caretaker here.
Grady:	I'm sorry to differ with you, sir, but you are the caretaker. You have always been the caretaker, I should know, sir. I've always been here.

Jack soon learns that he must "correct" his wife and son, if he wants to find his way back to the one good place—the Gold Room at the center of the maze.

Death by amazement

We may wonder if Jack's aides and advisors in the temporal creases of the Overlook are urging him to kill his family, to "correct" them for challenging patriarchy or to bring them along with him—like a Pharaoh or Sumerian King who has his court slaughtered—to the next world. Does Jack act as an avenger or a redeemer, a murderer or a sacrificial priest? The point remains, however, that whatever his motives, he fails: He manages his own death by misadventure and, presumably, returns to the timeless phantasmagoria of the Overlook Hotel. All of Danny's frightening moments of shining are not precognitive but retrospective warnings. In the end, Danny becomes the master of the maze, while his father becomes its sacrificial victim.

The concluding scene in the hedge maze reverses the earlier scene and fully exhibits its Oedipal themes. Now Jack is pursuing Danny in the maze and Wendy is searching for him inside the hotel. In the crisp clarity of the first scene, mother and son find their way easily into the center and then out. In the last scene, the maze is filled with snow and lit only by the low glare of lighting tucked into the hedges. In consequence of his improvisations on the Little Pigs and the Big Bad Wolf, Jack is now howling like a wolf. Limping,—axe in hand, Jack has passed beyond his human character to a mythic archetype of the murderous or castrating father. We realize soon enough that Danny has learned the layout of the maze the first time with his mother and effectively leads his father into it with the intention of leaving him there to die. Following the idyllic band music of the Gold Room, Jack's murderous, lupine pursuit of his son returns us to the atonal paroxysms of Penderecki, this time from his *Utrenja*. The low tracking shots of Danny and Jack emphasize the boy's perspective and the useless illumination of the hedge and its baffling pattern. Danny moves through it with assurance while Jack pursues him with increasing impatience and frustration.

Kubrick cuts back and forth between the maze and the hotel, contrasting the mother's loving search for her son and the father's homicidal pursuit. But instead of finding her son, she penetrates even deeper into the maze of the Overlook's perverse and criminal past. She sees a man in a pig costume fellating a guest in a dinner jacket and then encounters another party guest, drink in hand, with a split skull, who remarks: "Wonderful party!" She sees the cob-webbed Colorado room with skeletal guests, and finally the blood-emitting elevator that Danny saw in his first vision in the bathroom mirror in Boulder. In these intercut visions of figurative and literal mazes, Kubrick removes every bit of a familial and domestic repression: The family is now facing the abyss of timeless and terrifying mythical archetypes.

Kubrick seems to be playing with a rhyming theme of his crew's tracking shots and tracks of Jack and Danny in the snowy maze. The crew must leave none, Danny must leave his own clearly enough to find his way out, and Jack must try to distinguish between his own tracks and those of his son both to find him and to find his own way out. Tracking and trickery intermingle here. Danny, who has been studying the Roadrunner cartoons on television, turns his trickster's powers on his father, the way the roadrunner does with the coyote. Having penetrated the center of the maze, he steps backward into his footprints in the snow, jumps to the side, brushes the snow, and hides behind the hedge. Amazed by the disappearance of Danny and his tracks, Jack blunders about, dazed and confused, knocking into the hedge walls, howling in pain and frustration. His son follows his own tracks out of the maze and greets his mother with a kiss on her mouth. After they drive away in Halloran's Snow Cat, the camera tracks Jack's errant, pointless movements—and then cuts to a close up in the morning light of Jack's frozen features.

The Shining ends as it begins, with a long tracking shot across the hotel lobby toward a wall, just past a placard for the Gold Room, hung with framed photographs. Throughout the film, we have seen that the walls of the Overlook are hung with dozens of such records of its celebrated history. Now, for the first time, the camera moves purposely toward one photograph in a group of 21, ending with a close up of a crowd of July 4 revelers from the heady days of 1921. There, front and center, is the chief reveler—Jack Torrance, properly dressed for the occasion, a beatific smile on his face, as if for all time. Given the temporal warping, we can conclude either that Jack has *always* been in the photograph and its "time" or that he has just returned. Is the photograph a "factual" datum or is the audience itself now shining?

The artistic concerns of *The Shining* follow a parallel path, for in a sense any truly ambitious artist is seeking to escape from the banality of linear time into a realm of pure esthesis. If Jack Torrance wants to escape from such terminal existence, first through fiction writing and then through a mythic struggle with his merely generative powers, so Kubrick too wanted not only to make movies but to transcend the ordinary boundaries of what movies are supposed to be. His "obsessive" concerns for perfection and control, which no one would find odd in a poet, a painter, or a composer, manifest a nearly unique concern with what a film could be or mean. In one sense, Kubrick was taking a popular genre novel and turning it into a "blockbuster." In another sense, Kubrick was creating an esthetic realm beyond time, a masterpiece of cinematic poiesis drawn from a work of literary kitsch—elements of which persist, unfortunately, in the final cut.

To speak of this experience simply in terms of *story* or *scenario* ignores the deeper and stranger impact of imagery, music, dialog, and narration as they are woven into subjective experience. Cinematic poiesis seeks to flood the sensorium of its audience and displace its consciousness. The audience has paid money in the fervent hope that this will in fact occur: Each seat in the theater ideally becomes a kind of cinematic monad—a virtual realization of this poiesis. Yet a further complexity follows from the differing ways in which the eyes of the witness wander across the screen, the ears identify or recognize the music, the understanding detects irony or citation in narration or dialog. The ambiguity of cinematic poiesis may be limited or organized by plot and character, but its depth, resonance, and appeal are accomplished by these more ambiguous means that accomplish what Kubrick calls illumination. Kubrick is free to explore the reasons for Jack's escape from time through poiesis or "cinematic thinking"—a kind of meditation that is distributed among the media of film but is never presented in terms of a concept. The basic questions the film asks are these: What is time and how is "shining" related to it? But these questions can only be answered by its poiesis not its plot. The poiesis of *The Shining* haunts the sensorium with its alternate reality, bringing with it a different kind of thinking—as does *2001*, Kubrick's other distinctive affront to interpretation.

11

Transcendence

Homer's *Odyssey* has long inspired poets, artists, and philosophers. Porphyry, the neo-Platonic philosopher, saw in it the archetypal journey of the soul. From its home in the eternal realm, it journeys through the seas of time and space, resisting and then yielding to the lure of matter, but finally returning in triumph to its timeless home. This essential schema, described by Porphyry in "The Cave of the Nymphs," found expression in countless Gnostic forms in the Hellenic period and would be enshrined afterward in Christian metaphysics.[1] Dante, who did not know Homer's poem first-hand, made of Odysseus a figure of the rootless modern: His hero forsakes home because of an unrelenting desire for novelty and experience. In the modern era, James Joyce, Ezra Pound, and Stanley Kubrick have taken up this ancient mythos and made it the frame of their greatest works. Joyce's Leopold Bloom is a little man, short on heroism but long on humanity, who journeys through Dublin one day in June without notable accomplishment. Pound's Odyssean persona in *The Cantos* journeys through the centuries and across the earth, witnessing and engaging the rise and decline of civilizations. The temporal scope of Stanley Kubrick's *2001* exceeded all of these: It would dramatize the origin and destiny of human intelligence.

Kubrick's *Odyssey* holds a unique place in the arc of his films: It alone maintains a largely un-ironic vision of the human enterprise. Imagined as a "mythic documentary," it relies on the audience's ability to assimilate and respond intuitively to the play of symbol and sound:

> I tried [Kubrick said in 1968] to create a *visual* experience, one that bypasses verbalized pigeonholing and directly penetrates the subconscious with an emotional and philosophical content . . . I intended the film to be an intensely subjective experience that reaches the viewer at an inner level of consciousness, just as music does . . . You're free to speculate as you wish about the philosophical and allegorical meaning of the film—and such speculation is one indication that it has succeeded in gripping the audience at a deep level.[2]

This esthetic license and trust in the audience are in service to an epic theme, the high point in Kubrick's canon, recalling the mythological and psychological styles and premises of modern humanists such as Joyce and C. G. Jung. Like Joyce, Kubrick would reinvent a perennial myth in modern terms; like Jung, he would rely on the capacity of the unconscious mind to respond to symbols and the conscious mind to turn those responses into a powerful experience, what the film posters called "the ultimate trip."

Kubrick did an enormous amount of research for *2001* in astronautics, anthropology, mythology, and psychology. In putting his story of space travel into a mythic context, he sought, like the modernists, to locate contemporary parallels to Homer's world. This meant transforming the science fiction genre into something quite different:

> It occurred to us that for the Greeks the vast stretches of the sea must have had the same sort of mystery and remoteness that space has for our generation, and that the far-flung islands Homer's wonderful characters visited were no less remote to them than the planets our spacemen will soon be landing on are to us.[3]

Following this premise, Kubrick and Clarke studied Joseph Campbell's *The Hero with a Thousand Faces* (1949) in an attempt to open the symbolic material of the scenario to archetypal resonances.[4] Inspired as much by Joyce's *Finnegans Wake* as by Jung's works, Campbell attempted to create a universal and ahistorical grammar for the hero's journey. Setting out from an endangered home into the testing ground of a strange land, the hero endures various tests, overcomes a monstrous opponent—an aspect of his own fears—and thus gains a saving boon with which he returns homeward. One can recognize immediately how Dr David Bowman journeys far from home into a strange space, does battle with a monster, and returns homeward with—and as—a visionary boon. What makes Kubrick's film nearly unique is how it develops this heroic journey in powerfully implicit ways that are remarkably dependent on visual symbols and music. The relative absence of dramatic conventions works to activate archetypal symbols and stir a psychical movement toward a new synthesis of the conscious mind and its unconscious others—space, body, time, and origin. The film is a radical attempt to awaken a sense of human depth, distribution, timelessness, wholeness, and teleology. It was the perfect expression of the year 1968.

Kubrick relied on the numinous power of two images that have come to be universally recognized symbols: the monolith and the astral fetus. In an interview from 1970, Kubrick indicated that the monolith was "something of a Jungian archetype," that is to say, a universal psychic feature operating in all human beings that contributes to the collective unconscious.[5] These archetypes, Jung believed, are not themselves symbols; they are the universal and timeless psychic "potentials" that symbols can activate. Thus, the appearance of a woman's body to an infant can activate the mother archetype and its potentials are realized in a relationship of dependency and nurture.[6] Anthony Stevens has compared the archetypes to Levi-Strauss's "infrastructures" of human custom and Chomsky's "deep structure" of linguistic competence that directs speech performance. Jung's archetypes are an example of the rationalist tradition in Western thought that holds a largely ahistorical role for innate, collective, and unifying features of "human nature."[7] In linking his symbol with this heritage, Kubrick is suggesting that his film has a universal range of mythic significance.

Without disputing the influence of Freud, there is, nevertheless, a significant and pervasive Jungian element in Kubrick's films, by which I mean a dramatic interest in the emergence of buried or unconscious elements and the consequent attempt by the psyche to reconcile them to consciousness. Where Freud treated the expressions of the unconscious with a highly influential "hermeneutics of suspicion," Jung maintained that they offered the conscious mind the necessary elements for psychic wholeness. Crucial to this individuation, as Jung understands it, is the emergence of the psychic double, a manifestation of the conflict between the ideals of consciousness and the instincts of the unconscious. Among these polar features of identity, Jung argues, are the persona and the shadow. The persona is a mask that reflects an acceptance of social roles and functions; the shadow is the unseemly, obscene, or violent aspect of identity that is repressed and projected onto others. Each "compensates" for the partiality of the other and points to the need for either repression or individuation, the former acting simply to disguise the problem, the latter being the aim of Jungian analysis: the reconciliation of the conscious and the unconscious minds and the emergence of psychic wholeness.[8]

Kubrick's films provide an objective correlative for this psychological dynamic. We see versions of profound insight as well profound derangement—the emergence of the shadow—in the features of contorted faces: General Jack Ripper in *Dr. Strangelove* chomping his cigar and explaining his vision of the communist conspiracy; Private Pyle's lunatic expression as he prepares to kill Sergeant Hartman and himself in *Full Metal Jacket*; Jack Torrance's distorted and frozen expressions in *The Shining*; Dr Harford's twisted expressions as he broods on his wife's sexual fantasies in *Eyes Wide Shut*. We also see actual masks: Johnny Clay donning his clown mask during the heist in *The Killing*; Alex wearing his "Pinocchio" mask during his assault on the writer's wife in *A Clockwork Orange*; the gorgeous and sinister carnival masks in *Eyes Wide Shut*.

According to James Naremore, these faces and masks are examples of an "aesthetics of the grotesque" that emerges with an unsettling realization of the unseemly, frightening, and absurd fact of embodiment, corporeality, violence, and libido.[9] For Naremore, the grotesque finds expression in complex masks, artificial and natural, fearful and ludicrous, that lead to an affective aporia. The viewer does not know whether to laugh or scream and is paralyzed by a nameless feeling between empathy and disgust.

In a Jungian context, the grotesque can be considered another way of describing the overdetermined affect that emerges when the shadow emerges from the persona, when the pretensions of human dignity yield to the facts of human bestiality. The masks, both literal and figurative, are, in effect, internal, instinctual masks that supplant the external and performed masks of social adaptation. Gnostic or paranoid certainty, redemptive vision or patriarchal rage—all are detached from social constructions of time, space, and the self, tapping into an older "self." We see this dynamic in the last panel of *2001*, "Beyond the Infinite," when Bowman's carefully maintained mask of professional detachment makes way for masks of terror and illumination. As he journeys through the star-gate, we see Bowman's professional face collapse into open-mouthed horror and bliss as he discovers the shadow-side of "reality" itself.

The Jungian thing

Aspects of Jung's archetypal vision and the theme of the double of the persona and the shadow are evident in Kubrick's very first film, *Fear and Desire*. In a letter from 1952 to his distributor Joseph Burstyn, Kubrick writes:

> Its structure: allegorical. Its conception: poetic. A drama of "man" lost in a hostile world—deprived of material and spiritual foundations—seeking his way to an understanding of himself . . . He is further imperiled on his Odyssey by an unseen but deadly enemy that surrounds him; but an enemy who, upon scrutiny, seems to be almost shaped from the same mold.[10]

The individual characters are representative of human types who must fathom the shadow aspect that emerges most radically during times of war. Their "odyssey," then, consists of going from the world of civilized performance to the world of "the enemy" and then returning. While "behind enemy lines," the fundamental emotions of fear and desire are aroused and threaten their personae, but they also provide access to the shadow side.

Thrown behind enemy line into the mythic realm of tests and prodigies, Corby and Fletcher have discovered their shadows in the faces of the enemy. They escape by plane back to their own side, leaving Mac and Sidney behind. Later, as they await their comrades at the river, Corby says that they have "traveled too far from [their] own private boundaries" to be certain of anything anymore. Fletcher tells Corby that he wishes that he could still want what he wanted before. While the two men come to some insight about the meaning of their experiences, they see the raft floating toward them: Mac appears to be dead and Sidney is on all fours, apparently mad.

In another war film, *Full Metal Jacket*, Kubrick explicitly explores the universalizing aspect of Jungian thought while squarely establishing a historical setting in the Vietnam War between 1967 and 1968. The recruits in boot camp lose their personae and their names and assume archetypal identities: Private Joker, Private Cowboy, Private Gomer Pyle, and so forth. Gustav Hasford, Michael Herr, and Kubrick transform the generic "boot camp to battlefield" war film into an exploration of what Private Joker calls "The duality of man, the Jungian thing." Joker is the narrator and focus of the film's exploration of the conflict between empathic and violent impulses in ordinary men who have been conditioned by violence and shame. A journalist and a soldier, Joker is an exaggerated version of Corby, a man both in and out of his social role, serious and unserious, an example of the Jungian trickster who constantly interferes with social decorum. Thus, he can do a mocking impression of John Wayne (the star of *The Green Berets*, a propaganda film on behalf of the US mission) and also produce, on the command of Sergeant Hartman, a horrifying "war face," filled with rage and commitment. Likewise, Private Pyle undergoes a transformation from sad sack to top marksman, from infantile bungler to graduated killer. As he prepares to kill Hartman and himself, his ordinarily goofy expression is eclipsed by a mugging look of grotesque joy, both ludicrous and terrifying. Joker comes fully to understand this duplicity: In South Vietnam, he wears a peace button on his body armor and the scrawled confession, "Born to Kill" on his helmet. Joker offers his thesis about the "duality of man" to an uncomprehending Colonel who responds with the cliché, "How about getting with the program?" Protocol requires that Joker bury his self-knowledge of the "Jungian thing" and assume the appropriate "persona," the public mask of the United States Marine Corps.

Michel Ciment has said that "the anima-animus, the 'Jungian shadow,' is totally integrated into [*Full Metal Jacket* and] made concrete."[11] Where the unification of the shadow with the persona may prevent violent projections onto others, the recognition by the male of his own *anima* can likewise prevent destructive projections onto females. According to Jung, the *anima* or feminine component of masculinity, like the shadow, is an unrecognized but necessary component of male psychic wholeness that must be evoked and accepted for individuation to occur. In the last scenes of the film, Joker accepts the task of "wasting" a wounded, female, Viet Cong sniper who has decimated his platoon. Although she wants to be put out of her misery, Joker's motives for acceding to her request are complex. Like Sidney in *Fear and Desire*, Joker's gallantry is the flip side of his barbarism: Killing her will reconstitute him in the eyes of the other Marines. Susan White has analyzed the "violent rejection of the female" in *Full Metal Jacket*, while stipulating that the sniper is a complex figure that is not separable from male Marine identity.[12] She represents the warrior ideal, but she also recalls the feminine aspect the men were shamed into rejecting during basic training. In a sense, then, Joker meets his double (as Corby did) and kills her, the female (or *anima*) aspect that his training has failed to eliminate. Having finally gotten with the program and banished his "ambivalence," Joker concludes his narrative by claiming: "I'm in a world of shit . . . yes. But I am alive. And I am not afraid."

Although Freudian elements may predominate, Jungian themes are also apparent in *The Shining*: The Overlook Hotel is in effect a metaphor of the collective unconscious. (Jung tells of a dream he had in 1912 of a house whose stairs took him from his own story down through previous centuries and finally "into the depths."[13]) Unable to write his novel, Jack Torrance descends into his unconscious and instinctual abysses, living out a real fiction of a haunted hotel and a mad caretaker. Through the influences of his psychic son Danny and the Hotel's active history, Jack's conscious identity is gradually eclipsed by another Jack, a kind of archetypal caretaker and resident in the Hotel.

A powerful and concise postulate, the "Jungian thing" also motivates *Eyes Wide Shut*, a film very much about the shadow side of marital and professional personae. Bill's night journey is a compressed and domesticated urban Odyssey that takes him from the illusory safeties of home through a series of dangerous tests and back. The day after, Bill repeats his Odyssey by the light of day and rationality, learning of all the dangers he escaped. He is, as a tabloid headline claims, "Lucky to be Alive." The "duality of man" is thus neatly outlined, each from the contrasting point of the other. By the end of the film, "New York City" resembles a collective fiction behind which operates another city of inexhaustible erotic and violent potentials. When in the late scene in the billiard room, Victor Ziegler explains away Bill's romantic fantasies and tells him that he is "way out of [his] depth," a slow transformation occurs. Bill's chipper and smiling superficiality—his Tom Cruise face—is replaced by a twisted, petrified expression of frustration, rage, and shame.

In powerful contrast to the films just analyzed, *2001* comes close to being an explicitly successful individuation, a reconciliation and integration of the ego with its shadowy double, the cosmos itself. Jungian thought not only influenced its making but also provided a revealing way of interpreting it.

John Izod has argued that Jungian film criticism, in contrast to Freudian and Lacanian approaches, provides a more subtle means of appreciating the "fascination" of films that are "symbolic" rather than "symptomatic" in nature.[14] Freudian and Lacanian criticism, he claims, tends to place a nearly clerical barrier between the analytical mind of the critic and the richly various film experience of the "laity."[15] Freudian and Lacanian criticism seeks to discover and establish a traumatic symptomology, whether personal, cultural, or both, while Jungian analysis regards expressions of the unconscious as potentially leading to the harmonization of the psyche. Izod reads Kubrick's *Odyssey* in the context of Jung's book on UFOs and his late work on alchemy, which for Jung was a precursor, like Gnosticism, of his analytical psychology. He uses the latter work as a means of interpreting the transformative aspect of the monolith and the chromatic metamorphoses of Bowman's eye during his journey through the star-gate.[16] For Izod, the film is finally about the "encounter with the self" and the realization of the "God within."[17]

In fact, the film's relationship to Jung may be even closer than I have yet claimed. In his widely read memoir, *Memories, Dreams, Reflections* (1961), Jung relates two visions he had (as the result of a near-death experience in 1944) that seem to foreshadow Kubrick's central symbols in his *Odyssey*:

> It seemed to me that I was high in space. Far below I saw the globe of the earth, bathed in a gloriously blue light . . . Something new entered my field of vision. A short distance away I saw in space a tremendously dark block of stone, like a meteorite. It was about the size of my house, or even bigger. It was floating in space, and I myself was floating in space.
>
> Then I would come to myself and lie awake for about an hour, but in an utterly transformed state. It was as if I were in ecstasy. I felt as though I were floating in

> space, as though I were safe in the womb of the universe—in a tremendous void, but filled with the highest possible feeling of happiness.[18]

If the report of these two visions did not influence the formation of the two most impressive symbols in Kubrick's *Odyssey*, they certainly do suggest a common origin in the unconscious. They are the alpha and omega of existence, the archetypes of the originary abyss or God-concept and the divine child or *puer aeternus*.

According to Jung, the human psyche, no less than the body, is guided by a teleological drive for completeness. Jung calls this final achievement the "transcendent function." The central expression of the unconscious is our own corporeal nature, the fact that our bodies are the expression of millions of years of evolution. We cannot be conscious of the body's structural ancientness, but we sense it nevertheless through our responses to other bodies and to the world. The unconscious is, in the broadest sense, our shadow: a dark, unknown aspect that we do not recognize. Until the ego has discovered and allowed itself to form a complementary whole with the unconscious, until one has become individuated, one is not living so much as being lived. One is little more than the social role masking the chaos of instincts and impulses. For civilization and the particular self, individuation, the reconciliation with the shadow, is the great goal and demand of being-in-the-world.

Technology and Gnosis

Individuation is related to Jung's research into the Gnostic sects of the centuries before and after Jesus Christ. As opposed to those who held faith, *Pistis*, as the way to salvation, the Gnostics insisted on individual knowledge and experience, *Gnosis*. Gnosis, then, is an embodied knowing, the transcendence of verbal or conceptual cognition, and the recognition of immanence. Gnosis means seeing through the local conventions, past even the known God, to the eternal and unblemished, the unknown or alien god who has never been revealed but can only be encountered. For some Gnostics, then, the living world is necessarily a fallen world, the realm of *Creatura* that emerged, mournfully, from the uncreated *Pleroma*. The demiurges who engineered this world are befuddled and deluded beings who believe that they are creating the world when they are instead destroying eternity and chaining the fragmented souls of that ineffable realm to animal bodies who look longingly into space for confirmations of their confused but persistent intuition of a distant origin. For the Gnostics, creator gods, like Yahweh, are buffoon-like figures who operate out of an ignorance of their own secondary status.[19] In this, Yahweh is the prototype of the mystified technologist who misunderstands the significance of his own motives and ambitions.

The modern and Western approach is to seek technical solutions to our human situation. If we feel that we are alone in the cosmos, then we need to build machines to escape our alienation, create medicine that will lengthen our lives, and design robots that will do our work for us. Ironically, from a Gnostic perspective, the origins of our alienation were, in fact, the technical and misinformed interventions of the demiurges that have interrupted eternity and invented alienation. It seems that these technologists maintain the same premise that the ancient Gnostics did: that we are more or less abandoned or marooned, and that we need to transform ourselves. The Gnostic and technologist alike devise technologies meant to rectify the alienation that technology invented by ministering to the ego's demand to be freed from the unconscious, the body, and death.

The ancient Gnostics, the modern technologists, and Jung represent signal stages in the movement of human beings from animal, traditional, and alienated existence. Kubrick stages the first two of these phases: the hominids of the "Dawn of Man" and the technologists of 2001, while the film itself is a powerful expression of the third stage—a return to the origin. The film takes up the sixties' search for a spirituality that rejects sectarianism and sentimental atavism, while using modernist, nonlinear form to dramatize the possible destiny of technology in human self-realization.

The genesis and making of the film was an ever-deepening psychic excavation of rather routine materials. The original scenario and Arthur Clarke's novel preceding the making of the film are familiar science fiction fare. The film would have a narrator, a documentary prolog about aliens, a musical score by Alex North, and an explicit presentation of the alien role in human development, reflecting the film's origin in Clarke's story "The Sentinel." In the course of production and postproduction, the narrator disappeared, the score was replaced by a musical anthology of classical compositions, and the aliens retreated ever deeper into the dark matter of the monolith and of space and time. Kubrick and his team attempted mightily to find a way of representing aliens convincingly (avoiding the clichés of science fiction), but Kubrick finally decided it was not feasible. This is fortunate, because it allowed Kubrick to dispense with aliens as an instrument of human development and to ponder the void itself.[20]

In one sense, Kubrick delved into the psychological and symbolic possibilities of the film's evolving premises to make the film we all know. In another sense, Kubrick involved himself in a 4-year engagement with the psychological potentials of the symbols of planetary bodies, space, space travel, and whatever may lie beyond them. In Jungian analysis, this is called "active imagination," working with symbolic materials from one's dreams or art to sound out and solicit reconciliation with the unconscious mind.[21] There was, despite Kubrick's reputation for coldly intellectual filmmaking, no clear plan or concept that Kubrick set out to film. Even the ending, the rotating astral fetus, came very late to Kubrick. When Kubrick was asked by Michael Herr "where" he got the idea, he asked in turn, "I don't know. How does anybody ever think of anything?"[22]

Thus, Kubrick's film pushes beyond the narrative and generic premises of the original scripts toward a cinematic parallel to modernist works like Eliot's *The Waste Land*, Pound's *Cantos*, and Joyce's *Ulysses*. Like them, Kubrick's vision of totality is ironically accomplished by radical allusiveness and abrupt discontinuity. Like them, Kubrick's film is an account of modernity grounded in myth. Where Joyce discovers in Leopold Bloom an instantiation of the archetypal wanderer, of Odysseus, Kubrick will find in the genius ape Moon-watcher, Dr Heywood Floyd, Dr David Bowman, and the astral fetus examples of the embodied wandering of intelligence through time and space. Kubrick's form foregrounds image and symbol and backgrounds character and plot. Juxtaposition and montage replace linear development and running authorial narrative. This form will allow Kubrick to break with the ideological limitation of Clarke's science fiction realism and to invent a kind of cinematic tone poem.

Journey to the self

Kubrick not only dramatizes the Odyssey of intelligence from the "Dawn of Man" panel to "Beyond the Infinite," he also attempts to stimulate, through music and image, the same kind of experience of technology and gnosis in his audience. The sparse dialog deprives the audience of familiar conceptual and social handrails. They will have to find their own way. Working like an analytical psychologist bringing his client to an awareness of the unknown self, Kubrick alienates us from the earth in the title sequence. We witness the earth rising in alignment with the sun from the point of view of moon space. Other alignments will occur at crucial points in the film to signal a discontinuous leap in knowledge and a shift in temporality. The alignment or conjunction of celestial bodies symbolically presents an assimilation or reconciliation of different perspectives into a single totalizing moment.

Aligned with this opening conjunction is the dawn prelude to Richard Strauss's *Also Sprach Zarathustra*. The evolutionary drama implicit in Nietzsche's prophetic work can be concisely sketched with reference to the parable of "the three metamorphoses" from Nietzsche's introduction. The camel, like traditional human cultures, bends down to take on the load of transmitted values and demands. The lion, like enlightened technologists, confronts the dragon of tradition whose scales each bear the instruction: Thou Shalt. The final metamorphosis is that of the child acting out of its own impulse, free of tradition and free of resentment. The child, Nietzsche writes, is like "a wheel rolling out of itself."[23] These literary allusions may direct the filmgoer to Nietzsche's work, but Strauss's music presents us with a good deal more. Speaking to the body's acoustic registers, the music dramatizes dawn, the awakening of consciousness, but also expresses its ground in night, space, and the unconscious. According to Michel Ciment, the prelude to *Also Sprach Zarathustra* expresses the "world riddle" through the "ascending line of three notes . . . the same number three which is embodied in the presence of spheres after the credit titles, the moon, the earth and the sun."[24] The title sequence has presented in miniature the dynamics of the movie: the alignment of celestial bodies, the still point of the turning world, and the drama of the emergence of consciousness from the unconscious, of the sun from the abyss of space. Now these symbols must be "amplified," as Jung says, by following the ramifications of archetypes.

The hominids that live among the animals in the first panel of the film inhabit what we can call primordial or cyclical time. They have no history because there are no significant changes in their fate. Time is a cycle of repetitions: birth and death, dawn and dusk, waking and sleeping. Kubrick emphasizes the primordiality of time by long slow shots of eerie landscapes, without music or narrative cues, punctuated by long, dark transitions.

One hominid is set apart, his wondering and worrying eyes suggesting the awakening of conceptual powers. Moon-watcher is submerged in primordial time, but he is becoming conscious of it. As the hominids huddle together during the night, smacking each other occasionally and falling into resigned silence, it is Moon-watcher who is caught up in expectation and dread, waiting for the coming of another day. It is after his watchful night, and the long-anticipated coming of dawn, that the ape-men awaken to the monolith that has appeared overnight.

Seeing the featureless, black, "inert" monolith standing enigmatically amid the chaotic, geological formations, the hominids are roused and, filled with fear and desire, rush toward and away from it. With the swirling voices of Ligeti's *Requiem*, we and the hominids witness another alignment, a reversal of the alignment used in the opening sequence: We see the conjunction of the monolith, the sun, and a crescent moon.

In the black monolith, Kubrick has created his most startling and significant symbol which, we have seen, he understood in terms of a Jungian archetype, presumably of the "God-concept." As he told an interviewer in 1970, "the God concept is at the heart of the film."[25] "God-concept" is a Jungian term, like "God image" and "*imago Dei*," that indicates—without regard to the existence or nonexistence of "God"—psychic readiness for its symbolization:

> Although the God-concept is a spiritual principle *par excellence*, the collective metaphysical need nevertheless insists that it is at the same time a conception of the First Cause, from which proceed all those instinctual forces that are opposed to the spiritual principle . . . God would thus be not only the essence of spiritual light . . . but also the darkest, nethermost cause of Nature's blackest deeps.[26]

Even if one wants to read it, instead, as having strictly extraterrestrial origins, the monolith is an absence, like the dark part of the moon, the darkness of night, the unconscious. It is, one could say, a concretization of space itself, as well as the essential provocation toward conceptual thought and ego-formation. As God-concept, it expresses a superrational agency.

We may imagine that some kind of communication is taking place between the hominids and the monolith, but what we see and hear is their confrontation with a symbol. As a symbol, it does not impart information but draws out unconscious material. After his first analytic session with the monolith, Moon-watcher realizes, through playing with the remains of an animal, that a bone is not only a sign, but a symbol of death. Like Hamlet puttering with bones, the pensive Moon-watcher moves from play to insight. As he begins to see the possibility of the femur as a weapon, his grip tightens and conceptuality is attained. In other words, when objects are no longer seen as things in themselves but as constituents of thought, a revolution in cognition has occurred

In this scene, into which the monolithic alignment is spliced, Moon-watcher and the audience see the application of this tool in the killing of a tapir, but we will see it first deployed against the opposing clan of ape-men. Once the weapon has vanquished his enemies, it is exhibited to the defeated clan as a symbol of domination. With his tool as his magical baton and scepter, Moon-watcher becomes the first shaman-king as well as the inventor of technology—and the strategy of deterrence. In the famous montage joining the first two panels of the movie, we see how the bone becomes a satellite and ape-men become spacemen. In the broadest sense, "man" has dawned at the moment the ego emerges from primordial time and aligned itself with linear time and technical innovation.

The match cut from bone to satellite—which in the film treatments was explicitly meant to be an orbiting nuclear weapon—links the first and the second intervention of the monoliths in human affairs. Moon-watcher now makes way for Dr Heywood Floyd; the shaman-technician makes way for the technocrat; and imagination makes way for bureaucracy. Kubrick dramatizes the shift in human culture by leaving the earth behind: From this point on, all action is confined to artificial and space environments. An initial impression—although we are beguiled by the *valse mécanique* of satellites, *Space Station V*, and spaceships set to Johann Strauss's *By the Beautiful Blue Danube*—is that the realization of Moon-watcher's celestial longings has emptied them of vigor. Space, now inhabited and comfortably imprinted with corporate logos, has become an adjunct of the earth—another world that the Gnostic soul longs to escape. The discrete ego attained by Moon-watcher has been supplanted by the persona, the role required by social hierarchies. We see people devoid of spontaneity performing rather than experiencing humor, collegiality, duty, curiosity. This advance in social formations has been achieved by the domination of the persona over the body, the unconscious, and the shadow. There is a bright, hollow sound to everything and everyone in this artificial, indoor world. Identity is enforced through a generic protocol. "Voice-print identification" requires that Dr Floyd define himself according to destination, nationality, surname, Christian name, and middle initial. The unbearable lightness of constructed being is emphasized through scenes exhibiting the experience and look of weightlessness, culminating in the most arcane of human accommodations to space, the zero gravity toilet.

While Floyd awaits transport to the moon, he encounters a Russian friend and her colleagues. We see that the opposing hominid clan from the "Dawn of Man" has been supplanted by the Soviets; the opposing clans have now added deceit and hypocrisy to their history and promise of violence. The conversation between the Soviet scientists and Dr Floyd exemplifies the Cold War stalemate, the ways in which political and scientific technologies act to subvert the slightest expression of spontaneous existence.

During his briefing on the moon base at Clavius, Dr Floyd congratulates his colleagues for their discovery of the monolith—what may well be, he says, "among the most significant in the history of science." The scientists and bureaucrats at Clavius conclave do not realize that this is not only a *scientific* discovery—it is the discovery of science, its origin and destiny. Technology and science have progressed, without intention, toward a disclosure of their origins in the abyss, in the concretized symbol of the monolith.

When Floyd is flown out to inspect the monolith, we see just how banal human beings have become. The ape-people lived instinctively according to unconscious, organic demands. Their human descendants have had to construct their own substitutes for instinct: the ideologies of the persona, progress, and simulation. The monolith is officially designated "TMA-1" or "Tycho Magnetic Anomaly 1." The astronauts are more interested in the simulated ham and chicken sandwiches than in the sublimity their ancestors gazed at from earth. In the midst of their speculation about the sandwiches, Floyd's mind wanders back to the monolith, and he says, with just the right touch of bonhomie, "I don't suppose you know what the damn thing is?" Indeed they do not, because "the damned thing" is the shadow aspect of their glittering but empty world, the abyss out of which they and their inventions have emerged.

When they assemble before the excavated monolith in its flood-lit trench, one is reminded of a movie set. When Dr Floyd sees and touches the monolith, it is through the insulation of his space helmet and glove. There is no ecstatic mystical participation, as there was with the ape-men. Like tourists, the scientists gather round the monument for a group photograph. At this point, we see an alignment of the sun and the earth above the lunar monolith and a high-pitched tone pierces their ears, signaling to its counterpart in Jupiter space. We see now these baffled personae reacquainted with the unconscious element represented by the monolith, "deliberately buried 4 million years ago." It is a painful experience, a traumatic encounter. They cover their ears and retreat, reeling from the encounter.

The scenes on the moon and in the subsequent voyage to Jupiter emphasize the role of "security" in technical civilization: It is an attempt to prevent all forms of spontaneous activity from altering planned forms of existence. From the point of view of Valentinus and other Gnostics, "security" is enforced forgetting, an intentional alienation from the *Pleroma* or spiritual abyss beyond mundane existence—the creative but unpredictable void.[27] Dr Floyd has come to the moon to make sure that news of the discovery does not get out: normative scientific and religious accounts of human origins must remain "secure." The cover story—the leaked disinformation that the station at Clavius is under quarantine—must be maintained at all costs.

The opening scene of the third panel of the film, the Mission to Jupiter 18 months later, is one of the most melancholy in all of cinema. We see the *Discovery*, like a ganglion or a virus, as it penetrates space to a haunting dance from Khachaturian's *Gayne* Ballet Suite. These were once Pascalian spaces, terrifying voids between stars. Now they are merely distances to be covered with stolid patience and resolution. We see Dr Frank Poole boxing and jogging around the revolving deck of the bridge. He will later work on his tan, eat his simulated food, and watch his parents on television as they wish him a happy birthday. Here is a perfect picture, not of an intrepid voyager, but of a modern human being.

Throughout the film, we have seen other images of rotation and revolution, of planetary spheres crossing the rectangular frame of the screen, of satellites in orbit, and of a space station in orbit and revolving around its own axis. This primordial symbolism of the circle and the cycle reminds us that the movement forward and up must also accommodate itself to recursiveness: There is a limit to linear progression, at which point, lines begin to turn and time to bend. It is the cyclonic tedium of technological existence, this parody of eternity, which will be broken once the third monolith is discovered.

Although not a likely avatar of Odysseus, David Bowman does appear to be more intelligent than Poole. Bowman is the Greek archer, Poole the collective man. But Bowman is, at this point, equally remote and mechanized. Where Poole tries to beat the HAL at chess and loses rather gracelessly, Bowman's art elicits encouraging but surely insincere praise from the machine. Poole is not prepared for a leap ahead in consciousness and HAL will soon have him dispatched. Bowman's angelic, epicene appearance makes him a perfect candidate for a more profound kind of travel, and it is he who will take up Moon-watcher's odyssey and gnosis.

Although HAL would appear to some in the Artificial Intelligence and Robotics Community to be Moon-watcher's successor, it is important to remember that HAL fails to live up to his designers' specifications. If the astronauts are robotic, HAL becomes suspicious, emotional, vengeful, and human, all too human. It is Bowman who will take the next step in the circuitous human journey, while HAL ends up as gutted and abandoned hardware. Indeed, it is HAL's cold violence that awakens Bowman and prepares him for the psychic journey. Where HAL is returned to his machine childhood as he expires, Bowman is instead shot forward through his own experience of the complete life cycle and beyond.

When everyone on board, except Bowman, is either dead or dismantled, a video-recording finally announces the secret purpose of the mission. It is as if accident and planning, technology and the failure of technology, have positioned Bowman for his journey "Beyond the Infinite." By "forgetting" his helmet in his rush to save Poole, Bowman breaks with protocol. He acts spontaneously to save his colleague, forsaking the demands of "security" and thus opening the way for his total break with the secure "cover story" of scientific civilization. Leaving the hardware behind, the journey becomes entirely psychic and all the more real and significant because of that. It would seem that HAL is the final expression of a failed, utilitarian conception of intelligence. HAL is not only a caricature of intelligence and omniscience; he is a parody of gnosis: a cyclopean, one-eyed monster that must be heroically confronted and destroyed. Like Odysseus trapped in the cave of the Cyclops, Bowman outwits HAL and escapes to continue his odyssey homeward.

Bowman's *nostos* requires a harrowing initiation into the mysteries of the cosmos conserved in the unconscious mind. As Gilles Deleuze remarks, "If Kubrick renews the theme of the initiatory journey, it is because every journey in the world is an exploration of the brain."[28] The experience is triggered by the alignment of Jupiter, its moons, the space pod, the sun, and the monolith. Once again we see planetary alignment as a metaphor for psychic organization, insight, and individuation—what Jung called "the transcendent function." Gnosis or realization begins with a passage between suggestive luminosities and spectral planets. It is as if we—Bowman and the audience—are moving, not through time and space, but into a vision compressing both into a single dimension. Here again we have glimpses of Bowman's mask-like face as he witnesses the Big Bang, the expanding universe, the appearance of organic form, a zygote, and reconnaissance flights over planets shown in photographic negatives, as if to suggest that Bowman has moved from figure to ground, from individual to universal, from temporality to timelessness.

Because Bowman has been constrained by technical protocols, he is, paradoxically, the perfect candidate for a journey beyond time. Jung describes the relationship between depersonalization and the welling up of collective psychic material in a way that uncannily describes Bowman's journey:

> An infallible sign of collective images seems to be the appearance of the "cosmic" element, i.e., the images in the dream or fantasy are connected with cosmic qualities, such as temporal or spatial infinity, enormous speed and extension of movement, "astrological" associations, telluric, lunar, and solar analogies, changes in the proportions of the body, etc. The obvious occurrence of mythological and religious motifs in a dream also points to the activity of the collective unconscious. The collective element is very often announced by peculiar symptoms, as for example by dreams where a dreamer is flying through space like a comet, or feels that he is the earth, or the sun, or a star; or else is of immense size, or dwarfishly small; or that he is dead, in a strange place, is a stranger to himself, confused, mad, etc.[29]

After Bowman's pod comes to rest inside the baroque room, a series of transformations overtakes him, each mediated by his own act of perception: Bowman looks out of the pod and finds himself there. This process of identification with the "outer" or "unconscious" world leads him along the cycle of aging, death, and rebirth. The initiation and subsequent individuation requires a sacrifice in which Bowman's life is compressed according to the ritualistic demands of Gnosis. As in Nietzsche's parable of the three metamorphoses, Bowman is transformed from dutiful camel bearing the weight of scientific culture to heroic lion slaying the dragon of rules (HAL, computer protocols, the tradition, the limitations of terrestrial existence, the "thou shalt"), to the "astral fetus" or "star child." The *puer aeternus* is free of alienation and resentment alike.

Kubrick's film stops short of a complete visionary *nostos* or return to eternity, concluding with a symbolic tableau that anticipates the photograph, taken by Apollo 8, of the blue and watery earth afloat in space. It is, in fact, a new symbol for the oldest of mysteries, the appearance of life out of the void. It is a fetus floating in the abyss, an embryo secure in the womb of space. It is Bowman's final vision of himself, sublimely cast into space, without an umbilicus, anticipating his next metamorphosis. In analytical terms, this is symbolic of the individuated Self—the reconciliation of the unconscious, that is the cosmos, with the consciousness that it has produced, and by which it is finally known. In Gnostic terms, Bowman has realized his identity with the abyss that precedes creation, time, and space. Intelligence, via its technological inventions, is finally privileged to see itself in its absolute otherness and identity with the void. What began as a technical "conquest" of space bends backward into a journey into the unconscious motives of exploration.

The vision fades and the screen goes black. For a moment, we may be reminded of the monolith. Like Moon-watcher and Bowman, we have been gazing into the abyss, watching the play of symbols and listening, sometimes without knowing it, to music, words, and sound effects. Then we hear the reassuring, opening bars of the Strauss waltz *By the Beautiful Blue Danube* and see the credits rolling by—the music of psychic convention. We have been safely delivered from the realm of anagogic symbol made and exhibited by an esthetic technology and returned to the realm of sociable signs—and a roster of cast and crew. Kubrick's *Odyssey* ends as our temporal intelligence, exalted and baffled by an encounter with its origins in eternity, begins the task of interpretation—as the houselights come on.

At the high point of the arc of Kubrick's films, *2001* provides the boldest extrapolations of his philosophical themes and the fullest mastery of his formal qualities. Beginning with its dramatization of human corporeality and the dynamism of war, the film establishes the premises of civilization in the frightening premises which life presented to human beings in the beginning. The challenge of the will has here been sublimated by custom and an evident weariness with eros: In the male world of this film, the flight attendants represent its final transformation into a cool, detached performance. In the weightless environment of space, these epicene women only allude to sex: Their helmeted heads and magnetic slippers suggest the furthest remove from mere will and corporeality. Dominated as it is by the apparent triumph of technology, *2001* moves away from the instrumental purposes of machines toward a lyrical and balletic realization of their unforeseen esthetic and revelatory potentials. So with technology's triumphant reconfiguration as art, we witness also its confrontation with its own origins and motives. The monolith may be the civilizing instrument of aliens intent on leading hominids toward self-realization: more significantly, the monolith may be seen as a concretized symbol of the black mystery of space and time. It is in addressing this mystery that Moon-watcher and his ancestors are the authors of their own transcendence.

None of these philosophical abstractions would be of the slightest interest unless Kubrick had mastered and transformed time, light, music, speech, and their simultaneous enactment in cinematic poiesis. In essence, each of these formal qualities is subject to a questioning and a thinking through: None of them are accepted as givens or conventions for "story telling." As we have seen throughout this book, time has no absolute status: It contracts and expands according to its interplay with consciousness. So too, light—far from being simply a way of "getting the shot"—is enmeshed within the drama and theme and plays its role, like time, as an instrument of illumination. With respect to music and speech, one observes a kind of reversal wherein music is *heard* in its own medium and speech becomes in a sense *witnessed* or *overheard.* As music emerges from the vagaries of emotional supplementation, speech retreats into a deadened, nearly material form—far indeed from illumination or enlightenment. These formal elements are experienced simultaneously as a multi-media *poiesis* in all of Kubrick's films, but none more remarkably than in *2001*. Here Kubrick's total cinema comes into its own.

Feature films directed by Stanley Kubrick

Fear and Desire. Joseph Burstyn, Inc. 1953 (withdrawn).

Killer's Kiss. United Artists. 1955.

The Killing. United Artists. 1956.

Paths of Glory. United Artists. 1957.

Spartacus. Universal. 1960.

Lolita. MGM. 1962.

Dr. Strangelove or: How I Learned to Stop Worrying and Love the Bomb. Columbia Pictures. 1964.

2001: A Space Odyssey. MGM. 1968.

A Clockwork Orange. Warner Brothers. 1971.

Barry Lyndon. Warner Brothers. 1975.

The Shining. Warner Brothers. 1980.

Full Metal Jacket. Warner Brothers. 1987.

Eyes Wide Shut. Warner Brothers. 1999.

Notes

Chapter 1

1 Alexander Walker, *Stanley Kubrick, Director* (New York: Norton, 1999), 7.
2 Ibid., 15.
3 Kent Jones, "Un Conteur metaphysique," *Cahiers du cinema*, #534 (April 1999).
4 Thomas Allen Nelson, *Kubrick: Inside a Film Artist's Maze* (Bloomington: Indiana University Press, 2000), 16.
5 James Naremore, *On Kubrick* (London: BFI, 2007), 247.
6 Walker, *Stanley Kubrick*, 13.
7 Vincent LoBrutto, *Stanley Kubrick: A Biography* (New York: De Capo, 1997), 166.
8 Frederic Raphael, *Eyes Wide Open: A Memoir of Stanley Kubrick* (New York: Ballantine, 1999), 164.
9 Stanley Kubrick, "Words and Movies," *Sight & Sound*, Vol. 30 (1960/61), 14.
T. S. Eliot, "Hamlet and his Problems," in *Selected Essays* (New York: Harcourt Brace, 1952).
10 Ibid.
11 Ibid.
12 Ibid.
13 Naremore, *On Kubrick*, 3–4.
14 T. Pipolo, "The Modernist & The Misanthrope: The Cinema of Stanley Kubrick." *Cineaste*, Vol. 27, No. 2 (Spring 2002), 4.
15 W. K. Wimsatt, *The Verbal Icon: Studies in the Meaning of Poetry* (Lexington, KY: University of Kentucky Press, 1954); Cleanth Brooks, *The Well-Wrought Urn: Studies in the Structure of Poetry* (New York: Harcourt Brace, 1947).
16 Stanley Kubrick, *Interviews*, ed. Gene D. Phillips (Jackson, MS: University of Mississippi Press, 1995), 7.
17 Ibid., 192.
18 Ibid.
19 Ibid., 91.
20 Ibid., 87, 90.
21 Ibid., 130.
22 Stanley Kubrick, "Foreword" in Krzysztof Kieslowski and Krzysztof Piesiewicz. *Decalogue: The Ten Commandments*, trans. Phil Cavendish and Suzannah Bluh (London: Faber & Faber, 1991), vii.

23 Walker, *Stanley Kubrick*, 38.
24 "*Dr. Strangelove*: Stanley Kubrick's Shattering Sick Joke," *New York Times*, January 30 (1964), 24.
25 See LoBrutto, *Stanley Kubrick*, 361–3.
26 Arthur Schopenhauer, *The World as Will and Representation*, two volumes, trans. E. J. Payne (New York: Dover, 1969), passim.

Chapter 2

1 Mervyn Nicholson, "My Dinner with Stanley: Kubrick, Food, and the Logic of Images," *Literature/Film Quarterly*, Vol. 29. No. 4 (Winter 2001): 286
2 Ibid., 280.
3 Julia Kristeva, *Powers of Horror: An Essay on Abjection*, trans. Leon S. Roudiez (New York: Columbia University Press, 1982), 71.
4 Ibid., 2.
5 See J. Laplanche and J.-B. Pontalis, *The Language of Psychoanalysis* (New York: Norton, 1973), 314–19.
6 Walker, *Stanley Kubrick*,, 352.
7 See Gregory Bateson, *Steps to an Ecology of Mind* (New York: Ballantine, 1972), 271–8.
8 See Geoffrey Aggeler, "Pelagius and Augustine in the Novels of Anthony Burgess." *English Studies*, Vol. 55 (1974), 43–55.

Chapter 3

1 Walker, *Stanley Kubrick*, 17.
2 Nelson, *Kubrick*, 192.
3 Ezra Pound, *Literary Essays* (New York: New Directions, 1954), 4.
4 Ernest Fenollosa, *The Chinese Written Character as a Medium for Poetry* (San Francisco: City Lights, 1964).
5 LoBrutto, *Stanley Kubrick: A Biography*, 122–3.
6 Nelson, *Kubrick*, 131.

Chapter 4

1 Thomas Hobbes, *Leviathan* (Baltimore: Pelican Books, 1968), 185.
2 Immanuel Kant, *The Philosophy of Kant*, trans. Carl J. Friedrich (New York: The Modern Library, 1949), 120.

3 G. W. F. Hegel, *Elements of the Philosophy of Right*, trans. T. M. Knox (London: Oxford University Press, 1967), 210.

4 Gilles Deleuze and Félix Guattari, *Nomadology: The War Machine*, trans. Brian Massumi (New York: Semiotexte, 1986), 2.

5 Ibid., 73.

6 Victor David Hanson, *Carnage and Culture: Landmark Battles in the Rise of Western Power* (New York: Anchor, 2002), 1–5, 49.

7 Ibid., 5.

8 Lawrence H. Keeley, *War Before Civilization: The Myth of the Peaceful Savage* (New York: Oxford University Press, 1996), 3–24.

9 Martin M. Winkler, ed., *Spartacus: Film and History* (Oxford: Blackwell, 2007), 125.

10 Ibid., 127.

11 Baron von Clausewitz, *On War*, trans. Michael Howard and Peter Paret (Princeton: Princeton University Press, 1989), 75.

12 Nelson, *Kubrick*, 181.

13 Stanley Kubrick, *Napoleon: The Greatest Movie Never Made* (Köln: Taschen, 2009), 697.

14 See Gene D. Phillips and Rodney Hill, *The Encyclopedia of Stanley Kubrick* (New York: Checkmark, 2002), 14–16.

15 Walker, *Kubrick*, 69.

16 Raphael, *Eyes Wide Open*, 49.

17 Peter Sloterdijk, *Terror from the Air*, trans. Amy Patton and Steve Corcoran (New York: Semiotexte, 2009), 53.

18 http://b-29s-over-korea.com/SAC/sac1.html.

Chapter 5

1 A. R. Fulton, *Motion Pictures: The Development of an Art from Silent Films to Television* (Norman: Oklahoma University Press, 1960), 7.

2 Ibid., 80.

3 LoBrutto, *Stanley Kubrick: A Biography*, 234.

Chapter 6

1 Michael Herr, *Kubrick* (New York: Grove Press, 2000), 11.

2 Schopenhauer, *The World as Will and Representation*, Vol. 1, 110.

3 Ibid., 196.

4 Ibid., 197.

5 Ibid., 411–12.
6 Vladimir Nabokov, *Lolita* (New York: Putnam, 1958), 18.
7 Raphael, *Eyes Wide Open*, 39.
8 Michel Chion, *Eyes Wide Shut* (London: BFI, 2002), 36.
9 Ibid., 47.
10 Schopenhauer, *The World as Will and Representation*, Vol. 1, 330.

Chapter 7

1 Claudia Gorbman, "Ears Wide Open: Kubrick's Music" in *Changing Tunes: The Use of Pre-Existing Music in Film*, ed. Phil Powrie and Robynn Stilwell (Aldershot, England and Burlington, VT: Ashgate, 2006), 4.
2 Michel Ciment, *Kubrick: The Definitive Edition*, trans. Gilbert Adair and Robert Bononno (New York: Faber and Faber, 1999), 153.
3 Arthur Schopenhauer, *The World as Will and Representation*, Vol. 1, 257.
4 LoBrutto, *Stanley Kubrick: A Biography*, 308.
5 David Bordwell and Noel Carroll, *Post-Theory: Reconstructing Film Studies* (Madison: University of Wisconsin Press, 1996), 249.
6 See Anthony Stevens, *Jung: A Very Short Introduction* (Oxford: Oxford University Press, 1994), 38–42.
7 LoBrutto, *Stanley Kubrick: A Biography*, 353.

Chapter 8

1 Michel Ciment, *Kubrick: The Definitive Edition*, 75.
2 Martin Heidegger, "The Question Concerning Technology," in *The Question Concerning Technology and Other Essays*, trans. William Lovitt (New York: Harper, 1977), 34.
3 Ibid., 12–13.
4 Albert Borgmann, *Technology and the Character of Contemporary Life: A Philosophical Inquiry*, (Chicago: University of Chicago Press, 1984), 40–8.
5 Michael Mateas, "Reading HAL: Representation and Artificial Intelligence," in *Stanley Kubrick's 2001: A Space Odyssey: New Essays*, ed. Robert Kolker (New York: Oxford University Press, 2006), 105.
6 Friedrich Nietzsche, *The Birth of Tragedy and The Case of Wagner*, trans. Walter Kaufmann (New York: Vintage, 1967), 96.
7 Heidegger, *Question Concerning Technology*, 134.

Chapter 9

1 Naremore, *On Kubrick*, 124.
2 Anthony Burgess, *You've Had Your Time* (Harmondsworth: Penguin, 1991), 38.
3 Frederic Raphael, *Eyes Wide Open*, 178.
4 Chion, *Eyes Wide Shut*, 74.

Chapter 10

1 See Ezra Pound, *ABC of Reading* (New York: New Directions, 1960), 37, 42–3, 63.
2 Nelson, *Kubrick*, 1–19.
3 Alex Ross, liner notes, Bartok, *Concerto for Orchestra, Music for Strings, Percussion and Celesta*. Sony Recording 62598.
4 Garret Brown, "Commentary," Two-Disc DVD Special Edition of *The Shining* (Warner Bros, 2007).

Chapter 11

1 See Porphyry, "The Cave of the Nymphs," in *Selected Works*, trans. Thomas Taylor (London, 1823).
2 Kubrick, *Interviews*,, 47–8.
3 Ibid., 18.
4 LoBrutto, *Stanley Kubrick: A Biography*, 266.
5 Kubrick, *Interviews*, 93.
6 C. G. Jung, *Collected Works*, Vol. 1–21, ed. Sir Herbert Read, Michael Fordham, Gerhard Adler; trans. R. F. C. Hull et al. (Princeton: Princeton University Press, 1989), Vol. 7, 127–38; 9.I, 42–53.
7 Anthony Stevens, 52–5.
8 See Jung, *Collected Works*, Vols 9.II, 8–10; 9.I, 3–41; 6, 463–70.
9 Naremore, *On Kubrick*, 26–41.
10 LoBrutto, *Stanley Kubrick: A Biography*, 89–90.
11 Ciment, *Kubrick*, 251.
12 Susan White, "Male Bonding, Hollywood Orientalism, and the Repression of the Feminine in Kubrick's *Full Metal Jacket*," *Arizona Quarterly*, Vol. 44, No. 3 (Autumn 1988), 122, 130–1.
13 C. G. Jung, *Memories, Dreams, Reflections*, ed. Aniela Jaffe, trans. Richard and Clara Winston (New York: Vintage Books, 1989), 158–9.

14 John Izod, *Myth, Mind and the Screen: Understanding the Heroes of Our Time* (Cambridge: Cambridge University Press, 2001), 6–7.

15 Ibid.

16 Ibid., 185–203.

17 Ibid., 199.

18 Jung, *Memories, Dreams, Reflections*, 290, 293.

19 For a classic account of Gnostic principles, see Hans Jonas, *The Gnostic Religion: The Message of the Alien God and the Beginnings of Christianity* (London: Routledge, 1963), 31–97.

20 For an account of the making of the film, see LoBrutto, *Stanley Kubrick*, 255–308.

21 See Jung, *Collected Works*, Vol. 8, 67–91.

22 Michael Herr, *Kubrick*, 71.

23 Friedrich Nietzsche, *Thus Spoke Zarathustra*: *A Book for None and All*, trans. Walter Kaufmann (New York: Modern Library, 1995), 25–8, translation modified.

24 Ciment, *Kubrick*, 130.

25 Kubrick, *Interviews*, 92.

26 Jung, *Collected Works*, Vol. 8, 103.

27 Jonas, *The Gnostic Religion*, 174–97.

28 Gilles Deleuze, *Cinema 2: Image-Temps* (Paris: Minuit, 1985), 267.

29 Jung, *Collected Works*, Vol. 7, 160.

Bibliography

Abrams, Jerold J., Ed. *The Philosophy of Stanley Kubrick*. Lexington: University Press of Kentucky, 2007.

Aggeler, Geoffrey. "Pelagius and Augustine in the Novels of Anthony Burgess." *English Studies* 55 (1974): 43–55.

Bateson, Gregory. *Steps to an Ecology of Mind*. New York: Ballantine, 1972.

Baudrillard, Jean. *Simulations*. Translated by Paul Foss, et al. New York: Semiotexte, 1983.

Bingham, Dennis. "Kidman, Cruise, and Kubrick: A Brechtian Pastiche." In *More than a Method: Trends and Traditions in Contemporary Film Performance*. Edited by Cynthia Baron and Frank P. Tomasulo. Detroit: Wayne State University Press, 2004.

Bordwell, David and Noel Carroll. *Post-Theory: Reconstructing Film Studies*. Madison: University of Wisconsin Press, 1996.

Borgmann, Albert. *Technology and the Character of Contemporary Life: A Philosophical Inquiry*. Chicago: University of Chicago Press, 1984.

Brooks, Cleanth. *The Well-Wrought Urn: Studies in the Structure of Poetry*. New York: Harcourt Brace, 1947.

Brown, Blain. *Cinematography: Theory and Practice*. Amsterdam: Focal Press, 2002.

Brown, Gordon. "Commentary," Two-Disc DVD Special Edition of *The Shining*, Warner Bros, 2007.

Burgess, Anthony. *You've Had Your Time*. Harmondsworth: Penguin, 1991.

Castle, Alison. *The Stanley Kubrick Archive*. Köln: Taschen, 2005.

Campbell, Joseph. *The Hero with a Thousand Faces*. Princeton: Princeton University Press, 1968.

Chion, Michel. *Eyes Wide Shut*. London: BFI, 2002.

—. *Kubrick's Cinema Odyssey*. Translated by Claudia Gorbman. London: BFI, 2001.

Ciment, Michel. *Kubrick: The Definitive Edition*. Translated by Gilbert Adair and Robert Bononno. New York: Faber and Faber, 1999.

Clarke, Arthur C. *2001: A Space Odyssey*. New York: Signet Books, 1968.

—. *The Sentinel: Masterworks of Science Fiction and Fantasy*. New York: Berkeley Books, 1983.

Clausewitz, Baron von. *On War*. Translated by Michael Howard and Peter Paret. Princeton: Princeton University Press, 1989.

Cocks, Geoffrey. *The Wolf at the Door: Stanley Kubrick, History, & the Holocaust*. New York: Peter Lang, 2004.

Cocks, Jeffrey, James Diedrick, and Glen Perusek, eds. *Depth of Field: Stanley Kubrick, Film, and the Uses of History*. Madison: University of Wisconsin Press, 2007.

Crowther, Bosely. "*Dr. Strangelove*: Stanley Kubrick's Shattering, Sick Joke." *New York Times* January 30 (1964).

Dawkins, Richard. *The Selfish Gene*. New York: Oxford University Press, 1979.

Deleuze, Gilles. *Cinema 2: Image-Temps*. Paris: Minuit, 1985.

Deleuze, Gilles and Félix Guattari. *Nomadology: The War Machine*. Translated by Brian Massumi. New York: Semiotexte, 1986.

Eliot, T. S. "Hamlet and His Problems." In *Selected Essays*. New York: Harcourt Brace, 1952.

Falsetto, Mario. *Stanley Kubrick: A Narrative and Stylistic Analysis*. New and Expanded Edition. Westport: Prager, 2001.

Fenollosa, Ernest. *The Chinese Written Character as a Medium for Poetry*. Edited by Ezra Pound. San Francisco: City Lights, 1964.

Fry, Carrol L. "From Technology to Transcendence: Humanity's Evolutionary Journey in *2001: A Space Odyssey*." *Extrapolation* 44(3) (Fall 2003): 331–43.

Fulton, A. R. *Motion Pictures: The Development of an Art from Silent Films to Television*. Norman: University of Oklahoma Press, 1960.

Gorbman, Claudia. "Ears Wide Open: Kubrick's Music." In *Changing Tunes: The Use of Pre-Existing Music in Film*. Edited by Phil Powrie and Robynn Stilwell. Aldershot, England; Bulington, VT: Ashgate, 2006.

Hanson, Victor Davis. *Carnage and Culture: Landmark Battles in the Rise of Western Power*. New York: Anchor, 2002.

Hegel, G. W. F. *Elements of the Philosophy of Right*. Translated by T. M. Knox. London: Oxford University Press, 1967.

Heidegger, Martin. *The Question Concerning Technology and Other Essays*. Translated by William Lovitt. New York: Harper, 1977.

Herr, Michael. *Kubrick*. New York: Grove Press, 2000.

Hobbes, Thomas. *Leviathan*. Baltimore: Pelican Books, 1968.

Horkheimer, Max and Theodor W. Adorno. *Dialectic of Enlightenment: Philosophical Fragments*. Translated by Edmund Jephcott. Stanford: Stanford University Press, 2002.

Izod, John. *Myth, Mind and the Screen: Understanding the Heroes of Our Time*. Cambridge: Cambridge University Press, 2001.

Jenkins, Greg. *Stanley Kubrick and the Art of Adaptation: Three Novels, Three Films*. Jefferson, NC: McFarland and Company, 1997.

Jonas, Hans. *The Gnostic Religion: The Message of the Alien God and the Beginnings of Christianity*. London: Routledge, 1963.

Jones, Kent. "Un Conteur metaphysique." *Cahiers du cinema* #534 (April 1999): 25–7.

Jung, C. G. *Collected Works*, Vols 1–21. Edited by Sir Herbert Read, Michael Fordham, and Gerhard Adler. Translated by R. F. C. Hull et al. Princeton: Princeton University Press, 1989.

—. *Memories, Dreams, Reflections*. Recorded and edited by Aniela Jaffe. Translated by Richard and Clara Winston. New York: Vintage Books, 1989. Originally published in 1961.

Kagan, Norman. *The Cinema of Stanley Kubrick*. New York: Continuum, 2000.

Kant, Immanuel. *The Philosophy of Kant*. Translated by Carl J. Friedrich. New York: The Modern Library, 1949.

Keeley, Lawrence H. *War Before Civilization: The Myth of the Peaceful Savage*. New York: Oxford University Press, 1996.

Kieslowski, Krzysztof and Krzysztof Piesiewicz. *Decalogue: The Ten Commandments*. Translated by Phil Cavendish and Suzannah Bluh. Foreword by Stanley Kubrick. London: Faber & Faber, 1991.

Kristeva, Julia. *Powers of Horror: An Essay on Abjection*. Translated by Leon S. Roudiez. New York: Columbia University Press, 1982.

Kubrick, Stanley. *Drama and Shadows: Photographs 1945–1950*. Edited by Rainer Crone. New York: Phaidon, 2005.

—. *Interviews*. Edited by Gene D. Phillips. Jackson, MS: University of Mississippi Press, 1995.

—. *Napoleon: The Greatest Movie Never Made*. Edited by Alison Castle. Köln: Taschen, 2009.

—. "Words and Movies." *Sight & Sound* 30 (1960/61): 14.

Kubrick, Stanley and Frederic Raphael. *Eyes Wide Shut: A Screenplay*. New York: Warner Books, 1999.

Kubrick, Stanley, Michael Herr, and Gustav Hasford. *Full Metal Jacket: The Screenplay*. New York: Knopf, 1987.

Kurzweil, Ray. *The Singularity is Near: When Humans Transcend Biology*. New York: Viking, 2005.

Laplanche, J. and Pontalis, J.-B. Translated by Donald Nicholson-Smith. *The Language of Psychoanalysis*. New York: Norton, 1973.

LoBrutto, Vincent. *Stanley Kubrick: A Biography*. New York: Da Capo, 1997.

Mainar, Luis M. Garcia. *Narrative and Stylistic Patterns in the Films of Stanley Kubrick*. Rochester: Camden House, 1999.

Mateas, Michael. "Reading HAL: Representation and Artificial Intelligence." In *Stanley Kubrick's 2001: A Space Odyssey: New Essays*, Edited by Robert Kolker. New York: Oxford University Press, 2006.

Moravec, Hans. *Mind Children: The Future of Robot and Human Intelligence*. Cambridge, MA: Harvard University Press, 1988.

Nabokov, Vladimir. *Lolita*. New York: Putnam, 1958.

Naremore, James. *On Kubrick*. London: BFI, 2007.

Nelson, Thomas Allen. *Kubrick: Inside a Film Artist's Maze*. Bloomington: Indiana University Press, 2000.

Nicholson, Mervyn. "My Dinner with Stanley: Kubrick, Food, and the Logic of Images." *Literature/Film Quarterly* 29(4) (Winter 2001): 229–89.

Nietzsche, Friedrich. *The Birth of Tragedy and The Case of Wagner*. Translated by Walter Kaufmann. New York: Vintage, 1967.

—. *Thus Spoke Zarathustra: A Book for None and All.* Translated by Walter Kaufmann. New York: Modern Library, 1995.

Phillips, Gene D. and Rodney Hill. *The Encyclopedia of Stanley Kubrick*. New York: Checkmark Books, 2002.

Pipolo, T. "The Modernist & The Misanthrope: The Cinema of Stanley Kubrick." *Cineaste* 27(2) (Spring 2002): 4–15.

Porphyry. *Selected Works*. Translated by Thomas Taylor. London, 1823.

Pound, Ezra. *ABC of Reading*. New York: New Directions, 1960.

—. *Literary Essays*. Edited by T. S. Eliot. New York: New Directions, 1954.

Raphael, Frederic. *Eyes Wide Open: A Memoir of Stanley Kubrick*. New York: Ballantine, 1999.

Rice, Julian. *Kubrick's Hope: Discovering Optimism from* 2001 *to* Eyes Wide Shut. Lanham, MD: Scarecrow Press, 2008.

Ross, Alex. "Bela Bartók." Bartók: Concerto for Orchestra, Music for Strings, Percussion and Celesta, and Salonen. Sony Classical CD 62598, 1996.

Scheurer, Timothy E. "The Score for *2001: A Space Odyssey*." *Journal of Popular Film and Television* 25(4) (Winter 1998): 172–82.

Schopenhauer, Arthur. *The World as Will and Representation*. Two volumes. Translated by E. J. Payne. New York: Dover, 1969.

Siegel, Lee. "*Eyes Wide Shut*: What the Critics Missed in Kubrick's Last Film." *Harpers* October 1999: 29–32.

Soterdijk, Peter. *Terror from the Air*. Translated by Amy Patton and Steve Corcoran. New York: Semiotexte. 2009.

Spaatz, Carl. "SAC Mission Statement." http://b-29s-over-korea.com/SAC/sac1.html.

Stevens, Anthony. *Jung: A Very Short Introduction*. Oxford: Oxford University Press, 2001.

Stork, David, ed. *HAL's Legacy: 2001's Computer as Dream and Reality*. Cambridge, MA: MIT Press, 1997.

Tipler, Frank J. *The Physics of Immortality: Modern Cosmology, God, and the Resurrection of the Dead*. New York: Doubleday, 1994.

Walker, Alexander. *Stanley Kubrick, Director*. New York: Norton, 1999.

White, Susan. "Male Bonding, Hollywood Orientalism, and the Repression of the Feminine in Kubrick's *Full Metal Jacket*." *Arizona Quarterly* 44(3) (Autumn 1988): 120–44.

Wimsatt, W. K. *The Verbal Icon: Studies in the Meaning of Poetry*. Lexington, KY: University of Kentucky Press, 1954.

Winkler, Martin M. (ed.) *Spartacus: Film and History*. Oxford: Blackwell, 2007.

Index